THE ENCYCLOPEDIA OF
DECORATIVE
STYLES
1850   1935

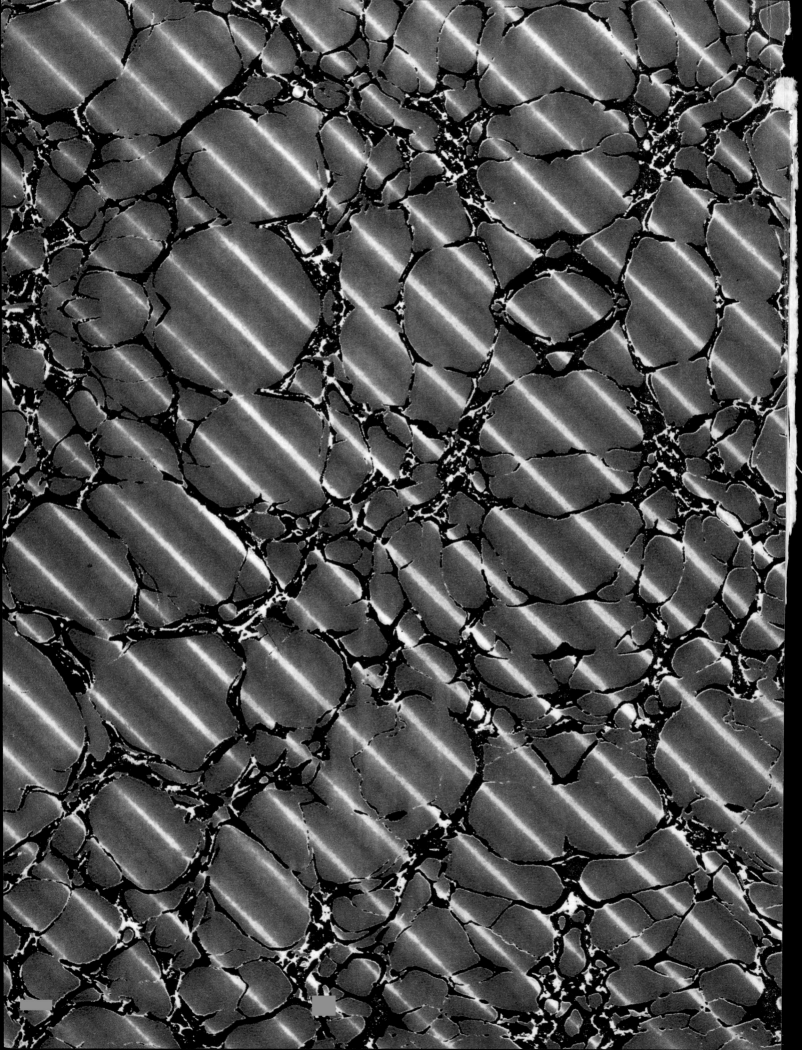

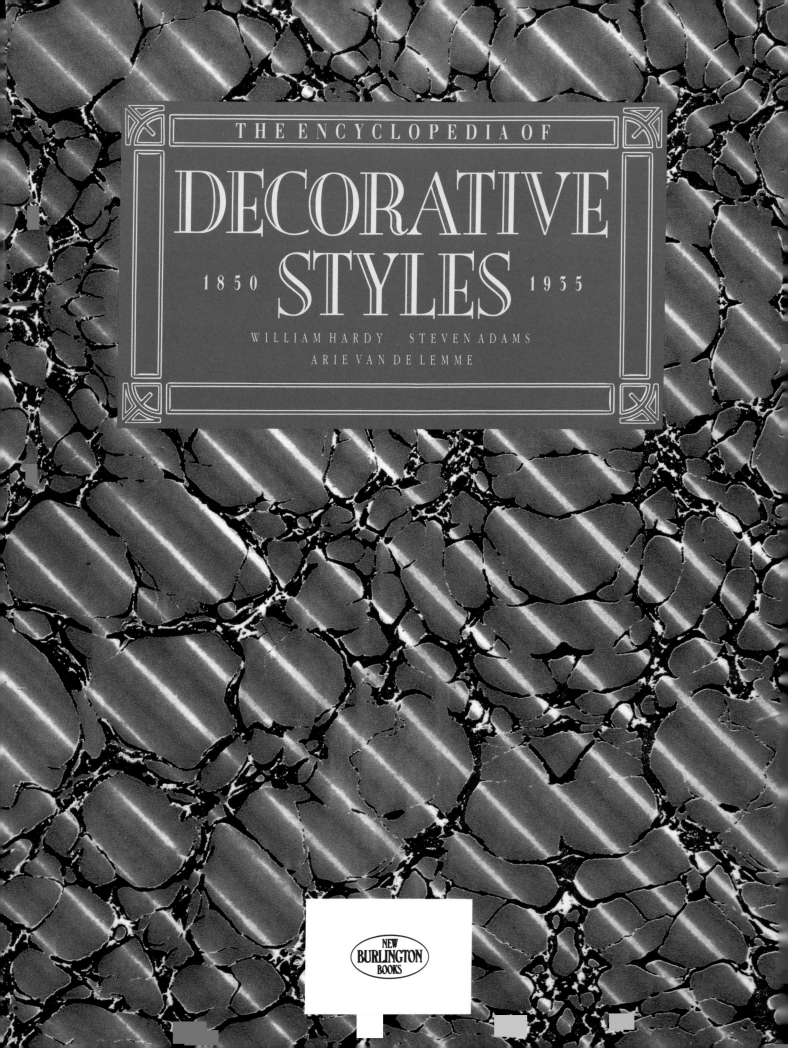

THE ENCYCLOPEDIA OF

DECORATIVE
STYLES

1850   1935

WILLIAM HARDY · STEVEN ADAMS
ARIE VAN DE LEMME

NEW
BURLINGTON
BOOKS

A QUINTET BOOK

Published by New Burlington Books
6 Blundell Street
London N7 9BH

ISBN 1-85343-039-8

This book was designed and produced by
Quintet Publishing Limited
6 Blundell Street
London N7 9BH

Art Director: Peter Bridgewater
Designer: Linda Moore
Editors: Nicholas Law, Josephine Bacon, Patricia Bayer,
Judith Simons, Sarah Goodwin
Illustrator: Lorraine Harrison
Picture Researcher: Anne-Marie Ehrlich

Typeset in Great Britain by
Central Southern Typesetters, Eastbourne
Manufactured in Hong Kong by Regent Publishing
Services Limited
Printed in Hong Kong by Leefung-Asco Printers Ltd

The author and publishers would like to thank the
following publishers for permission to reproduce
quotations: The Architectural Press, London; Brooklyn
Museum, New York; Chapel Publishing, London; The
Frank Lloyd Wright Foundation, Arizona; Garland
Publishing, New York; Harper Row, London; Lawrence &
Wishart, London; Open University, Milton Keynes;
Phaidon, Oxford; Routledge & Kegan Paul, London; P
Smith, Santa Barbara.

The assistance of Stephen Astley of the Furniture and
Interior Design Department, Victoria and Albert Museum,
and of Patrick Cook of the Bakelite Museum of London, in
the production of this book is greatly appreciated.

CONTENTS

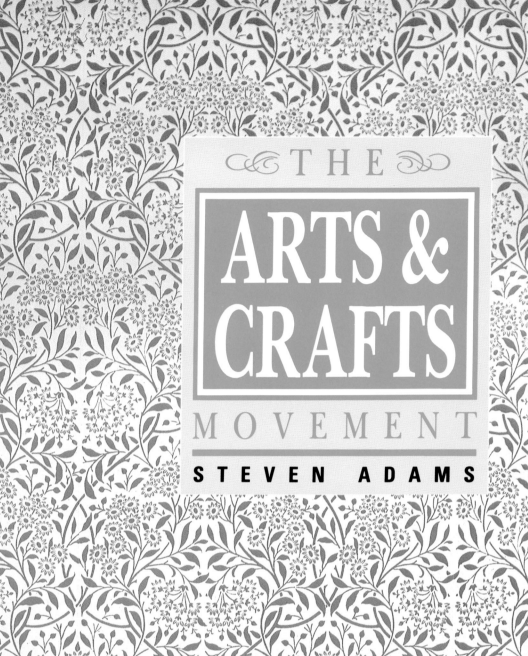

THE
ARTS &
CRAFTS
MOVEMENT

STEVEN ADAMS

*RIGHT Thomas Carlyle
by A.C. Armytage, after
Samuel Lawrence.*

The Arts and Crafts Movement evolved and developed during the second half of the 19th century. It incorporated a wide variety of artists, writers, craftsmen and women, so wide that it is difficult to define 'Arts & Crafts' with any accuracy. One has only to consider that some of its precursors were deeply conservative and looked wistfully back to a medieval past, while others were socialists and ardent reformers. Some, like John Ruskin (1819–1900), identified the Arts and Crafts aesthetic with Protestantism, while others, such as the architect Augustus Welby Pugin (1812–52), saw clear affinities between the revival of medievalism and the Catholic cause. Moreover, the craftsmen and women connected with the movement were active within a wide cross-section of crafts: as architects, printers and bookbinders, potters, jewellers, painters, sculptors, and cabinetmakers. Some members of the movement, such as the designers William Morris (1834–96) and C.R. Ashbee (1863–1942), cherished handicraft and tended to reject the opportunity to produce for a mass market. Others, such as the architect Frank Lloyd Wright (1867–1959), positively relished the creative and social advantages of machine production.

The Arts and Crafts Movement became even more diverse in the 1870s, when the revival of an interest in the Arts and Crafts in Britain was exported and grafted onto indigenous traditions abroad. In the United States, the revival of craft traditions had a resonant appeal for a nation with a strong political affinity with individualism and for things handmade and homespun. It is interesting to note that decades before critics such as Thomas Carlyle (1795–1881) or Ruskin were writing about the horror of industrialism and the idyll of rural medieval England, Shaker communities in the United States were producing simple furniture and buildings that echoed many of the creative and social ideals of the Arts and Crafts Movement. Friedrich Engels (1820–95) dissociated himself from the religious faith of the Shakers but admired the near-socialist conditions under which their work was produced and sold.

The revival of Arts and Crafts in the second half of the 19th century embodied a rich and varied tradition of political, religious and aesthetic ideas that found form in a variety of media, yet there were some principles and articles of faith common to the Arts and Crafts Movement in general. The belief that a well-designed environment – fashioned with beautiful and well-crafted buildings, furniture, tapestries and ceramics – would serve to improve the fabric of society for both producers and consumers is a theme common to the Arts and Crafts Movement in both the 19th and 20th centuries. The idea was expressed by William Morris in the middle of the 19th century and repeated constantly thereafter by kindred spirits in Europe and the United States.

Together with the idea that the material and moral fabric of society were connected, there existed an interest in the working conditions under which the artefacts were produced. A building or a piece of furniture true to the aims of the Arts and Crafts tradition had not only to be beautiful but also to be the result of contented labour, in which the craftsman or woman could reject the drudgery and alienation of factory work and delight in simple handicraft. The movement's precursors, Carlyle, and more particularly Ruskin and Morris, had virtually characterized labour as a sacrament. It was through the medium of work, they maintained, that men and women expressed not only their individual creativity but also the essence of their humanity. In his *Lectures on Socialism*, Morris wrote that 'Art is Man's expression of his joy in Labour', an expression that the pressure of industrialized factory work had rendered impossible. Morris continues: 'Since all persons . . . must produce in some form or another it follows that under our present system most honest men must lead unhappy lives since their work . . . is devoid of pleasure'. Or, put more succinctly, that in Victorian society, as far as Morris was concerned, 'happiness is only possible to artists and thieves'.

It was the desire to improve both aesthetic standards and working conditions that generated a further article of faith shared by many active within the Arts and Crafts Movement: the belief that the material and moral fabric of society had been infinitely better some time in the past, be it the England of the Middle Ages or the America of the pioneer age. The ethos of industrial capitalism demanded production for profit rather than need and had generated

*RIGHT John Ruskin,
from an early
photograph in the
Mansell Collection,
London.*

shoddily designed goods in the process at the expense of both their aesthetic appeal to consumers and the well-being of the workforce. These miserable conditions were in stark contrast to those of a pre-industrialized past in which, it was generally believed, production took place under far more wholesome conditions. The crafts of medieval society had none of the 'engine-turned precision' of modern industry, but they retained the sense of humanity that Ruskin so admired. Writing on 'The Nature of Gothic' in the second volume of *The Stones of Venice*, published in 1853, Ruskin insisted that: 'You must make either a tool of the creature or a man of him. You cannot make both. Men were not intended to work with the accuracy of tools, to be precise and perfect in all their actions. If you will have that precision out of them, and make their fingers measure degrees like cog-wheels, and their arms strike curves like compasses, you must unhumanize them.'

Pre-industrial society, then, was understood to retain precisely that element of humanity that industrial capitalism lacked. Men and women were not bound by the relationship of 'master' and 'wage-slave', based on alienating and mechanized factory labour, but lived as a human community centred upon the workshop, where they were employed on useful and creative tasks. The admiration for some romanticized, pre-industrial Utopia was endemic among 19th-century critics of industrialism – so endemic, in fact, that an echo of the sentiment even permeates the *Economic and Philosophical Manuscripts* of Karl Marx (1818–83). Not generally known for his romanticism, Marx found and admired in the working con-

ditions of medieval society – 'an intimate and human side' that was resolutely absent in the factory sweatshops of the industrialized 19th century.

Not all of the ventures that took place under the banner of Arts and Crafts were an unqualified success. William Morris, towards the end of his life, expressed profound doubt about the real value of his work and maintained that the undeniably beautiful work produced by his company was undertaken only for the wealthy. There were, in turn, numerous other well-intentioned craft ventures that began with great optimism only to end in bankruptcy. Morris had stumbled on a paradox that affected all evangelistic craftsmen and women active within the movement in Europe and the United States: objects made by hand are far more expensive than those made by machine and necessarily exclude the disadvantaged masses

for whom they were intended. Ultimately, there came to the Arts and Crafts Movement the realization that the social reform demanded by many craftsmen and women could not be achieved by Arts and Crafts alone, and there was a catalogue of attempts to resolve this paradox. In fact, the history of the Arts and Crafts Movement is, in many respects, a history of compromises, and the various solutions to this paradox form the framework of this present study. It begins with the romantic refuge from industrialism sought by the Pre-Raphaelites and their circle in the mid-19th century and goes on to chart the development of the craft fraternities and sororities on both sides of the Atlantic and ends with the establishment of the European and American design factories in this century that compromised earlier romantic ideals and came to terms with mechanized industry.

LEFT American clock in the Gothic style by Brewster and Co., c. 1860. The Gothic style became increasingly important in 19th-century American culture. It is evident in domestic goods and architecture and was seen by some as a less pretentious style than the classical idiom common in the 18th and early 19th centuries.

CHAPTER ONE

THE FOUNDING FATHERS

Title page from Clarence Cook's The House Beautiful, *1878.*
The House Beautiful *introduced tasteful art and design to an
American bourgeoisie cut off from recent cultural developments in
Europe.*

RIGHT *Exterior view of
Joseph Paxton's Crystal
Palace, constructed in
1851 to house the
Great Exhibition,
London.*

 On 1 May 1851, Britain celebrated its industrial might with the opening of the 'Great Exhibition of all Nations'. The exhibition took place in Joseph Paxton's Crystal Palace, erected in London's Hyde Park. The glass and iron construction, some 1,800 ft (549 m) long, 140 ft (43 m) high and with a volume of 33 million cubic ft (934,000 cubic m), was erected in less than eight months. Sir Matthew Digby, Secretary to the exhibition's Executive Committee, saw this vast undertaking as a reflection of the national character. The size of the venture represented national courage and the nation's strength could be seen in the speed with which it was built. National wealth was displayed in the resources used in the building and the country's intellect symbolized by its architectural complexity. Moreover, the beauty of the Crystal Palace, according to Digby, demonstrated that 'the British are by no means indifferent to the beautiful in fine arts'. The building housed the work of 15,000 exhibitors, which was displayed in four categories: raw materials; machinery; manufactures; sculpture and the fine arts. Queen Victoria summed up

BELOW LEFT Interior view of the Crystal Palace showing a display of moving machinery. The illustration is taken from the exhibition catalogue.

the exhibition's purpose in her reply to her husband's opening address. She hoped that it would 'conduce to . . . the common interests of the human race by encouraging the arts of peace and industry', and that it would promote 'friendly and honourable rivalry . . . for the good and happiness of mankind'.

Many of Victoria's subjects did not share her appreciation for the fruits of industry and free international trade, and saw the onslaught of industrialization as detrimental to the nation. Since the beginning of the century many commentators had realized that industry had the capacity to generate wealth and misery in equal quantities. William Cobbett, writing as early as 1807, observed that the industrialized city of Coventry maintained a population of 20,000, almost one half of whom were paupers. Industry had generated wealth but concentrated that wealth in the hands of a few people, serving to create 'two nations'. One of the most vivid descriptions of the extent to which wealth had been polarized is given by Friedrich Engels. Writing in *The Condition of the Working Class in England*, he gave a graphic account of the conditions of the urban poor. He stated,

RIGHT
The Guild Hall,
London, and the Hôtel
de Ville, Paris, from
A.W.N. Pugin's
Contrasts, *published*
in 1836.

Heaps of garbage and ashes lie in all directions, and the foul liquids emptied before the door gather in stinking pools. Here live the poorest of the poor, the worst paid workers with thieves and the victims of prostitution indiscriminately huddled together, the majority Irish, or of Irish extraction, and those who have not yet sunk in the whirlpool of moral ruin which surrounds them, sinking daily deeper, losing daily more and more of their power to resist the demoralising influence of want, filth, and surroundings.

The sense of loyalty and social responsibility that was understood to have existed between the various levels of society in the previous centuries was now absent. The creed of *laissez-faire* utilitarianism relieved the wealthy from any responsibility toward the poor. Some economists saw the conditions Engels described as an unfortunate but necessary evil. Social life in England was, in the eyes of many critics, gradually being undermined to generate a nation of masters and wage-slaves.

The climate of dissent in the late 18th and 19th centuries took on a variety of forms. At one end of the spectrum was the romantic, celibate 'Brotherhood', dedicated to art and chivalry, conceived by William Morris and Edward Burne-Jones (1833–98) while at Oxford. This fraternity devoted itself to things of the spirit and determined to mask the horrors of industrialism beneath a veneer of art. At the other end of the spectrum Karl Marx and Friedrich Engels saw within industrial society's class-struggle, inevitable revolution and the seeds of its own destruction. At various points between these extremes a host of other critics argued for democratic freedom and the emancipation of the industrial working classes or saw national salvation in the revival of the feudal ideals of a lost past. In many instances there was very little love lost between the factions. These dissenters, whether revolutionary or romantic, were, however, bound by the deep suspicion that was to be shared by artists and artisans of the Arts and Crafts Movement, the suspicion that society under industrialism was getting worse rather than better.

In the first half of the 19th century protests against the horror of the Industrial Revolution were common. The tone of these protests was often ineffectual, serving to create a means of escape from the unpleasantness of Victorian

life rather than a remedy for its social ills. Aspects of the work of John Keats (1795–1821), some of the earlier paintings of Dante Gabriel Rossetti (1828–82) and his contemporaries, and the poetry of William Morris serve as examples in which refined artistic sensibilities were used to eclipse the realities of the world. In essence, imagination afforded a romantic shelter from real life. Protests against industrialism attained a stronger and intellectually more coherent character in the writings of two of the most important catalysts of the Arts and Crafts Movement, Thomas Carlyle and John Ruskin. Both Carlyle and Ruskin were read avidly by the young Morris while at Oxford, and Ruskin in particular was to exert a strong influence upon the Pre-Raphaelites, their counterparts in the United States, and on the development of the Arts and Crafts Movement on both sides of the Atlantic. Neither Carlyle nor Ruskin shared the socialist convictions of many of those active within the Arts and Crafts Movement. Both writers were conservative and Carlyle, at times, was deeply reactionary. The Movement, however, gleaned from them a marked distaste for modern industrial capital-

ism that went beyond the sentimental and gradually began to take on a practical, philosophical form.

Carlyle's invective against the horrors of the modern age was directed at the twin evils of mechanized industrial society and the radical movements that had risen to oppose it. In *Sayings of the Times*, written for the Edinburgh Review of 1829, Carlyle attacked utilitarianism, the prevailing idea that the economic policy could not afford to be burdened with concern for the poor and should only be influenced by the laws of supply and demand. Utilitarianism demanded that if machinery proved a more efficient instrument of profit it should be used regardless of the consequences to less efficient human labour. An extension of Carlyle's distaste for the money-grabbing middle classes was an equal dislike of the democratic working-class movements that had evolved to oppose them. Democracy, for Carlyle, would only serve to spread *laissez-faire* notions and create a nation of competing individuals fuelled by greed and ambition. Absent in both utilitarianism and its Chartist antidote was the old feudal notion of social responsi-

CHAPTER ONE
■

BELOW LEFT Maiolica plate designed by A.W.N. Pugin, c. 1850. Pugin, like the later architects associated with the Arts and Crafts Movement, designed both buildings and their contents. Pugin is also noted for his fabric designs, tiles, metalwork and stained glass, many of which were displayed at the Great Exhibition of 1851.

bility and a sense of community explained by Carlyle in *Chartism*, written a decade later. The demands for democracy made by the working classes were, Carlyle explained, really only demands for leadership from an unled class. The solution could be found in the restoration of a socially responsible hierarchy led by the 'strong of heart' and 'noble of soul'. In essence, the solution could be found in a return to the chivalric ideals of medieval England. The restoration of these conditions would ensure that the serf would work under the paternalistic protection of the lord; labour would be dignified and bonds of mutual cooperation would replace the chains of industry wherein 'wage-slaves' were bound to inanimate machines and a desperate need for cash.

Ruskin placed a similar emphasis on the value of work, in particular on the value of creative work. The Machine Age, he argued, had created a division of labour in which it was impossible for men and women to find fulfilment in work. In the second volume of *The Stones of Venice*, written in 1853, Ruskin wrote:

Look round this English room of yours, about which you have been so proud so often, because the work of it was so good and strong, and the ornaments of it so finished. Examine again all these accurate mouldings, and perfect polishings, and unerring adjustments of the seasoned wood and tempered steel. Many a time have you exulted over them, and thought how great England was, because her slightest work was done so thoroughly. Alas! if read rightly, these perfectnesses are signs of slavery in our England a thousand times more bitter and degrading than the African, or helot Greek.

Ruskin objected to the refinement of contemporary Victorian design because it was dependent upon machinery, and machinery necessarily destroyed the creativity of human labour. Ruskin was less sentimental than many of his contemporaries about the charms of a medieval past. He nonetheless maintained that work in the Middle Ages, although hard and often unpleasant, was undertaken voluntarily by men and women and retained its dignity. The dignity found in simple and unsophisticated craftsmanship explains Ruskin's unbridled admiration for medieval building. He recognized the 'fantastic ignorance' of the sculptors that decorated medieval churches and conceded the sophistication of his age in comparison to that of the past. He nonetheless

saw the conditions under which medieval craftsmen worked as infinitely more wholesome than the mechanized drudgery of industrialism, and maintained that it was to the spirit of this medieval model that 19th-century society must turn for salvation. Production, he insisted, would be for use rather than profit and the machine-like precision exchanged for an imperfect human finish. Ruskin explained his ideal of creative work in writing:

Let him but begin to imagine, to think, to try to do anything worth doing; and the engine turned precision is lost at once. Out come all his roughness, all his dullness, all his incapability; shame upon shame, failure upon failure, pause after pause: but out comes the whole majesty of him also.

One of the first architects and designers in Britain to give practical form to an antipathy for the modern industrial environment was Augustus Welby Pugin. Pugin employed an architectural style reminiscent of that of the Middle Ages. He distinguished himself from many other late 18th- and early 19th- century Gothic revivalists by equating the appearance of medieval building with the spiritual refinement of the Middle Ages. The Gothic had long been employed either for its picturesque characteristics or as a nationalistic antidote to the international classical style. Pugin, however, maintained that Gothic was less a style than an architectural representation of Christian sentiment, and was starkly contrasted to the crass and spiritually vacuous utilitarian building of his own age.

In 1835 Pugin wrote *Contrasts: or a Parallel between the Noble Edifices of the Middle Ages, and Corresponding Buildings of the Present Day, shewing the Present Decay of Taste*. The work was an indictment not only of 19th-century taste but also the degenerate industrialized social system from which it emerged. The 'Contrast' between a Catholic town of 1440 and the same town some 400 years later illustrated the sorry state of contemporary building. The 19th-century town showed despoiled medieval churches interspersed among iron and gas works, an asylum and prison. The indictment continued with further contrasts between medieval and modern society: one illustration showed a benign community of well-fed and -clothed poor housed in a medieval monastery, the other the misery of the modern panopti-

*RIGHT Grace Church,
on New York's
Broadway and Tenth
Street, by James
Renwick, Jr.;
completed in 1846.*

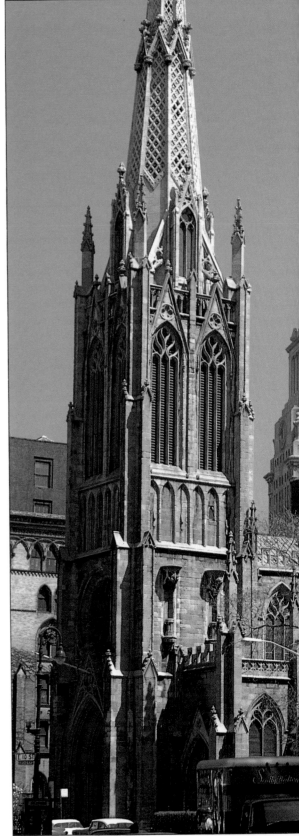

con. Although Ruskin and Morris dissociated themselves from Pugin (respectively for his Catholicism and his antipathy to working-class movements), the notion that art and architecture carry the capacity to redeem and improve society was an important departure in Gothic revivalist architecture and one that was to recur in many manifestations of the Arts and Crafts Movement both in Europe and in the United States.

Mid-19th-century America began to share the European taste for Gothic architecture. In most cases American builders used the Gothic purely for its picturesque and visual appeal. James Renwick Jr, for example, designer of Grace Church on New York's Lower Broadway and the Smithsonian Institution in Washington, D.C., used the Gothic with little regard for the historical associations the style retained in Britain. Some architects, however, began to adapt and lend their own meaning to the style. The Gothic was seen by some as less pretentious than the sophisticated Greek revival style that had dominated building in the early 19th century. Andrew Jackson Downing (1815–1851), a landscape gardener and writer, saw within the Gothic style an element of honesty and practicality. The style was, he maintained, far better suited to the homespun aspirations of American citizens and could also serve to refine uneducated American tastes, cheapened by the mass-produced *objets d'art* that had flooded markets in the wake of the Industrial Revolution in the United States. Downing's *Cottage Residences*, published in 1842, expressed a strong sense of artistic independence and an affinity with old pioneer values. He wrote:

... every man either builds or looks forward to building a home for himself, at some period of his life; it may be only a log hut or a most rustic cottage, but perhaps also, a villa or a mansion. As yet, however, our houses are mostly either of the plainest and most meagre description, or if of a more ambitious, they are frequently of a more objectionable character – shingle palaces, of very questionable convenience, and not in the least adapted, by their domestic and rural beauty, to harmonise with our lovely natural landscapes.

Downing advocated, in some instances, the use of a more elaborate Gothic style in the design of homes for the wealthy. In general, good domestic American architecture could take its

LEFT Design for a small cottage from Andrew Jackson Downing's Cottage Residences, *published in 1842.*

BELOW LEFT Detail, Grace Church, by James Renwick, Jr.

[Fig. 87.]

ANDERSON Sc.

802

RIGHT Lyndhurst by Alexander Jackson Davis; built in Tarrytown, New York, in 1838 for William Paulding.

lead from the example set by more modest Tudor Gothic or Tuscan building, simple but soundly built architecture appropriate to the independent lifestyle of most rural Americans.

The notion of a specifically American sense of design and architecture was developed in the writings of the art collector and critic James Jackson Jarves (1818–1888). Jarves, a keen collector of late medieval Italian paintings, disliked the way in which European styles were being inappropriately used for American building to create 'chaotic, incomplete, and arbitrary' architecture. Eschewing both 'Bastard Grecian' and 'Impoverished Gothic', Jarves advocated a quite independent path that was to be followed by architects associated with Arts and Crafts in both Europe and the United States. Building, Jarves insisted, must be in harmony with its surroundings. He maintained that architecture grew out of the wants and ideas of a nation and could not be imported at will from a well of European styles and influences, be they Greek, Roman or Gothic. Writing in 1864, Jarves stated:

Our forefathers built simply for protection and adaptation. Their style of dwelling houses was suited to the climate, materials at hand, and social exigencies. Hence it was true and natural. They could not deal in artifice or plagiarism, because they had no tricks of beauty to display and nothing to copy. Over their simple truth of expression time has thrown the veil of rustic enchantment, so that the

farmhouses still standing of the period of the Indian wars are a much more pleasurable feature of the landscape than their villa-successors of the 19th century.

The development of a sense of artistic independence and the return to the common-sense values of the pioneer primarily occurred in writing rather than shingle, bricks and mortar. There are some exceptions: the architects Alexander Jackson Davis and Richard Upjohn, in particular, stand out. Davis, a friend of Downing, abhorred the symmetry of Greek classicism, preferring the more modest Gothic style: two contrasting examples of his work are the large mansion Lyndhurst, built in Tarrytown, New York, and the less ambitious Rotch House, a comparatively small cottage in New Bedford, Massachusetts. Richard Upjohn – architect of Trinity Church on New York's lower Broadway, believed by some to be the 'greatest church erected in America' – contributed to a more sophisticated understanding of Gothic architecture not dissimilar to that of Pugin. Interpreting church architecture not as a mere style but as a medium for religious devotion, Upjohn, a high churchman, professed to have no interest in the style of a building as an end in itself, but saw the Gothic as an idiom uniquely able to communicate Christian feeling. Architecture was seen as a medium of faith.

ABOVE LEFT *Shaker chair, 19th century. Shaker furniture anticipated many of the concerns of the Arts and Crafts Movement in the United States.*

ABOVE RIGHT *Reconstruction of a Shaker interior.*

By the middle of the 19th century there was a body of opinion that had begun to question the cultural dominance of Europe, a process that was to continue in one form or another until the Second World War. The antidote to the influence of European taste was a return to homespun values. It is worth noting, however, that these values, which were to provide so fertile an environment for the Arts and Crafts Movement to adapt and evolve in the second half of the century, had existed unchanged in some quarters for well over a century. The Quakers (some of whom later became 'Shaking Quakers' or 'Shakers') who had left England to escape persecution in the 17th and 18th centuries had, as pioneers, established a number of religious and economic communities that anticipated many of the aesthetic and social ideals of the Arts and Crafts Movement. Labour was seen as a sacrament (a sentiment shared by Ruskin, himself connected with the low-church Presbyterians). Some of the socialist ideals in Arts and Crafts workshops had, in turn, echoes in Shaker convictions: wealth was held in common by the community as a whole; work undertaken by men or women was understood to be of equal value, and craft activities took place within a secluded community reminiscent of the craft guilds of the second half of the 19th century. Consistent with an Arts and Crafts aesthetic, Shaker furniture and architecture were simply made, functional and without excessive decor-ation, and much of it bears a marked resemblance to later ventures by more self-conscious artists and craftsmen. It is interesting to consider that the Industrial Revolution, studious-ly ignored in the produc-tion of much Arts and Crafts furniture, is actu-ally absent in the historical evolution of Shaker crafts. The pre-industrial tradi-tions of the Shakers, im-ported from 17th-century England, were in many instances the very tradi-tions to which men and women of the Crafts Movement were returning.

24

We can conclude by saying that the Arts and Crafts Movement in Britain and the United States was built on separate but by no means independent cultural traditions. In Britain, the idea of a pre-industrial, medieval past articulated through the writings of Ruskin, Carlyle and Pugin provided the British Arts and Crafts Movement with a strong sense of the artistic, moral and social refinements of a technologically less sophisticated age. This British ideal of a feudal past has an American counterpart in the image of the pioneer. The traditions on which American arts and crafts developed were those of a respect for work, independence and self-sufficiency, and the desire to fashion a national culture remote from the fanciful notions and historical traditions of Europe. These two separate but linked traditions, which shared a distaste for sophistication, a strong sense of independence and a belief in the sanctity of work, were respectively to determine the shape of Arts and Crafts in Britain and the United States throughout the remainder of the 19th and 20th centuries.

CHAPTER TWO

PRE-RAPHAELITES IN ENGLAND AND THE UNITED STATES

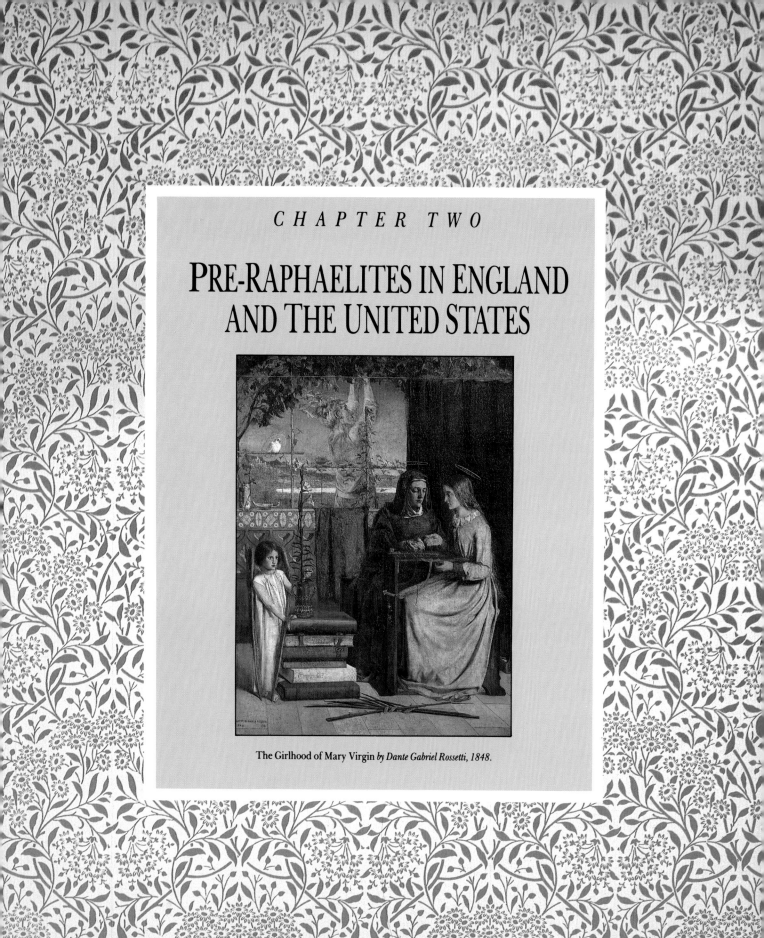

The Girlhood of Mary Virgin *by Dante Gabriel Rossetti, 1848.*

The Arts and Crafts Movement in Britain emerged, in part, from the works of the Pre-Raphaelite Brotherhood, a group of dissident artists who rejected the conventional artistic opinions of the academic establishment and sought inspiration in the arts, and later in the crafts, of the Middle Ages.

The accepted wisdom in conventional academic circles of the 19th century was that art gradually began to recover from the ignorance of the Dark Ages around the 14th century, steadily to become more refined until it virtually attained perfection during the High Renaissance. For the most part, the ideals of 16th-century painting became enshrined in the Royal Academy, to the extent that those ideas still had enormous influence almost a century after its foundation in 1768. Many of the young painters associated with the Pre-Raphaelite Brotherhood began to reject this academic sophistication in favour of medieval simplicity. Art, they maintained, should be based not upon the refined, philosophical idealism of the Academy but on the less affected and simpler style of painting found in Europe in the 14th and 15th centuries, or in the straightforward appreciation of nature itself. Ford Madox Brown's *Seeds and Fruit of English Poetry,* painted shortly before the formation of the Brotherhood (*c.* 1848), typifies the archaic but still naturalistic style of the Pre-Raphaelites. Brown's picture is divided by Gothic tracery into three sections to resemble a medieval triptych and, following medieval convention, the backgrounds of two of the panels are painted gold. Despite such conventions, the painting is intensely and naturalistically detailed, with great attention afforded to components of relatively minor importance. A suitable medieval and nationalistic subject is also used in preference to the international stock of tired classical subject matter considered suitable for academic painting. In this instance Chaucer reads aloud to Edward the Black Prince, flanked by a pantheon of British poets.

Rejecting the establishment canon that the principles of art were based upon timeless academic ideals embodied in the example of Raphael, the Pre-Raphaelites professed 'to have no master except their own powers of mind and hand, and their own first hand study

of Nature'. The Brotherhood's secretary, William Michael Rossetti, had succinctly recorded the aims of the movement in an account of the Rossetti family memoirs published in 1895. They were 'to have genuine ideas to express'; 'to study nature attentively'; and 'to sympathise with what is direct and heartfelt in previous art, to the exclusion of what is conventional and self parading and learned by rote'.

The Pre-Raphaelite Brotherhood was founded in London. Initially called 'Early Christian', the movement abandoned the name for fear of Roman Catholic associations. The

Brotherhood consisted of seven members: Dante Gabriel and William Michael Rossetti, John Everett Millais, William Holman Hunt, F.G. Stephens and Thomas Woolner, together with a handful of fellow-travellers, among them Burne-Jones and Morris.

One of the first pictures to bear the enigmatic stamp PRB (Pre-Raphaelite Brotherhood) was Dante Gabriel Rossetti's 'symbol of female excellence', *The Girlhood of Mary Virgin*, painted in 1848. Following the advice given by Ruskin, the broad and generalized impression of nature found in academic painting was rejected and every item in the picture depicted in

minute detail. A contemporary account of Rossetti at work recorded him painting in oils with fine watercolour brushes on a perfectly smooth white surface to achieve the detailed and translucent effect gained by 'primitive' artists of 15th-century Italy. Again, the choice of subject was unconventional. The picture shows an adolescent Mary surrounded by symbols that pre-figure her role as 'Mary, pre-elect God's Virgin'. A sonnet accompanying the picture when it was first exhibited at the Free Exhibition of 1849 explained the intense symbolism within the picture: the red cloth in the background – a symbol of Christ's passion –

RIGHT A Converted
British Family
Sheltering a
Christian Missionary
from the
Persecution of the
Druids *by William
Holman Hunt, 1850.*

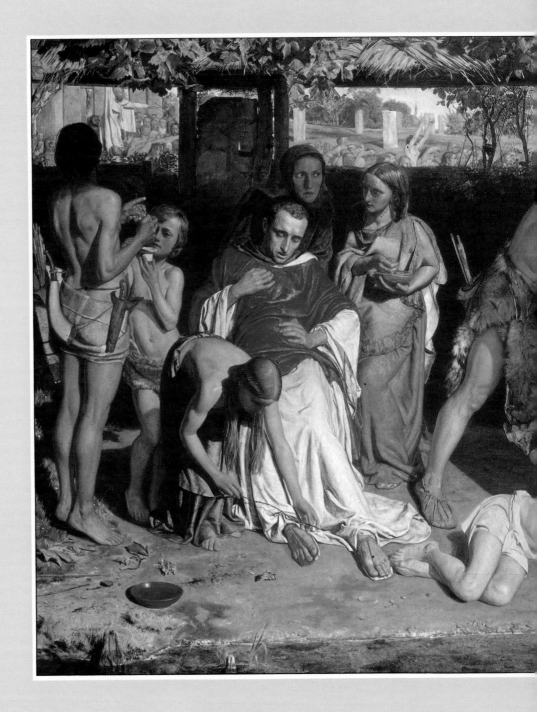

carries a tri-point, 'perfect each except the second of its points, to teach that Christ is not yet born'; the books represent the Virtues; the lamp – Piety; the lily symbolizes innocence and the vine pre-figures Christ's coming.

Other paintings in a similarly archaic, but invariably naturalistic style followed. John Everett Millais' *Isabella,* the first of his pictures to bear the insignia PRB, was taken from Keats' reworking of Boccaccio's account of the love affair between Lorenzo and Isabella from the *Decameron.* Millais painted the work in intricate detail and, in keeping with demands for historical accuracy, took the costume designs from recently published historical accounts of medieval Italian dress. Equally detailed is Millais' *Christ in the House of his Parents,* painted in 1849 and exhibited the following year at the Royal Academy. Pre-figurative symbols abound: among them nails, stigmata, baptismal bowls, sheep, doves and so on. Similar components are found within William Holman Hunt's *A Converted British Family Sheltering a Christian Missionary from the Persecution of the Druids* of 1850. The sheltered missionary serves as the figure of Christ, and the boy with the bowl to the left as John the Baptist; the water and bowl in the foreground again symbolize baptism, and the thorn and sponge held by the two young girls symbolize the Passion. The turn of mind of many Pre-Raphaelite painters of the period was such that in the search for a more meaningful 'heartfelt' style of painting to up-stage conventional academicism, the absence of symbolism became more remarkable than its presence – an arcane literary or religious backdrop was an invariable component of British Pre-Raphaelite painting.

Many of the characteristics of Pre-Raphaelite painting, its admiration for the sentiments of a medieval past, its tendency toward simplicity and its emphasis on individual, personal expression rather than established convention, began to find their way into crafts. The main catalyst in this process was the catholic interests of William Morris.

Morris came into contact with the Pre-Raphaelites in 1856, having read of the movement in *The Germ,* the Brotherhood's short-lived magazine, while at Oxford. Heavily under Rossetti's influence, and convinced that painting was the only proper medium to express one's disapproval of industrialism,

RIGHT Attic bedroom of William Morris's Kelmscott Manor, containing examples of green-stained furniture designed by Ford Madox Brown, c. 1861. In an attempt to unite the fine and applied arts, a number of Pre-Raphaelites tried their hand at a variety of crafts with varying degrees of success.

BELOW RIGHT Gothic sideboard designed by Philip Webb, c. 1862. Ebonized wood with painted and leather panels.

Morris and Burne-Jones set up a studio in Red Lion Square in London. Morris's abilities as a painter were somewhat limited (as his only extant oil painting, that of *Queen Guenevere*, indicates), and his interest in the medium was temporary. It was, however, around this period that Morris began designing some items of 'intensely medieval' furniture for the studio at Red Lion Square, and Pre-Raphaelite interest in art began to stray into other media. Several chairs and a table were made, together with an oak settle so large that Burne-Jones complained that it took up one-third of the studio. Rossetti decorated the panels on the settle with scenes depicting *Love between the Sun and the Moon* and *The Meeting of Dante and Beatrice in Florence*. More ambitious collaborative schemes soon followed when Morris moved from Red Lion Square into the Red House, near Bexleyheath in Kent.

LEFT **Queen Guenevere** *by William Morris, 1858.*

THE RED HOUSE

The Red House, one of the first examples of Arts and Crafts architecture, was completed for Morris and his new wife Jane Burden in 1860 by Philip Webb, a student of the architect George Edmond Street, to whom Morris had also once been articled. It was originally intended that the Red House be the home of a romantic community of artists and craftsmen, although the idea seems not to have been taken seriously by anyone other than Morris. The style of the house is very simple. The exterior is of the local plain red brick and is capped by a steeply pitched tile roof reminiscent of domestic Tudor buildings. The interior of the house is equally restrained. Consistent with the utilitarian Arts and Crafts aesthetic that no undue effort should be made to disguise materials or structure, the staircase was originally left unpanelled to render its structure visible, and the construction of the roof can be clearly seen from the rooms on the first floor. The general simplicity of the white-washed interior was offset by opulent pieces of furniture, painted glass, embroidery and fresco painting, collaboratively designed by one or more

of the artists and craftsmen associated with the Pre-Raphaelites. The furniture of the period echoed many of the features found in contemporary Pre-Raphaelite painting. Contemporary taste for refined machine-finished furniture was rejected and craftsmen used a heavy, rugged style reminiscent of the then unfashionable Tudor or Caroline periods. In some instances, such as the settle designed by Webb for the hall at the Red House, the furniture was very simple. In other examples, the furniture was decorated with minutely detailed painting. Other contributions to the house included

a variety of *métiers*, from furniture-making to fresco painting. The Pre-Raphaelite *oeuvre* and its 'Palace of Art' at the Red House had, as yet, only served to create a secluded community and a means of escape from Victorian social ills. Protected by Morris's independent income from mines in Cornwall, the painters and craftsmen and women active at the Red House were able to ignore the political revolutions throughout Europe. Like many romantics, Morris and Rossetti had expressed an aristocratic disdain for politics and current worldly events. Instead, their attention was focused on the design of an imaginary medieval world of chivalrous rather than practical values. The revolutionary spirit and desire for social change on which subsequent Arts and Crafts ventures were predicated had yet to appear in the works of Morris and his contemporaries. The desire to challenge rather than avoid the horrors of industrialism was, however, beginning to emerge and was among the ideals of the 'Fine Art Workmen' active in Morris, Marshall, Faulkner and Co.

Burne-Jones' painted glass designs in the long gallery and wall paintings in the drawing room. The ceiling contained decorations by Jane and William Morris and the former had embroidered hangings for the walls. Rossetti painted scenes from Dante's *Divine Comedy* on some items of furniture and contributed fragments to the painted ceiling.

The work produced by Morris and his associates, although original and very impressive, was, at this stage, still very romantic. The Pre-Raphaelites had tilted at Victorian convention, and their distaste for prevailing aesthetic standards found expression in

While the first ventures in Arts and Crafts were being undertaken at the Red House, another community of painters inspired by Ruskin's example was forming in the United States, a society called the Association for the Advancement of Truth in Art. The Association, often overlooked in accounts of Pre-Raphaelite painting, is interesting as it anticipates the direction of the Arts and Crafts Movement in the United States, a direction based not upon the medievalism of the British Arts and Crafts Movement, but rather on the search for an independent aesthetic conducive to American geography, culture and ideology. *The New Path*, the Association's journal, clarified some of these intentions in its first issue of 1861. Its opening statement read:

The future of art in America is not without hope . . . . The artists are nearly all young men; they are not hampered by too many traditions, and they enjoy almost inestimable advantage of having no past, no masters and no schools. Add that they work for an unsophisticated and, as far as art is concerned, uneducated public, which whatever else may stand in the way, will not be prevented by any prejudice or pre-conceived notions from accepting any really good work which may be set before it!

The Association had been founded on Ruskinian principles and modelled itself on the British Brotherhood. Although medieval subject matter did not really appeal to artists 'with no past', the notion that Nature rather than old academic tradition (and in this instance old European academic tradition) should serve as the prime source of inspiration in art had a strong appeal for artists searching for a cultural identity of their own.

The Association was established through a series of meetings around 1863, along lines similar to its British counterpart. Many of the painters and critics who were connected with the Association had long been aware of the Pre-Raphaelites through a magazine entitled *The Crayon,* published between 1855 and 1863. The magazine carried articles on Pre-Raphaelite painting and contained extracts of articles by Ruskin, already known in the United States for two enthusiastically received works, *Modern Painters* and *Elements of Drawing.*

The Association was established under the direction of Charles Farrer, a painter educated, in part, by Ruskin and Rossetti at the Working Men's College in London. It was Farrer who established a committee and the Association's articles. In essence, the Association was to be a fraternity dedicated to educating American artists and their public. Like its British counterpart, members of the Association were often declamatory and stridently anti-establishment. Its professed aim was to generate an air of dissatisfaction with the American art establishment and the academic theories to which it subscribed. Academic painters and sculptors were frequently subjected to savage criticism in *The New Path*. For example, the works of Thomas Cole, a painter of genteel landscapes in the English picturesque tradition and a pillar of the academic establishment, were dubbed as not being worth the canvas they were painted on. Cole was violently censured for his dependence on an out-

moded and alien tradition. Contrasted against the works of Cole and his peers were the intensely naturalistic pictures of Henry Hills; Charles Moore, Jonathan Sturgis, Farrer and a group of artists and critics that by the end of 1863 was to number well over 20. Hills' 1863 study, *Buttermilk Falls*, consistent with Ruskin's demands, selects and rejects nothing. Whereas more conventional American painters, like their European counterparts, sought to give general impressions of a landscape, Hills painted in such detail that it was possible to identify the geology of a landscape through the factual detail in the painted rock. No one particular part of Hills' pictures ever assumes importance. Painters connected with the Association invariably worked in an almost mechanical fashion, thereby giving each component the most minute attention.

Farrer's *Gone Gone* epitomizes an equally naturalistic but more anecdotal facet of American Pre-Raphaelite-inspired painting. The picture was painted in 1860 but appears originally to have escaped the notice of the press. It was brought to public attention several years later by the critic Clarence Cook, a staunch supporter of the Association and its work. Unlike its British equivalents, such as Millais' *A Huguenot on the Eve of St. Bartholomew's Day* – a print of which appears in the corner of Farrer's painting – *Gone Gone* is not extracted directly from a known literary source or historical event. The painting only alludes to some loss or tragic parting. Symbolism, again, abounds, with images of loss or death such as autumn leaves, the setting sun, and an extract from the Gospel according to St Matthew.

The Association lost much of its impetus by the late 1860s, although individual painters continued to work along similar lines. Clarence Cook, who had hitherto supported the Association, stated that he considered the achievements of Farrer and his contemporaries to be limited and that their painting, although superficially impressive, lacked real depth. By this time *The New Path* had ceased publication and artists connected with the Association failed to show works at the American Watercolor Society, a venue it had helped to establish. It eventually disbanded and Farrer and Moore left for Europe.

The achievements of the Association for the Advancement of Truth in Art were limited. Unlike the Pre-Raphaelite movement in Britain, it did not act as a springboard for a wealth of further developments in the arts and crafts. However, the advent of an American response to Ruskin's theories lends weight to the existence of a gradually evolving nationalistic artistic consciousness on which subsequent Arts and Crafts ventures were nurtured.

BELOW LEFT Wall cabinet designed by Philip Webb, c. 1861– 62, and painted with scenes from the life of St George by William Morris.

MORRIS AND CO.

Christ Suffering the Little Children, *designed by Edward Burne-Jones in 1862 in collaboration with the firm of Morris, Marshall, Faulkner and Co., for the Church of All Saints, Selsley, Gloucestershire.*

The firm of Morris, Marshall, Faulkner and Co. was established in April 1861. The company was of unparalleled importance in the Arts and Crafts Movement and established theoretical and practical precedents that were followed by similar communities in Europe and the United States. The beginnings of Morris, Marshall, Faulkner and Co., however, were rather uncertain. Rossetti, one of the founder members of the firm, recounted some years later that the idea of this business venture began as little more than a joke. A discussion began among some of the painters and architects who had designed and decorated the Red House regarding the way in which artists of the Middle Ages undertook not only painting and sculpture but also many other *métiers*. A small sum of money was raised as capital and Rossetti, Madox Brown, Burne-Jones, Webb, P.P. Marshall, C.J. Faulkner and Morris decided to establish their own community of 'fine art workmen'. Faulkner was to be the firm's bookkeeper and Morris, the only member with sufficient time and money to devote himself entirely to the company, was elected manager. The firm's prospectus declared its intentions. Diversely working in stained glass, mural decoration, carving, metalwork, furniture and embroidery, Morris, Marshall, Faulkner and Company lent its weight to the reform of the decorative arts in England.

Morris was later to explain the importance of the decorative or 'Lesser Arts' in a lecture given to the Trades Guild of Learning in 1877. He maintained that it was only comparatively recently that these 'lesser' decorative arts had become divorced from the fine arts of painting and sculpture. The division between these two forms of creative labour had, he maintained, served to trivialize the decorative arts and reduce the finer arts of painting and sculpture to a 'dull adjunct to unmeaning pomp'. The decorative arts, properly reconstituted according to old medieval traditions, had a noble calling. They were, for Morris, akin to a democratic, popular art. 'Our subject', he wrote, 'is that great body of art, by means of which men have at all times striven to beautify the familiar matters of everyday life'.

Morris described decorative art historically as a natural form of human feeling and expression, as an 'art of the unconscious intelli-

LEFT A Scene from the Annunciation *by Edward Burne-Jones, 1860, for St Columba's Church, Topcliffe, Yorkshire.*

gence'. 'Everything', he wrote, 'made by man's hand has a form which must be either beautiful or ugly'. If the craftsman or woman follows the example of Nature on his or her design, the result, Morris maintained, will necessarily be beautiful. If Nature's example is ignored, the product will turn out to be ugly. Morris neatly described beautiful decoration as an 'alliance with nature'. The craftsman or woman must work in the way that Nature does 'till the web, the cup or the knife, look as natural, nay as lovely, as the green field, the river bank, or the mountain flint'.

The decorative arts had a formidable opponent in the philistinism of the Victorian middle classes. Since the Great Exhibition of 1851, which, incidently, the young Morris refused to visit, English taste had been dominated by an eclectic style not dissimilar to the bourgeois taste prevalent in the United States. The furniture of the period was absurdly decorative, with gilt, veneers, and marble used at every opportunity. Moreover, such goods were invariably machine-made and often of very poor quality. For Morris, the source of this 'design debauchery' (as Walter Crane was later to describe Victorian taste) was twofold. Firstly, ill-educated and penny-pinching consumers were anxious to get sumptuous furniture at the lowest possible price. This in turn provided a ready market that avaricious manufacturers were only too eager to supply. Using the ingenuity of machine production and the aesthetics of the counting-house, Britain therefore turned out a constant supply of goods of dubious quality and even more dubious taste. The mission of the handicraftsman was a formidable one: to educate and reform public taste and also to reform the means of production and consumption. This socialist aesthetic is neatly summarized in *The Lesser Arts*, in which Morris wrote:

To give people pleasure in the things they must perforce *use,* that is one great office of decoration; to give people pleasure in the things they must perforce *make,* that is the other use of it.

Several of the design projects of Morris, Marshall, Faulkner and Co. well illustrated this statement, especially the joint endeavours involving their own domiciles that were undertaken by the firm's principals and assorted friends and relatives.

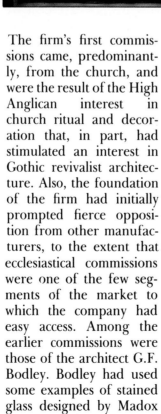

The firm's first commissions came, predominantly, from the church, and were the result of the High Anglican interest in church ritual and decoration that, in part, had stimulated an interest in Gothic revivalist architecture. Also, the foundation of the firm had initially prompted fierce opposition from other manufacturers, to the extent that ecclesiastical commissions were one of the few segments of the market to which the company had easy access. Among the earlier commissions were those of the architect G.F. Bodley. Bodley had used some examples of stained glass designed by Madox Brown, Burne-Jones and Rossetti for his newly built churches of St Michael's, Brighton, E. Sussex; All Saints, Selsley, Gloucestershire; St Martin's on the Hill, Scarborough, Yorkshire, and All Saints in Cambridge. Messrs Morris and Co. had also decorated other parts of the interior of St Martin's, contributing a painted mural and two painted panels on the pulpit. Other ecclesiastical commissions followed, among them Madox Brown's work for St Oswald's Church, Durham, and one of the few examples of stained glass by Morris himself – a figure of St Paul, for the Church of St Giles in Camberwell, London.

FAR LEFT Stained-glass window depicting *Miriam, the sister of Moses and Aaron, by Edward Burne-Jones, 1872.*

CENTRE LEFT Part of a scene depicting the Flight into Egypt, *designed by Edward Burne-Jones in collaboration with Morris and Co., for St Michael's Church in Brighton.*

LEFT Detail of Flight into Egypt *by Edward Burne-Jones, St Michael's Church, Brighton.*

FAR LEFT, BELOW Stained-glass window showing King David, from a design by William Morris.

BELOW Scenes from the Life of Christ *by Burne-Jones and Morris, 1864.*

One of the company's first secular commissions was the decoration of a massive cabinet to the design of the architect J. P. Seddon. Madox Brown, Rossetti and Burne-Jones collaborated on the decoration for the cabinet: an allegory of the arts in the form of a series of scenes from the honeymoon of King René of Anjou. Around this period Philip Webb designed several pieces of similarly elaborate furniture. Characteristic of the firm's early style was the ebonized and painted sideboard with illuminated panels that had been included in the company's catalogue of 1862. Experiments in other media followed. A series of designs for wallpapers was produced and printed. Morris initially attempted to expand the technique of printing and master the craft himself, although difficulties occurred and the work was sent to an independent contractor. In 1864 Webb had helped to design some of the wallpapers.

'Trellis', an early design inspired by the garden at the Red House, contains a climbing rose, a trellis and a bird by Webb. Morris's wallpaper design 'Daisy', produced in the same year, was inspired by a French illuminated manuscript and was also used both as a design for a piece of embroidery and ceramic tiles. Several other artists and designers had contributed some ceramic designs on plain tiles imported from the Netherlands, among them Rossetti, Burne-Jones, Brown, Kate and Lucy Faulkner and, not least, William De Morgan. Jane Morris and her sister Elizabeth Burden had also supervised the production of embroidered cloth and silk, one of the few skills undertaken by women employees.

The fortunes of the company were at first precarious. J.W. Mackail, Morris's biographer, mentioned that the firm failed to make any substantial profits during its first years. Its fortunes changed, however, after the International Exhibition of 1862, to which the company contributed specimens of glass, ironwork, embroidery and furniture. Important secular commissions to decorate the Dining Room at the South Kensington Museum (now the Victoria and Albert Museum) and the Tapestry and Armoury Room at St James's Palace followed the exhibition, after which the firm seems to have prospered.

The majority of the company's earlier work was expensive. The South Kensington

RIGHT *Oak cabinet designed by J. P. Seddon and decorated with scenes from the honeymoon of King René of Anjou by Madox Brown, Burne-Jones, Morris and Rossetti, 1862.*

BELOW RIGHT *The William Morris Room in the Victoria and Albert Museum, London. The windows are by Burne-Jones; the screen by Jane and William Morris; the piano's gesso work by Kate Faulkner, and the walls by Philip Webb.*

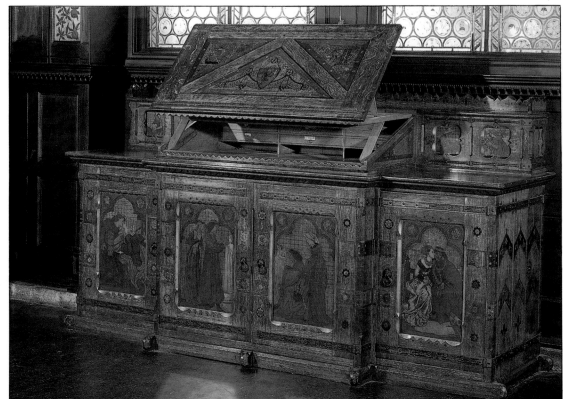

Museum had complained about the cost of the Green Dining Room and other observers had noted that 'it required a long purse to live up to the higher phases of Morrisean taste'. In addition to the opulently decorated settles and wardrobes produced by Webb and Burne-Jones, there were attempts to produce for those of more modest means. Madox Brown produced some items of simply made 'artisan' furniture, objects of straightforward utility with virtually no decoration whatsoever. Some of these items were, in fact, produced before the foundation of the firm. However, the most famous example of the simpler form of furniture produced by Morris and Co. was the 'Sussex' range of chairs. This 'Good Citizen's' furniture, as it was also known, was based on vernacular designs of country furniture that dated back to the 18th century. The Sussex range was very much cheaper than many of the company's other products, costing from seven to thirty-five shillings, and was certainly within the pockets of the middle classes. It is interesting to observe, however, that the Sussex range, contrary to the ethos of the Arts and Crafts Movement, was produced using some very sophisticated techniques: the wood used for the furniture, for instance, was ebonized, a technique used in 19th-century furniture production to disguise cheap materials.

In 1874 Morris began some of his first experiments in dyeing silk and woollen yarns for embroidery. In keeping with the best Arts and Crafts traditions, the dyestuffs came from natural sources such as indigo, cochineal and madder, the latter a dye with unusual chemical properties rendering it difficult to use with consistency and precision. The first of the famous 'Marigold' designs, printed in madder by Thomas Wardle, followed in 1875. Under Wardle's supervision, Morris tried his hand at the craft during the following year, having researched traditional dyeing methods from old French and English technical manuals. It was around this period that Morris also began to

experiment with woven textiles and carpets. A French weaver helped set up a Jacquard loom and Morris began research into the tapestry collection at the South Kensington Museum. His designs were often taken from early Renaissance needlework, with Morris expressing a characteristic dislike of the more sophisticated patterns and techniques of the 17th and 18th centuries.

In 1874 the firm was reorganized under Morris's sole direction. In recent years the company had prospered and began to influence the work of its competitors. Showrooms for its products were opened in 1877 in Oxford Street and the company had also expanded its interests to incorporate commercial weaving, dyeing and printing with its other activities. In 1881 attempts were made to find more spacious premises to accommodate all of the firm's work under one roof. Morris had initially favoured the conversion of a picturesque disused mill near his country home Kelmscott Manor, Oxfordshire, although its distance from London made it economically less viable than the premises at Merton Abbey, Surrey, only seven miles from the centre of the capital.

LEFT Chair produced by Morris and Co. in ebonized wood with original woollen tapestry with bird motif. Chairs of this design were widely copied both in England and the United States.

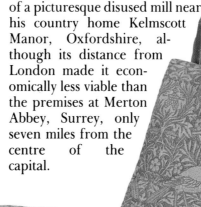

*RIGHT 'Trellis'
wallpaper designed by
Morris and Webb; first
produced in 1862.*

Production began at Merton Abbey at the end of 1881 and marked the beginning of one of the firm's most prolific periods. A variety of chintz patterns was produced with the use of old printing techniques. In addition, a series of tapestries was made at the Abbey. Morris had especially trained three young assistants, finding that small fingers were better suited to the craft, and purposely selected average rather than gifted recruits on the Ruskinian premise that creative ability was latent in any intelligent worker. A variety of artists and designers collaborated on the tapestries: the painter and illustrator. Walter Crane designed 'Goose Girl' in 1883; Morris, with the assistance of Webb, designed the 'Woodpecker' and 'Forest' tapestries, and Burne-Jones was instrumental in the design of a series on the subject of the Holy Grail for Webb's Standen Hall, in W. Sussex. William De Morgan worked, albeit temporarily, at Merton Abbey producing ceramic tiles, and stained-glass designs were undertaken with the proviso that the firm would only accept contracts working for newly built churches. Morris had recently been instrumental in founding the Society for the Pro-

tection of Ancient Buildings, an organization that had successfully prevented the restoration or demolition of a number of famous buildings, from Canterbury Cathedral to San Marco in Venice. The Society demanded that the restoration of ancient monuments be undertaken with the minimum of alteration to the existing fabric. Morris's firm, consequently, declined any offer to contribute modern additions to old buildings; the last recorded stained-glass contract for anything other than a comparatively recent example of church architecture, according to Philip Henderson's monograph on Morris, was Burne-Jones' work at Salisbury Cathedral in 1878.

The working conditions at Merton Abbey described by a number of contemporary observers were nothing short of idyllic. The accommodation was light and spacious and set in the countryside beside the river Wandle. Like the craftsmen and women of the Middle Ages, Morris's workers were, according to one observer, free to interpret and add their own personality to many of the designs. Men were involved in the production of most crafts save carpets, which were hand-made by women at

CHAPTER THREE
■

LEFT 'Michaelmas Daisy' wallpaper designed by Morris and Co., first produced in 1912.

Both illustrations show an armchair from the 'Sussex' range by Morris and Co.

the cost to the customer of no less than four guineas per square yard. Morris's workers apparently went unhurriedly about their respective crafts, striving, unlike similar industries in Victorian society, for standards of excellence and beauty rather than quantity.

By the end of the 1880s, Morris and Co. had become something of a nursery for the Arts and Crafts Movement, with many of its artists and craftsmen going on to work independently or to form guilds or associations inspired by Morris's aesthetic and social ideals. Walter Crane, for example, carried out designs for Morris and in 1883 joined the Socialist League and was instrumental in the founding of the Art Workers' Guild. Also active in the Guild was W.A.S. Benson, a designer, metalworker and director of Morris and Co. George Jack, the American-born architect and designer responsible for some of the more sophisticated mahogany furniture produced by the firm in the 1880s, later succeeded Webb in his archi-

LEFT The Orchard, *left-hand fragment of high-warp tapestry by William Morris and J.H. Dearle, c. 1890.*

BELOW LEFT Painting of the pond at Merton Abbey, Surrey, by Lexdon Lewis Pocock (1850–1919). Morris signed the lease for the converted print works 7 June 1881, and thereafter it was a centre for much of his company's work.

tectural practice. Arthur Heygate Mackmurdo's Century Guild, established in 1882, was inspired by the examples of Morris and Ruskin, as was the architect and designer Ernest Gimson. However, the 1880s, the period during which the firm was commercially most successful, also marks an important shift in Morris's opinion on the value of the Arts and Crafts. His interest in the Utopian ideals of the ever-expanding ranks of artists and craftsmen had begun to vacillate. When, for example, T.J. Cobden-Sanderson, a disaffected lawyer eager to work with his hands, entertained the idea of taking up bookbinding at Jane Morris's suggestion, the surprised lawyer found Morris scathing about the purpose of some Utopian guilds of printers dedicated to the production of beautiful books.

The firm had originally been established as an antidote to and buttress against the shoddy philistinism of the upper and middle classes, yet, decades after its foundation, little had visibly changed in Victorian society. Morris and Co. may have been commercially successful, yet the 'holy crusade' waged against the age was far from won. Industrial society continued to produce shoddy goods and had perversely warmed to, and imitated, Morris's work, often with the aid of machinery. His patrons, moreover, ironically came from that section of society that had some responsibility for perpetuating the social conditions he so hated, for good design made under humane and fulfilling working conditions was – as critics had already noted – nothing if not expensive. Morris eventually realized that the capacity of the arts alone to challenge industrial society was severely limited, and so his attitude to the other ventures in the arts and crafts that imitated his example (among them Cobden-Sanderson's 'Dove Press') became, at times, less than enthusiastic. Morris, it appears, still strongly upheld the principles that formed the bedrock of the Arts and Crafts Movement. Beautiful, often simple, handmade objects were invariably preferable to anything that profit-mongering, industrial capitalism could offer, yet Morris continued to nurse the nagging doubt that art on its own was merely a palliative. Writing to Georgiana Burne-Jones in 1882, Morris described the bulk of his efforts as nothing but make-believe. Action was therefore required in a sphere outside the

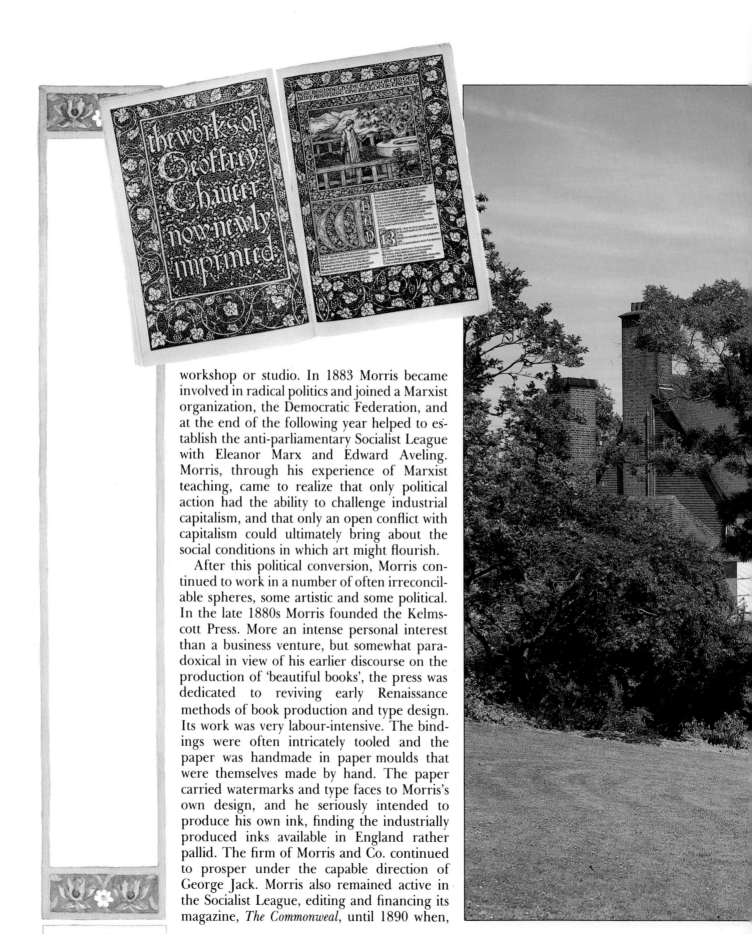

workshop or studio. In 1883 Morris became involved in radical politics and joined a Marxist organization, the Democratic Federation, and at the end of the following year helped to establish the anti-parliamentary Socialist League with Eleanor Marx and Edward Aveling. Morris, through his experience of Marxist teaching, came to realize that only political action had the ability to challenge industrial capitalism, and that only an open conflict with capitalism could ultimately bring about the social conditions in which art might flourish.

After this political conversion, Morris continued to work in a number of often irreconcilable spheres, some artistic and some political. In the late 1880s Morris founded the Kelmscott Press. More an intense personal interest than a business venture, but somewhat paradoxical in view of his earlier discourse on the production of 'beautiful books', the press was dedicated to reviving early Renaissance methods of book production and type design. Its work was very labour-intensive. The bindings were often intricately tooled and the paper was handmade in paper moulds that were themselves made by hand. The paper carried watermarks and type faces to Morris's own design, and he seriously intended to produce his own ink, finding the industrially produced inks available in England rather pallid. The firm of Morris and Co. continued to prosper under the capable direction of George Jack. Morris also remained active in the Socialist League, editing and financing its magazine, *The Commonweal*, until 1890 when,

FAR LEFT The title page and first page of The Works of Geoffrey Chaucer, *printed by Morris's Kelmscott Press in 1896. Known as* The Kelmscott Chaucer, *the book was hand-printed in red and black and bound in pigskin.*

LEFT Standen, near East Grinstead, Sussex. Designed by Philip Webb in 1892 for James Beale, a London solicitor. The house contains works by Morris, W.A.S. Benson and George Jack, together with a number of other employees of Morris and Co.

after a schism with an anarchist faction, he established the Hammersmith Socialist Society. He also continued to write poetry and prose. During this period he wrote *News from Nowhere,* the novel that elaborated precisely the revolutionary society to which Morris had aspired in his art and politics.

Morris died in 1896, having made a vast contribution to the practical and intellectual development of the principles of the Arts and Crafts Movement. In fact, so substantial was Morris's contribution, that his progression from the romanticism of the 1860s to his revolutionary opinions of the late 1880s and 1890s pointed to many of the contradictions that subsequent artists and craftsmen were to face in the 19th and 20th centuries. Long after Morris, many craftsmen and women continued to nurse the romantic hope that art still had the ability to challenge the *bête noire* of capitalist industry. Morris, however, had clearly demonstrated that the conditions necessary to create a wholesome and popular art, craft and architecture demanded the overthrow of industrial society. It is no accident that in *News from Nowhere* the Utopian simplicity to which he had aspired was achieved only after a violent revolution.

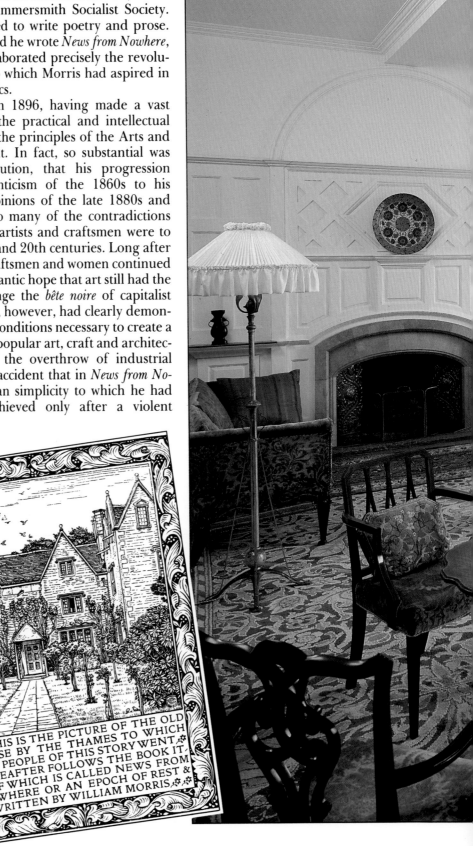

■

*LEFT The Drawing
Room at Standen.
The chair with cushion
in the foreground is by
Morris and Co., as are
the hand-knotted carpet
and the wallpaper. The
lighting fixtures are by
Webb and Benson.*

*RIGHT The Morning
Room at Standen.
The table in the
foreground is by Webb;
the wallhangings are in
'Daffodil' chintz by
Morris and Co.*

LEFT First page from William Morris's Utopian novel, News from Nowhere.

CENTRE LEFT A gathering of the Hammersmith Socialist League of 1889. The league was later reconstituted into the Hammersmith Socialist Society, whose object was 'the spreading of the principles of Socialism, especially by Lectures, Street meetings, and Publications . . . and that object only'.

BELOW LEFT Escritoire and stand by George Jack for Morris and Co., 1893.

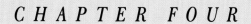

C H A P T E R   F O U R

THE CRAFT GUILD IN BRITAIN

Design by William Burges for St Mary's, Aldford-cum-Studley,
Yorkshire, c. 1872. Watercolour by Axel Naig.

RIGHT Earthenware painted dish with peacock motif by William De Morgan.

In the decades following the foundation of Morris and Co., a number of craft guilds were created in Britain, the majority by young architects from established practices, eager to revive craft traditions and to reconcile architecture with the decorative arts. They all insisted upon the dignity of work, and those such as Crane and Ashbee mobilized socialism to render labour as a predicate upon which not only healthy and beautiful art was based but also a healthier and more wholesome society. As before, all those involved insisted upon the dignity of work. Ruskin was among the first to try his hand at one such Utopian guild community. However, his Utopia was based not so much upon socialism but upon the romanticized feudalism discussed above. Despite his importance to the Arts and Crafts Movement, Ruskin's efforts to challenge in the form of the paternalistic Guild of St George were by far the most impractical and unsuccessful of the cluster of communities that developed in the wake of Morris and Co.

The foundation of Ruskin's Guild was announced in the eighth of a series of letters written 'to the Workmen and Labourers of Great Britain', the *Fors Clavigera* of May and August 1871. The community was to appeal to 'all holy and humble men of heart' sufficiently

disillusioned with the state of society to help establish an alternative. The alternative proposed by Ruskin was very far removed from the socialism of Morris. The Guild was to be an authoritarian community with Ruskin as its master, below whom came the Guild's three social orders: the *comites ministrantes*, companion servants or administrators; *comites militantes*, or labourers, and finally *comites consilii*, friends active in the world outside, making donations of one-tenth of their income to the Guild. In theory, however, the Guild was to sustain itself by working the land, notably without the aid of steam machinery. The eight clauses of the Guild's charter demanded, first, a love of God. The love of any god was sufficient: the community accommodated all faiths and excluded only atheists. Other demands included a love of one's country and one's fellow man; a respect for labour, beauty and beasts. Ruskin also made a list of appropriate reading material to be included in all of the Guild's homes and aimed to establish a museum. The achievements of the Guild, despite Ruskin's persistent efforts, were modest. He had initially hoped that his pseudo-feudal communities would spread throughout England and beyond. In fact, they were established only near Sheffield, in Barmouth in Wales, and on the Isle of Man.

*LEFT A series of
underglazed
earthenware tiles by
William De Morgan.*

THE CENTURY GUILD

Inspired by the example of Ruskin, Arthur Heygate Mackmurdo's Century Guild was infinitely more successful than that of his mentor. A pupil in Ruskin's Oxford drawing class and a companion on his visits to Italy, Mackmurdo established the Guild on the advice of his teacher in 1882. In the following year the Century Guild's workshops were opened in partnership with another of Ruskin's associates, Selwyn Image. Image, a former curate, worked in several media, including graphic design (he designed the title page for the Century Guild's magazine, *The Hobby Horse*), embroidery and stained glass. Other members of the Guild included the potter William De Morgan, the designer Heywood Sumner, the sculptor Benjamin Creswick, the textile designer and metalworker H.P. Horne, and the metalworker Clement Heaton. Mackmurdo had trained as an architect but had, in addition, attempted to learn several crafts himself, trying his hand at brasswork, embroidery and cabinetmaking. The purpose of the Century Guild was to accommodate craftsmen active in a number of *métiers* and unite the traditionally separate disciplines of architecture, interior design and decoration.

Whereas Morris had attempted to level the disciplines of painting and sculpture to the rank of democratic handicrafts, Mackmurdo's Century Guild aimed to raise the status of crafts such as building, fabric design, pottery, and metalworking in order that they might take their place alongside the professionally respectable 'fine' arts.

The work of Mackmurdo and the Century Guild tended to be more stylistically eclectic than that of Morris and Co., although it aspired to the same ideal of artists, architects and designers co-operatively undertaking the design of a home and its contents. Unlike the many medievalists associated with the Arts and Crafts, Mackmurdo admired Italian Renaissance and even Baroque architecture, and used the styles in his designs for several houses, including his own, Great Ruffins, in Essex. The furniture produced by the Guild was equally eclectic, ranging from the restrained and utilitarian to a style of decoration that anticipated the asymmetrical arabesques of the Aesthetic Movement and Art Nouveau. In fact, Mackmurdo associated with artists and literary figures connected with the cult of Aestheticism, artists of a quite different persuasion to many of those active in the craft guilds. Mackmurdo was an associate of J.A.M. Whistler and Oscar Wilde, both of whom had insisted upon the autonomy of the arts, that painting and design could be produced entirely for their own sake and need make no concession to social utility or the concerns of the audience. The party line among the crafts fraternity, by contrast, was often centred upon the social mission of art and its role to rescue the world from the ugliness of industry and capitalism. The catholic interests of the Century Guild and its ability to reconcile artists, architects and designers of a variety of persuasions, are evident in the contributors to *The Hobby Horse*. Editions of the Guild's magazine during its first years included contributions from Ruskin, Wilde, Rossetti, Paul Verlaine, Matthew Arnold, Herbert Gilchrist, W.S. Blunt, Selwyn Image and May Morris, covering items on art, literature and music.

BELOW Great Ruffins, Wickham Bishops, Essex, by Arthur Heygate Mackmurdo, c. 1904.
Mackmurdo, unlike other architects associated with the Arts and Crafts Movement, often admitted Renaissance, or in this instance Baroque, motifs into his building. Such sophisticated styles were anathema to William Morris.

RIGHT Frontispiece to Wren's City Churches *by A.H. Mackmurdo, 1883.*

FAR RIGHT Frontispiece for the Century Guild's magazine, The Hobby Horse.

BELOW RIGHT Oak writing desk by A.H. Mackmurdo, c. 1886.

■

*RIGHT Church of All
Saints, Leek,
Staffordshire, by
Gerald Horsley. Pen
and watercolour,
1891.*

The Century Guild was eventually dissolved in 1888. Although financially successful, many members of the Guild had pursued their own various interests. Horne, for example, continued his architectural practice and retired to Florence in 1900 to work as an art historian. Selwyn Image undertook independent work in several media, among them stained glass, typography, embroidery and mosaic, and Clement Heaton established his own business producing cloisonné enamel, later working in Europe and eventually settling in the United States. Mackmurdo continued his work as an architect and, like others in the Arts and Crafts Movement, strayed from work connected with the material fabric of society, its art, architecture and so on, to more theoretical concerns, in this instance monetary theory and sociology.

Selwyn Image, the co-founder of the Century Guild, was later active in another fraternity, the Art Workers' Guild. The Guild was established in 1884 and was, in part, formed from a group of young architects employed in the architect Richard Norman Shaw's practice, among them William Richard Lethaby – Shaw's chief clerk, Gerald Horsley, Ernest Newton, E.S. Prior and Mervyn Macartney. Encouraged by Shaw, his assistants were, like their counterparts in the Century Guild, interested in raising the status of the applied arts and breaching the division of labour that separated them from institutionalized notions of architecture and the fine arts of painting and sculpture that prevailed in the Royal Academy and at the Royal Institute of British Architects. In 1884 Shaw's assistants merged with a group of writers, designers and theorists known as 'The Fifteen', led by Lewis Forman Day. The Guild also included Walter Crane, John Sedding and Henry Holiday. The Art Workers' Guild shared most of the concerns of other Arts and Crafts ventures: it sought a handcrafted, well-designed environment in which artists, architects and craftsmen would assume collective responsibility for buildings and their contents. It is, however, difficult to discern within the Guild any clear sense of social purpose. The conspicuous radicalism that motivated the work of, say, Morris, is absent in the Art Workers' Guild. The Guild seems to have kept a deliberately low profile. It avoided controversy and in 1889 declared itself against 'public action', preferring, it seems, to influence the artistic establishment by stealth, for many of those active in the Guild were, over the next decade, to play prominent roles in art schools and public administration.

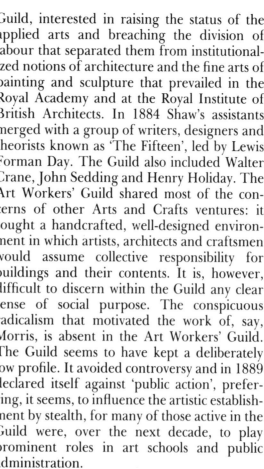

CHAPTER FOUR
■

LEFT St Osmund's Church, Poole, Dorset, by E.S. Prior.

*RIGHT Perspective
drawing of Ernest
Newton's Fouracre at
West Green,
Hampshire, by Thomas
Hamilton Crawford,
1902.*

The Guild's reticence to maintain a public presence led in 1888 to the foundation of the affiliated but more militant Arts and Crafts Exhibition Society. The first members of the Society had been active either in the Art Workers' Guild or in business and were well known in the Arts and Crafts milieu. Crane, Webb, Benson, Cobden-Sanderson, Day, Lethaby and De Morgan were prominent in the Society and its exhibition accommodated the work of other like-minded guilds and crafts fraternities. The Society's first exhibition, held in the New Gallery in 1888, contained contributions both from its own members, from the Century Guild, Morris and Co. and C.R. Ashbee's nascent Guild and School of Handicraft. William De Morgan, active within the Society until 1906, exhibited a substantial amount of ceramic work, inspired by Islamic pottery, and W.A.S. Benson's hand-crafted metalwork was also well represented. Benson was a fierce critic not only of capitalist methods of mechanized production but also the equally capitalist methods of distribution through the medium of high street stores. He had established his own workshop in 1880 on Morris's advice, producing household products such as teapots and kettles in an often

simple style with clear evidence of the craftsman's handiwork left on the product. Society exhibitions over the next two years included submissions from Lethaby and Ernest Gimson, who, with D.J. Blow, had established a small shop in Bloomsbury for the sale of their own furniture, plaster and metalwork. Walter Crane, a regular exhibitor in a variety of media, re-asserted the radical calling of Arts and Crafts by exhibiting an Irish Nationalist Banner of his own design, and the Keswick School of Industrial Art submitted some characteristically simple examples of metalwork. In addition to providing a platform to exhibit a wide spectrum of crafts from an ever-expanding body of artisans, the Society's exhibitions also afforded the opportunity for theoretical discussions and practical demonstrations in a variety of crafts, including printing, bookbinding, design and tapestry weaving.

The Arts and Crafts Exhibition Society exhibited annually for the first three years. Thereafter it exhibited every three years. The quality of many of the submissions – particularly those by the London stores and the plethora of provincial guild fraternities and sororities that had been formed in the wake of Arts and Crafts ventures – was often poor. The

LEFT **Sleeping Beauty** *wallpaper designed by Walter Crane.*

Society was, however, enormously influential in providing a platform for the exhibition of progressive design of a variety of aesthetic persuasions.

A more aggressively rustic style of furniture reminiscent of some of the first sorties into crafts made by the Pre-Raphaelites was evolved by Ernest Gimson and Sidney and Ernest Barnsley. Together with William Richard Lethaby, Reginald Blomfield and Mervyn Macartney, Gimson and Sidney Barnsley founded Kenton and Co. in 1890. The firm, which traded for less than two years, employed professional cabinetmakers to produce furniture to the designs of its founders, with each product carrying the initials of its maker. The style of Kenton and Co.'s work varies, although there is a marked return to some of the more simple and elegantly proportioned styles of the 18th century. After the company closed in 1892, Ernest Gimson, together with Sidney and Ernest Barnsley, moved to the Cotswolds, the first of many artists and craftsmen to settle in the district. The furniture designed around this period was unpretentious both in design and construction. The joinery is deliberately left visible and decoration is reduced to a minimum, a style that seems to have exasperated contemporary trade journals. A similar vernacular style permeated the architecture designed and built by Gimson and the Barnsleys. In fact, at Stoneywell in Markfield, Leicestershire, Ernest Gimson virtually succeeded in making vernacular architecture an organic part of the natural landscape. Built from materials such as uncut local stone and thatch, the elevation of this cottage literally follows the incline of the site on which it is built, with its massive chimney appearing to rise out of the landscape. Interior joinery forming the staircase and roof is equally simple, as was the rustic furniture designed for the cottage.

Another guild later to take up residence in the English Cotswolds was Charles Robert Ashbee's Guild and School of Handicraft. The Guild evolved from a Ruskin reading class held at Toynbee Hall in the East End of London under the direction of Ashbee, a Cambridge graduate and an associate of Morris and H.M. Hyndman. Whereas much of the produce of Arts and Crafts in the 1880s and 1890s had become increasingly eclectic in style and inten-

tion, often employing highly refined standards of craftsmanship and, in some instances, mechanized production, Ashbee's Guild marked a distinct return to the Ruskinian and socialist principles that characterized the earlier work of the Arts and Crafts Movement. The product of one of the most lucid of the second generation of artists and craftsmen, Ashbee's declaration of the Arts and Crafts ideal is stirring stuff. In *Craftsmanship in Competitive Industry,* published in 1908, he stated:

The Arts and Crafts Movement ... assumes through its contact with the realities of life, an ethical significance of the greatest moment. It touches both producer and consumer alike, and so it touches everybody. It brings ... into modern industry a little of that Soul, that imaginative quality in which our civilisation is so lacking. It reminds us that the imaginative things are real things, and shows us that when they are expressed in man's handiwork, they must come into immediate contact with material actuality.
What I seek to show is that this Arts and Crafts movement, which began with the earnestness of the Pre-Raphaelite Painters, the prophetic enthusiasm of Ruskin and the Titanic energy of Morris is not what the public has thought it to be, or is seeking to make it: a nursery for luxuries, a hothouse for the production of mere trivialities and useless things for the rich. It is a movement for the stamping out of such things by sound production on the one hand, and the inevitable regulation of machine production and cheap labour on the other.

The shoddy practice of industrialized production had been stamped out on several fronts. Ashbee insisted that crafts should be self-taught, the skill of the craftsman gradually evolving as his familiarity with the medium increased. He deliberately recruited unskilled workers in preference to tradesmen, educating them through the Guild's classes. Labour within the Guild workshops was undivided, with each craftsman involved with the whole production process. There was an emphasis on handicraft – 'the winged spirit we want to embody', wrote Ashbee, 'flies away at the touch of a duplicating machine'. Moreover, Guild members were encouraged to work cooperatively, each one in appreciation of the strengths and weaknesses of his or her comrades. In 1898, when the Guild became financially stable, Ashbee limited the liability of the company and offered his employees representation on the company's newly formed board.

OPPOSITE Design for a dado by Walter Crane.

RIGHT The Magpie and Stump by C.R. Ashbee in Cheyne Walk, Chelsea, London. The design and decoration of the house attracted the attention of The Studio *magazine and of the German Hermann Muthesius, author of* Das Englische Haus.

OPPOSITE ABOVE Sketchbook design for a ladderback chair by Ernest Gimson.

OPPOSITE BELOW Ladderback chair in ash by Ernest Gimson, c. 1895.

He also started a scheme in which a percentage could be deducted from the wages of his employees to give them a financial interest in the Guild.

The work produced by the Guild was simple in design. Its metalwork, in the form of jewellery, cutlery, plates and vases, was often inspired by medieval sources, with the addition of semiprecious stones and modest decorative devices similar in appearance to Art Nouveau. Ashbee, however, disliked the association and saw a marked distinction between the high socialist and craft ideals of the Guild and the self-consciously artistic sensibilities of the Art Nouveau products that permeated fashionable high street stores. Equally simple was the furniture produced by the Guild. Cabinets were usually constructed from oak or walnut, with large masses of unadorned wood offset by decorative metal handles and hinges. In fact, a late example of the Guild's cabinetmaking, shown at the Arts and Crafts Exhibition of 1896, had virtually all of its surface decoration removed, a style that was increasingly to dominate turn-of-the-century design.

In 1902 the fortunes of the Guild and School of Handicraft changed after it moved from its workshops at Essex House in the East End of London to Chipping Campden in Gloucestershire. The countryside was a more appropriate setting for a craft fraternity and Ashbee established workshops in the run-down village with some 50 of his craftsmen and their families. He offered the residents of Chipping Campden – few of whom warmed to his overtures – classes in his Campden School of Arts and Crafts, a counterpart to the educational programme offered in London. The curriculum included lectures by Walter Crane, among others, and practical instruction in subjects such as needlework, gardening, physical education and starching laundry. By 1905 the Guild's finances were looking precarious, with the year's business returning a loss of almost one thousand pounds, a loss that was virtually doubled during the following year. A manager was appointed to run the business and attempts were made to raise capital from shareholders, but the company eventually went into voluntary liquidation. The reasons for the Guild's demise were thought to be various. In a letter to his shareholders, Ashbee partly attributed the Guild's downfall to its

58-59 CHEYNE WALK. CHELSEA : S.W.

C.R. ASHBEE · MA · ARCHITEC
MAGPIE & STUMP HOUSE : ES
37 CHEYNE WALK · CHELSE

location. Craftsmen were unable to find alternative work in the countryside when orders declined and the cost of operating a business remote from urban markets was prohibitive. The problems were further exacerbated by the mechanized techniques used by market competitors. The Arts and Crafts style had become very fashionable by the turn of the century, although few of those that exploited its appearance felt it necessary to apply the same high standards of workmanship. Ashbee, nonetheless, struck a defiant note in the letter written to shareholders in the company on the eve of its collapse, defending the ideals of the enterprise and its achievements.

From the financial point of view, the Guild and School of Handicraft had failed. In *Craftmanship and Competitive Industry*, Ashbee presented an astute interpretation of its failure. He wrote: 'and since it has definitely been shown that it is impractical to carry on the arts and crafts upon any large scale, under existing industrial conditions, we must set to and devise other ways in which the work we want to do can be done'. Not for the first time had well-intentioned socialist craftsmen met head on with the megalith of industrial capitalism.

The Guild and School of Handicraft had

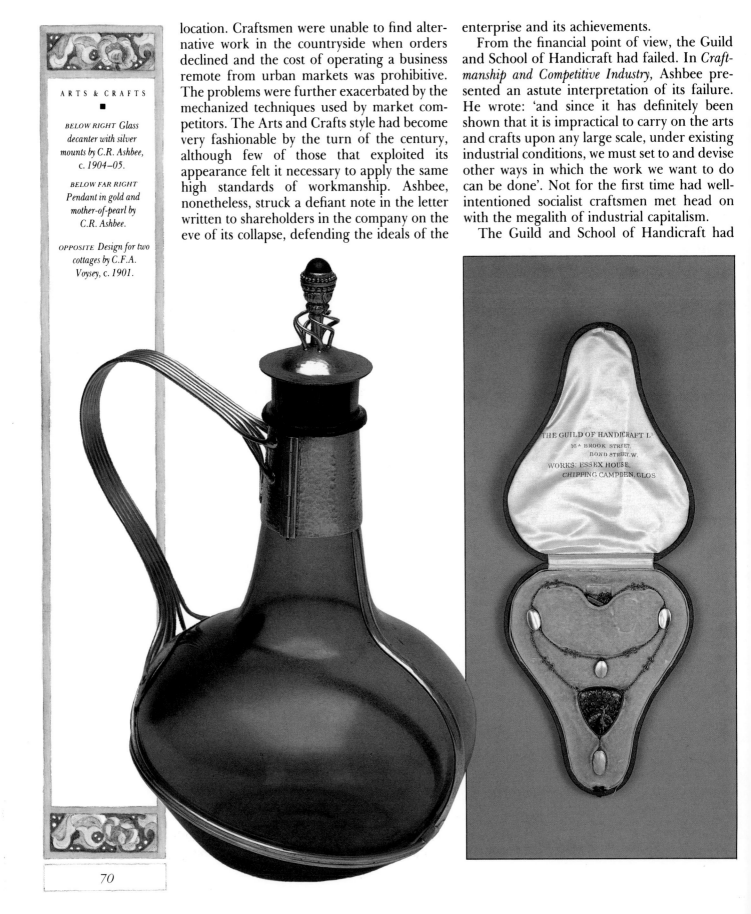

made various complaints against unfair competition, be it from mechanized industry or amateur sororities undercutting the Guild by failing to charge for their labour. Guilds such as those of Ashbee and Mackmurdo were, by the last decades of the 19th century, no longer operating in isolation. Beautifully produced handmade products, as contemporary art magazines such as the *Art Journal* and *The Studio* indicate, had permeated the public consciousness. Liberty and Co. had distributed Arts and Crafts products to a wider clientele and the demand for and interest in Arts and Crafts had risen accordingly.

At the lower end of the social scale, the Home Arts and Industries Association, established in 1884, had sought to protect country crafts and traditions and to encourage rural workers to put their leisure time to good use. The Association, a charitable body, was run on the whole by upper middle-class women and had the patronage of the local aristocracy. Its aim had been to raise standards of aesthetic taste and afford ailing parts of the rural economy an alternative source of income through the Victorian ideal of self-help. The Association was founded by one Mrs Jebb, with the support of A.H. Mackmurdo, and taught metal- and woodwork, together with knitting, embroidery and spinning. Women workers, largely absent in the more famous crafts guilds, at least as shop-floor producers, were common in the Association both as local organizers and workers. The Association had helped distribute the work of a number of smaller provincial crafts guilds and adult-education associations, among them the Keswick School of Industrial Art, a small design school established in Cumberland, in 1884, and which was eventually to sustain itself as a business venture through the sale of its work. Another sorority motivated by a patrician concern for the poor was the Royal School of Needlework, established in Kensington, London, to help women in distressed circumstances to earn a living from needlework. Some idea of the nature of the school was given by Tiffany's associate, the American fabric designer Candace Wheeler. Visiting England prior to establishing her own counterpart to the Kensington School, she is recorded as being shocked to see the vivid class divisions between the benign middle-class organizers and the women workers.

Women workers were also instrumental, as Anthea Callen observes, in the revival of the Langdale linen industry, founded in Langley, Cumberland, around 1885. The work of the Industry is eulogized in the 1897 edition of the *Art Journal*. Picturesque but sturdy homes contain a welcoming kitchen complete with an open fire over which a kettle boils. The scene 'once common throughout England but now an object for curiosity in shops and museums', could, at first glance, spring from any Arts and Crafts vision of socialist Utopia, but, in this instance, the craft revival is depicted as a model of a Victorian obsession with cleanliness, hard work and self-discipline as the antidote to poverty. The industry 'has brought increased comfort and orderliness into many a home, whose mistress is now to be found busily engaged by her own fireside instead of gossiping beside a neighbour's', the writer (a woman) stated. She continued:

When cottage mothers are engaged in the production of really beautiful fabrics, the whole family must benefit, thereby learning unconsciously to appreciate beautiful things, and also receiving a much needed training in conscientious work, no mean advantage in these days of scamping.

The original craft ideal had been turned on its head as public interest in the beautiful and handmade grew. Resonant Victorian themes of hard work, thrift and a benign and deserving poor upstaged the idealism of the movement by embracing the form of the Arts and Crafts but nothing of its socialist and democratic content. Women of little visible wealth communally producing handicrafts of excep-

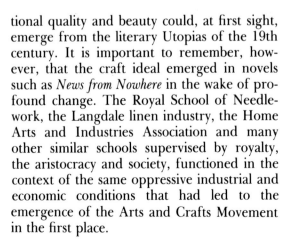

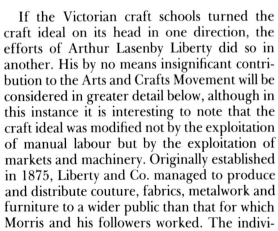

tional quality and beauty could, at first sight, emerge from the literary Utopias of the 19th century. It is important to remember, however, that the craft ideal emerged in novels such as *News from Nowhere* in the wake of profound change. The Royal School of Needlework, the Langdale linen industry, the Home Arts and Industries Association and many other similar schools supervised by royalty, the aristocracy and society, functioned in the context of the same oppressive industrial and economic conditions that had led to the emergence of the Arts and Crafts Movement in the first place.

If the Victorian craft schools turned the craft ideal on its head in one direction, the efforts of Arthur Lasenby Liberty did so in another. His by no means insignificant contribution to the Arts and Crafts Movement will be considered in greater detail below, although in this instance it is interesting to note that the craft ideal was modified not by the exploitation of manual labour but by the exploitation of markets and machinery. Originally established in 1875, Liberty and Co. managed to produce and distribute couture, fabrics, metalwork and furniture to a wider public than that for which Morris and his followers worked. The indivi-

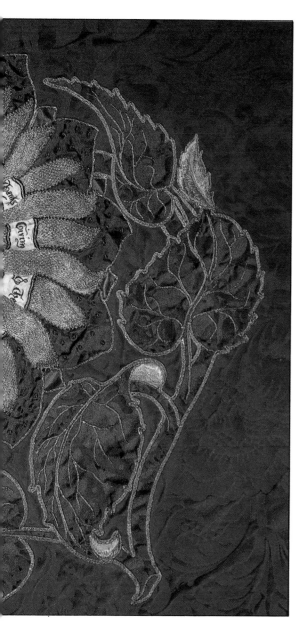

dual handicraft and creative expression of the artisans, the majority of whom worked anonymously, disappeared, to be replaced by a coalition with manufacturers who produced goods mechanically at a fraction of the cost of competitors. It is significant that C.R. Ashbee took exception to the cheap labour of poor amateurs and mechanical production, for both afforded a quick and easy route to the exterior appearance of the craft ideal. Absent on both accounts, however, was the radical change in social conditions that would enable the arts and crafts to be humanely made and enjoyed by the whole of society.

THE CRAFT IDEAL IN THE UNITED STATES

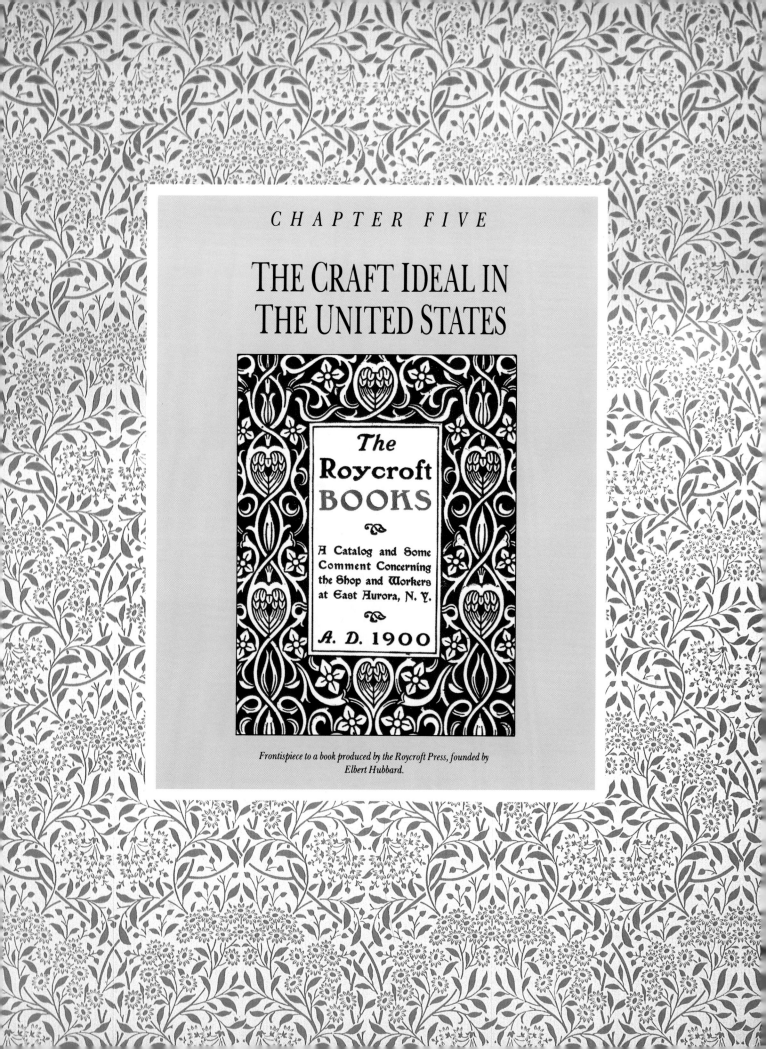

The Roycroft BOOKS

A Catalog and Some Comment Concerning the Shop and Workers at East Aurora, N. Y.

A. D. 1900

Frontispiece to a book produced by the Roycroft Press, founded by Elbert Hubbard.

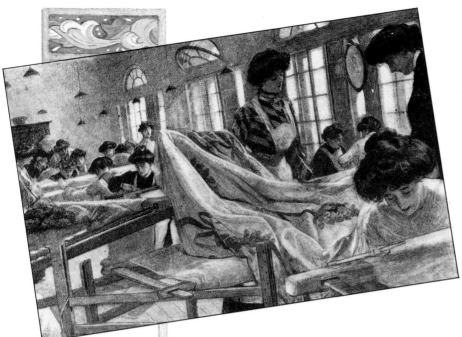

ABOVE *View of the Royal School of Needlework's workroom in 1904.*

bust of a young woman sculpted to order in butter in less than two hours.

Interest in the Arts and Crafts Movement in the United States was, for the most part, inspired by British contributors to the exhibition. Richard Norman Shaw, from whose studio the Art Workers' Guild had in part emerged, exhibited several influential designs for buildings in the 'Queen Anne' style. Shaw's vernacular building bore something of a resemblance to a colonial style and had a strong appeal to architects eager to abandon not only the classical style but also the equally European Gothic idiom. There was, independent of Shaw's influence, a developing additional interest in America's colonial past. *Harper's Magazine* had recently included articles on colonial architecture, and the Centennial Exposition contained a tableau of a kitchen from the period before the Revolution. It was from this network of influences, both home-spun and foreign, that a vernacular style of architecture developed, known as the 'Shingle style'. Architects such as William Ralph Emerson, H.H. Richardson, and firms such as McKim, Mead and White rejected many of the more obviously mainstream European influences in building and returned to a rustic, timber-built colonial idiom. Richardson had adopted this vernacular Shingle style around 1880 in preference to the classical manner he had acquired in France as a student and, in keeping with the work of British Arts and Crafts architects, assumed responsibility not only for the exterior of the building but also its contents. The office of H.H. Richardson produced examples of simple furniture designed, in most cases, by assistants and made by professional contractors.

Equally important in the evolution of an American craft ideal were the other British Arts and Crafts exhibits at Philadelphia. Jeffrey and Co. – the firm that had printed Morris's first wallpapers, Fairfax Murray, Walter Crane and the Royal School of Needlework had all contributed to the exhibition. In addition, the work, and to a lesser extent the ideals, of Morris were becoming increasingly well known in the United States. The company's ironwork and versions of his Sussex chair were commercially distributed and a number of designers confessed to having been influenced by his example.

Contact between the British Arts and Crafts Movement and artists, architects and designers in the United States was, at first, limited. The work of Downing, Renwick and Jarves had been influenced by the revival of a Gothic style in Britain in the late 19th century and Ruskin's writing had been enthusiastically received by some American painters and critics. A more substantial grasp of the Arts and Crafts Movement and its possible application to American culture did not really occur, however, until the Centennial Exposition held in Philadelphia in 1876.

The exhibition demonstrated the economic and political virility of the United States as the home of private enterprise and liberal democracy. It was apparent, however, that in the spheres of art, architecture and the decorative arts, the United States had yet to fashion a culture of its own. While a few notable and original examples of American work were included in the exhibition – Shaker furniture and the work of various Cincinnati potters, for instance – the majority of the industrial arts was dominated by the novel and decorative machine-produced Empire style so criticized by Downing. American popular taste for novelty perhaps achieved its apotheosis in the Centennial Exposition in the form of the

LOUIS C TIFFANY & ASSOCIATED ARTISTS

One such designer who claimed to be influenced by Morris was Louis Comfort Tiffany (1848–1933). Tiffany had established Louis C. Tiffany and Associated Artists in 1879 with Lockwood de Forest, Samuel Colman and Candace Wheeler. They had planned to run a studio following the example of a Renaissance workshop, with Tiffany as the creative centre surrounded by assistants working in a variety of media. The company worked mainly in the fields of glass and fabric design; its original purpose was to establish an alliance between art and industry and to revive standards of domestic taste in the United States. Despite Tiffany's ambitions, his company had few parallels with Morris's experiment. Tiffany never established any clear idea about the way in which art might combat philistinism and appears to have operated, like some designers on the other side of the Atlantic, on the general understanding that art was indiscriminately good for society. The exact mechanics of the conditions under which art was produced and consumed, the very stuff of Morris's concerns, were not considered. Tiffany's venture was nonetheless commercially very success-ful and the company quickly acquired prestigious commissions, not least of which was the contract to decorate the White House for President Chester A. Arthur. The company split early in the next decade, with Tiffany and Wheeler working independently, the one trading as Louis C. Tiffany and Co. and the other (Wheeler) as Associated Artists. Louis C. Tiffany's work is well documented. Less well known, and more germane to the Arts and Crafts tradition in the United States, was the work of his associate. Candace Wheeler had, following the example of the Royal School of Needlework, established the Society of Decorative Art in New York, which became the model for other sororities in Philadelphia and Boston. Among the aims of the Society was to represent a craft with which women had traditionally been associated not as some domestic pastime but as an activity that reflected what Wheeler understood to be women's innate creativity and sense of design.

ABOVE Photograph of Candace Wheeler, one of the most prominent designers in the American Arts and Crafts Movement.

BELOW Examples of glass produced by Louis C. Tiffany between 1890 and the 1920s. Tiffany's firm, although without Tiffany's direct involvement, continued to produce glass until 1938.

RIGHT Rookwood earthenware jar with coloured underglazes, decorated by Hattie E. Wilcox, 1900.

One of the most conspicuous developments in American Arts and Crafts – and one developed again by craftswomen rather than men – occurred in the field of ceramics. In Cincinnati a group of socially prominent women amateurs attended the city's School of Art and rapidly became equally prominent in their field, exhibiting at the 1876 Women's Pavilion at Philadelphia, where their work was also used for the Centennial tea party. One student from the Cincinnati school, Mary Louise McLaughlin, was particularly influential. In 1879 McLaughlin, who also claimed to have been influenced by the example of William Morris, established The Cincinnati Pottery Club with Clara Chapman Newton and evolved what became a characteristically American style of decoration based on a French technique of ceramic underglazing first seen by McLaughlin at the Centennial's French Pavilion.

The same technique was used by McLaughlin's contemporary, Maria Longworth Nichols, the founder of the Rookwood Pottery. Rookwood (the name was meant to evoke Wedgwood) was founded in 1880 by Nichols with money given by her father, a dealer in real estate and a local phil anthropist in the arts.

Maria Longworth Nichols claimed, as Anthea Callen observes, that Rookwood had been established mainly for her own gratification, although the venture was both large and financially successful. Some idea of the scale of the pottery is given when one considers that Rookwood absorbed a number of craftsmen from local industries to throw the clay for the mainly female contingent of decorators. The year after its formation, Rookwood lent its facilities to a number of skilled women amateurs and began supporting classes in ceramics. Tuition was offered (at the very expensive rate of three dollars per week) with the aim of training prospective ceramicists for the firm. The project was abandoned, however, on the advice of Rookwood's business manager, W.W. Taylor, on the grounds that the company was openly fostering competition in its own field. The pottery's excellent facilities were denied to the very skilled ceramicists connected with the Pottery Club and Rookwood had a virtual monopoly on underglazing, a difficult technique requiring mild firing to maintain the characteristic warm-coloured glazes. After her second marriage Maria Longworth Storer, continued to practise as a potter but left the running of Rookwood to Taylor.

The company continued, however, and trained an impressive stable of both male and female ceramicists, among them Shirayamandi, one of the company's few foreign craftsmen, Artus Van Briggle, Laura Fry and Matthew Daly.

The notion that creative work enabled women to turn their hands to a useful trade appropriate to their sex was one that occurred on the periphery of the Arts and Crafts Movement time and again. In the United States it appears in the Paul Revere Pottery in Boston, where classes were held for immigrant women workers, and in the Newcomb College Pottery attached to the women's section of Tulane University in New Orleans. The Newcomb College Pottery was established in 1895 and at first attempted to imitate the work of Rookwood, although it found the specialist glazing techniques too difficult to copy. Under the direction of Mary G. Sheerer, Newcomb began to evolve its own peculiar style based upon not only the use of local clays but also local decorative plant motifs common to the Southern states. A sense of geographical identity is very common in American crafts and appeared in Susan Frackelton's work at Newcomb, which evolved from a style peculiar to her native Wisconsin.

The demand for and interest in Art Pottery appeared to be nationwide. The

Chelsea Keramic Art Works in Massachusetts had produced traditional pottery since its foundation in 1866, and after the Centennial Exposition began to produce work influenced by Japanese and French ceramics. Lustre and matt glazes were the speciality of Clara Louise Poillon's Pottery, established in 1901, and the Boston-based Grueby Faience Co., which evolved a simple form of pottery decorated in a distinctive matt green glaze. Research indicates that the United States made a distinct contribution to the field of pottery, yet despite the 'good works' of Candace Wheeler, Newcomb College and the Paul Revere Pottery, the missionary zeal associated with creative labour that is so resonant within the British Arts and Crafts tradition is largely absent in most examples of American ceramics. American pottery is often aesthetically very pleasing, although it is never really used as a vehicle to challenge the artistic or social status quo. The zeal absent in the work of most American art potters appeared with a vengeance toward the end of the 19th century with the Rose Valley Association near Philadelphia, an artistic community that had tried to embrace not just the visible part of the craft ideal but also aspects of its socialism. In 1901 two architects, William L. Price and H.H. McLanahan, had attempted to establish a fraternity outside Philadelphia in disused mill buildings.

LEFT Vase produced by the Paul Revere Pottery, Boston, after 1908.

*RIGHT Empire-style
sofa and chairs in
laminated rosewood
and white pine by John
Henry Belter, c. 1855.*

Modelled on the communal ideals practised by Morris and Ashbee in England, the community was partly supported by Swarthmore College. Craftsmen from Switzerland were used to train local labour and the Association made pottery and furniture distributed through a retail outlet in Philadelphia. The Association foundered after eight years, apparently beset by the same problems of the cost of handcraftsmanship that dogged the many other idealistic Arts and Crafts communities. However, the craft ideal appears in far more robust form in the example of Gustav Stickley.

Gustav Stickley had originally been apprenticed to Schuler C. Brandt, his maternal uncle. After managing Brandt's small furniture factory, Stickley began to produce work of his own. His earliest examples of furniture appear to have met the popular demand for reproductions of European styles, although these were apparently done under duress. 'At first', Stickley wrote, 'in obedience to public demand, I produced in my workshops adaptations of foreign styles, but always under silent protest; my opposition developing, as I believe, out of a course of reading, largely from Ruskin and Emerson which I followed in my youth'. Stickley thought that the popular taste for European-inspired furniture was theatrical and out of context when applied to American homes. He understood that the European styles were peculiar to individual national identities, growing out of their own respective cultures. He considered it anomalous to take, say, the Empire style, which was the adequate expression of the aspirations of 19th-century France, and transport it to the other side of the Atlantic where its historical and social context would be lost. The excesses of the ornate Empire style were an easy target for criticism,

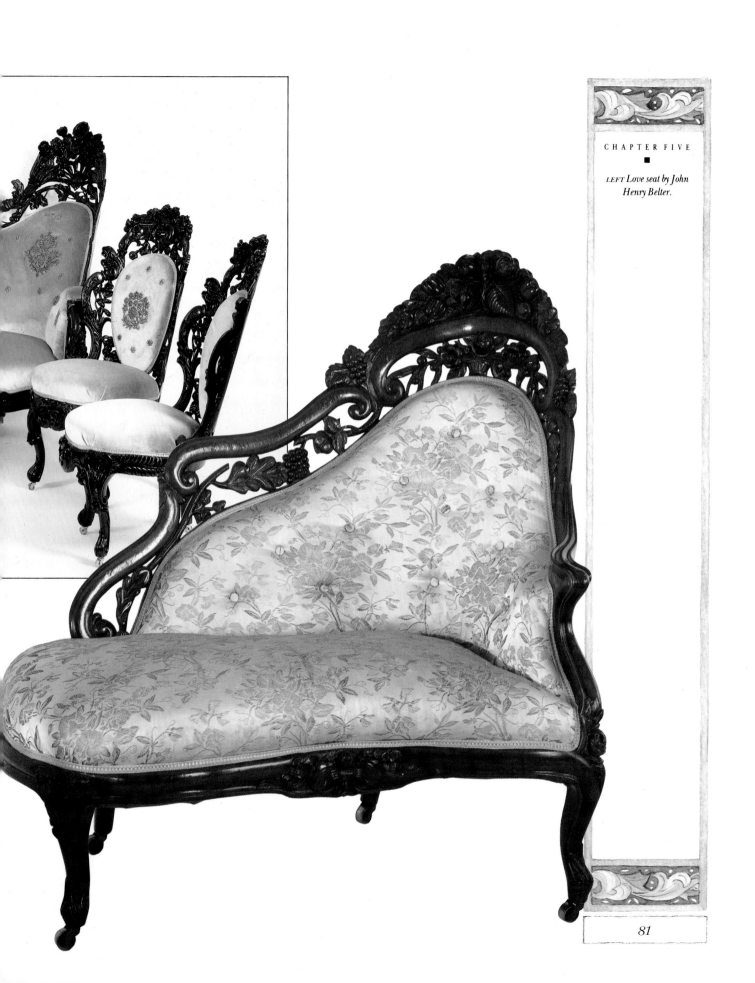

LEFT Love seat by John Henry Belter.

*RIGHT Sideboard
produced by the
workshops of Gustav
Stickley, of oak and oak
veneer with hammered
copper hinges and
handles, c. 1910–16.*

but Stickley rejected not just these but also the stylistic alternatives current in the late 19th century, including Japonisme, Gothic revival and even the work of the Modern Movement. Stickley's remedy was to abandon any influence motivated by appearance alone. 'I became convinced', he wrote 'that the designers of cabinet making use their eyes and their memories too freely and their reasoning powers too little'. The style, or more properly, the method Stickley used in cabinetmaking, he dubbed 'Structural'. This was a functional and austere style, similar in character to the Shaker furniture he had seen at the Philadelphia Centennial Exposition, and devoid of virtually any form of decoration.

Whereas individual styles of Empire, Gothic or Modern furniture represented various strands of European national culture, Stickley's aggressively simple furniture became an expression of American aesthetic values expressed in American terms. The furniture was made well but was simple and unpretentious. Constructed from humble, local materials, usually oak, it was inexpensive and within the reach of the average American consumer. Moreover, the furniture owed no stylistic debts to European models. Such independence and straightforward 'common-sense' resonate through American culture. Stickley stated:

They [the Americans] are the great middle classes, possessed of moderate culture and moderate material resources, modest in schemes and action, average in all but virtues. Called upon to meet stern issues, they have remaining little leisure in which to study problems of other and milder nature. But as offering such great and constant service, these same middle classes should be the objects of solicitude in all that makes for their comfort, their pleasure and mental development. For them art should not be allowed to remain as a subject of consideration for critics. It should be brought to their homes and become for them a part and parcel of their daily lives. A simple, democratic art should provide them with the material surroundings conducive to plain living and high thinking, to the development of the sense of order, symmetry and proportion.

Stickley gave attention both to the form of his furniture and the manner in which it was made. He set great store by Morris's demand that the labour of the craftsman should be free and contented. To this end his firm of United Craftsmen attempted to evoke the communal

fraternities of the Middle Ages. Stickley even adopted a medieval device, *Als Ich Kan*, taken from the painting of the 15th-century artist Jan Van Eyck and used in its English translation – If I Can – in some of the works of William Morris. Stickley's craftsmen were also incorporated into a profit-sharing scheme and regular meetings were held at the workshops, where 'friendly debate, brief addresses and genial discussion will be used as methods to secure harmony and unity of effort.' Machinery was used in the workshops, but only to liberate the craftsman from unnecessary work.

The aims of United Craftsmen were catalogued in the company's magazine, *The Craftsman*, published for the first time in 1901. The first edition was dedicated to Morris and subsequently contained contributions on the Arts and Crafts from both sides of the Atlantic, together with a cross-section of liberal critical essays on subjects from Native American songs to Art Nouveau. Later editions of the magazine increased in size and format and included articles by Stickley on education and social reform, an interest that found form in Craftsman Farms, a working agricultural venture under Stickley's direction wherein a school for

boys was established to supplement the short-comings of traditional academic education.

In the first decade of the 20th century United Craftsmen appeared to go from strength to strength. In 1902 the company took larger premises in Syracuse, where workshops and showrooms adjoined a library and a lecture hall. Metalwork and fabric were produced in addition to woodwork. Three years later Stickley's furniture was being widely imitated under trade names deceptively similar to United Craftsmen. The name was accordingly changed, first to United Crafts and later to Craftsmen Incorporated and the company moved to New York, where showrooms, a permanent exhibition, a lecture hall, a library, the equivalent to a modern supermarket and a restaurant were centralized in a large twelve-storey building. The rapid growth of the company caused its decline and eventual collapse. Its assets were gradually stripped and Stickley's interest in the company was terminated. Despite an ignominious end, United Craftsmen represented a radical departure in the American Arts and Crafts Movement. Stickley had followed not simply the outward signs of craftsmanship but also the spirit. The work was pleasing to look at, well and sensibly made by creatively fulfiled craftsmen who were getting something like proper remuneration for their labour. Moreover, Stickley's products owed no stylistic debt to European influences, save that of notions of common-sense crafts-manship pioneered originally by Ruskin and Morris. United Craftsmen furniture thereby became a fitting medium to reflect the modest democratic ideals of American citizenship.

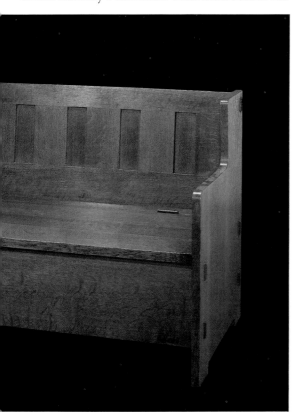

LEFT Photographs published in The Craftsman *of Gustav Stickley's Craftsman Workshops, c. 1902–03.*

BELOW LEFT Oak hall bench produced by Gustav Stickley, c. 1910.

RIGHT Front page of the first edition of The Craftsman, *published by Stickley's United Crafts, 1904.*

THE CRAFTSMAN

VOL . VI   APRIL 1904   NO. 1

COPY 25 CENTS   PUBLISHED MONTHLY BY THE UNITED CRAFTS SYRACUSE·N·Y· U·S·A·   YEAR 3 DOL LARS

LEFT Artist's impression of a Craftsman House, one of a series of homes in an American vernacular style published in The Craftsman, *1904.*

BELOW LEFT Artist's impression of a dining room, published in The Craftsman, *1904.*

The Arts and Crafts ideal was applied with equal enthusiasm (if not equal reverence) by Stickley's contemporary Elbert Hubbard. Hubbard, in his own words educated at the University of Hard Knocks (his presence there is noted in *Who's Who*), originally made a living as a travelling salesman and later tried his hand, with little initial success, at writing novels. The lack of enthusiasm shown by local publishers was however put to good use. Hubbard was later to sponsor the *Philistine*, one of numerous and usually short-lived pocket-sized magazines with the sole aim of settling a few scores with those editors too blind or stupid to appreciate his literary talents. The magazine ran for a number of years, returning a profit from its very first edition.

Hubbard's foray into the Arts and Crafts Movement had been inspired by the Kelmscott Press. He had met Ruskin and Morris in England in 1894 and set up a press at East Aurora on his return to New York. The Roycroft Press took its name from two English bookbinders of the 17th century, Samuel and Thomas Roycroft. The venture began with the publication of one book, the first of a long series of biographical essays written by Hubbard, entitled *Little Journeys*, the

Journey in this instance being to the home of George Eliot. Many of the first books produced at Roycroft were very lavish. The typeface had been designed in imitation of 17th-century-style lettering, printed using a hand press on handmade paper imported from Europe and finally bound in leather. Some editions contained decorative borders and a few early examples were even illuminated by hand.

In 1901 Roycroft began producing earnest-looking, Mission-style furniture similar to that produced at United Craftsmen, together with equally simple ceramics and household items in metal. Some examples were produced in brass or silver, although Roycroft was better known for its hand-beaten copperware, often made to the designs of the ex-banker-turned-artisan Karl Kipp.

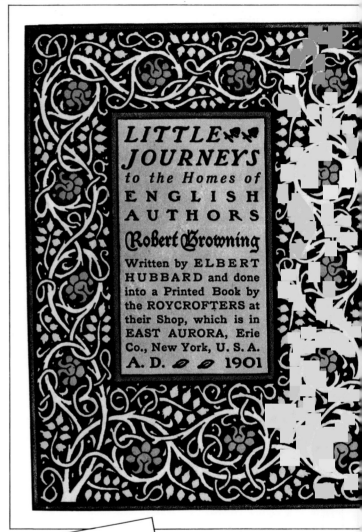

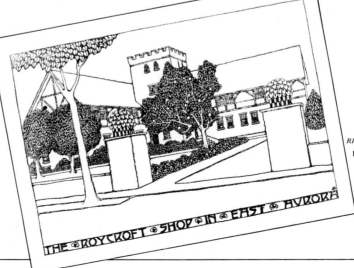

ABOVE *Illustrated frontispiece to* Little Journeys to the Homes of English Authors, *one of a series published by Elbert Hubbard, 1901.*

LEFT *Print of the Roycroft Shops at Hubbard's crafts community in East Aurora, near Buffalo, New York.*

ABOVE RIGHT *Photograph of Elbert Hubbard.*

RIGHT *Frontispiece from* Little Journeys to the Homes of Great Teachers *by Elbert Hubbard, 1908.*

Like United Craftsmen, Roycroft had democratic pretensions; its catalogue proudly declared that beautiful objects should be available to everyone. Hubbard had hoped to be able to encourage his craftsmen to work without the aid of machinery although, like countless other craftsmen, he found that the well-intentioned aim of pricing household goods within the reach of the average income was incompatible with the aim of respecting the creative integrity of the artisan. Hubbard, like others active in the Arts and Crafts Movement in the United States, compromised by using mechanized processess. However, despite such heresies, he gave great attention to the working practices and conditions at East Aurora. Individual craftsmen, where possible, maintained a considerable degree of autonomy in their daily work. Examples of Roycroft furniture tended to be individually made by one craftsman, and apprentices, having mastered one craft, were encouraged to move to another to further develop their skills. Extending the medieval guild system to characteristically extreme limits, Hubbard dubbed himself 'Fra Hubbard', the leader of a putative band of brothers recruited in the main from the locality around East Aurora.

RIGHT Robie House, Chicago, by Frank Lloyd Wright, 1908.

One of the principal features of the American Arts and Crafts Movement evident in the work of both Stickley and Hubbard was its increasing ability to be able to compromise with mechanized production. In England, where the Industrial Revolution had created social conditions comparable to the urban life-styles of some of today's Third World countries, it is easy to appreciate the fear generated by mechanization. The United States, however, was not witness to anything comparable to the social changes that occurred in England, and welcomed the creative possibilities of machine production. One of the chief figures responsible for assimilating the ideals of the Arts and Crafts Movement with those of mechanized production was the architect and designer Frank Lloyd Wright.

Wright trained as an architect in the offices of Joseph Silsbee and the firm of Adler and Sullivan. His first architectural designs were in the 'Prairie' style and on first sight appear to have little in common with Arts and Crafts architecture in England. Wright's buildings nonetheless observe some important aspects of the Arts and Crafts canon. Morris had insisted upon an honesty anticipating the modern pre-occupation with 'truth to material' and suggested that buildings should be an intrinsic part of their environment. Members of the second generation of the movement in England had, in addition, insisted upon the relationship between the design of the building and its contents. All of these features are evident in Wright's work, the principal difference being that the geography of the Cotswolds was exchanged for that of the prairies of Illinois. The

buildings of the Prairie School consequently stress flat, open geography by constantly drawing attention to the horizontal dimension of the architecture with the use of low overhanging roofs and water tables that extend well beyond the walls of the house. Overhanging roofs were not simply matters of stylistic caprice – they afforded excellent protection from the extremes in weather conditions. The height of each individual storey, in turn, was determined by the scale of the human figure. Wright had also sought to reconcile the design of the exterior of his buildings with furniture and household items, ambitions shared by his contemporaries Greene and Greene, active mainly on the West Coast.

Wright had first come into contact with the

CHAPTER FIVE

■

left Exterior of the
Gamble House,
Pasadena, California,
by Greene & Greene,
1908.

Arts and Crafts Movement through the works of Ruskin, and in 1898 became one of the founding members of the Chicago Arts and Crafts Society. Chicago was, in fact, an active centre for arts and crafts. Hull House, a settlement under the direction of social reformer Jane Addams, included an art gallery and studio and was inspired by London's Toynbee Hall (Ashbee and Crane both had connections with Hull House). In addition, Chicago maintained a William Morris Society, established by Joseph Twyman, and the Industrial Art League, under the direction of Oscar Lovell Triggs, was designed to promote Arts and Crafts ideals. Wright distinguished himself from other craftsmen in the city by his attitude to machine production. Triggs, for example,

had reservations about mechanized industry and thought that beauty was contingent upon the human hand. Wright, however, saw the creative, technical and social possibilities afforded by machinery. The division that separated the factions in the Chicago Arts and Crafts Society was not that which divided Ruskin and Morris from the capitalist industrialists of the mid-19th century. Rather, the issue concerned the extent to which men and women could control the machine and the way in which it could be used to make good and affordable items. Wright maintained that properly deployed machines could produce objects that were simple and truthful to their respective materials, criteria demanded by the Arts and Crafts Movement decades earlier. In

addition, he pointed out that mechanized processes had also been used to turn out 'machine-made copies of handicraft originals', pale and ludicrous imitations of the Empire style – 'the whole mass a tortured sprawl supposed artistic'. Machinery, used with intelligence, had the capacity to show wood in a more truthful and flattering light; not as a phoney work of machine-made 'handicraft' but as something simply but well turned out, using the machine as a logical tool. Wright stated his position in a famous lecture given at Hull House, entitled 'The Art and Craft of the Machine'. 'American Society', Wright said, 'has the essential tool of its own age by the blade, as lacerated hands everywhere testify!' He continued:

The machines used in woodwork will show that by unlimited power in cutting, shaping and smoothing, and by the tireless repeat, they have emancipated beauties of wood-nature, making possible without waste, beautiful surface treatments, clean and strong forms that veneers of Sheraton or Chippendale only hinted at with dire extravagance. Beauty unknown even to the middle ages. These machines have undoubtedly placed within reach of the designer a technique enabling him to realize the true nature of wood in his designs harmoniously with man's sense of beauty, satisfying his material needs with such extraordinary economy as to put this beauty of wood in use within the reach of everyone.

Wright, in many respects, compromised and renegotiated the ideals of the Arts and Crafts with the pressing demands of the Machine Age, and did much to wean the movement from an obsessive and unrealistic concern with the hand-made. The *bête noire* of mechanization was introduced into the prospectus of the Arts and Crafts, a move that was anathema to the movement. It is, however, important to recognize that one of the long-standing democratic aims of the Arts and Crafts Movement was to place inexpensive but well-designed products within the range of the common man, and this could only be achieved with methods of production that were less costly than handcraftsmanship. Perhaps Wright's most significant achievement was to accept this compromise and re-invent a concern for truth to material with the machine as an integral part of the process. Machinery simply became another tool in the hands of the craftsman, an ideal that was to be subsequently developed by the German craft workshops.

LEFT Dining room of
the Gamble House by
Greene & Greene.

BELOW LEFT Armchair
by Frank Lloyd Wright.

THE AESTHETIC BACKDROP

*Numbers 5 and 7 Blenheim Road, Bedford Park, London, two of a
substantial number of houses on the estate designed by Richard
Norman Shaw.*

RIGHT Sideboard in the Japanese style designed by E.W. Godwin and made by William Wyatt, c. 1867.

For the majority of craftsmen and women referred to so far, the Arts and Crafts were seen as a vehicle for change or reform, and implicated a host of historical, political, social and cultural ideas and opinions. However, relatively few of the observers of the artistic scene would have been aware of the lofty aims of the Arts and Crafts Movement. 'Art' had suddenly become very fashionable among the upper middle classes, and the patrons of Arthur Lasenby Liberty's Regent Street store or the residents of Richard Norman Shaw's Bedford Park, in London, would have embraced all things 'artistic' irrespective of their theoretical pedigree. In the latter part of the 19th century, styles such as the Gothic, the Japoniste or the aggressively modern Art Nouveau current in Europe appear to have been received with equal and uncritical enthusiasm. Art had, as the painter J.A.M. Whistler observed, become a common topic for the tea table.

Art had initially become a popular subject for conversation among the upper middle classes through the influence of high street stores. A number of these had opened in the 1870s selling fashionable fabrics and *objets d'art* inspired by or imported from the Orient. Stores such as Debenham's and Swan and Edgar sold fabrics, and the designer Christopher Dresser had visited Japan in 1877 and opened a warehouse of Japanese imported goods.

By far the most important vehicle bringing art to the tea table was Arthur Lasenby Liberty's store, opened in London's Regent

BELOW LEFT Liberty and Co.'s bamboo bookcase lined with gold leather paper, from the firm's illustrated catalogue.

BELOW RIGHT Bamboo folding card table, produced by Liberty and Co.

CENTRE RIGHT Wallpaper design by C.F.A. Voysey, one of a number of floral paper and fabric designs produced after Voysey established his own architectural practice in 1882.

Street in 1875. Liberty sold fashionable imported silk from the Orient, Japanese blue-and-white porcelain and furniture inspired by oriental models. Its products proved immediately popular and later other items were sold, including furniture, fabrics, clothes, metalware, carpets and pottery. The store boasted an impressive list of craftsmen. Archibald Knox designed the famous Celtic-inspired 'Cymric' and 'Tudric' metalwares and Walter Crane and C.F.A. Voysey were associated with some of Liberty's fabrics. George Walton designed much of its furniture, and couture was produced and sold under the supervision of the architect E.W. Godwin. Many of the craftsmen and women active for the store worked without attribution. Their designs were often modified, and mechanized techniques were used to produce goods in quantity. Liberty had ridden roughshod over many aspects of the Arts and Crafts credo and his skills as a merchant were formidable. His intentions, however, rose above mere commerce. One of the store's aims had been to refine public taste and aesthetic standards in England. Liberty couture was famous for its light silks printed in softly coloured patterns and was praised by the 1883 exhibition of the Rational Dress Association. Its informal designs made in natural 'art fabrics' were in stark contrast to formal women's dress produced in the fashion houses of Paris, a bastion that was stormed in 1884

when Liberty opened a store in the capital and 'Le Style Liberty' momentarily eclipsed French couture. Liberty supplied virtually everything for the fashionable *fin-de-siècle* aesthete, a pretension that was gently pilloried in the opening of Gilbert and Sullivan's operetta *Patience,* in which languid young ladies were found in precisely the sort of 'aesthetic draperies' bought by fashionable upper middle-class women of finer sensibilities.

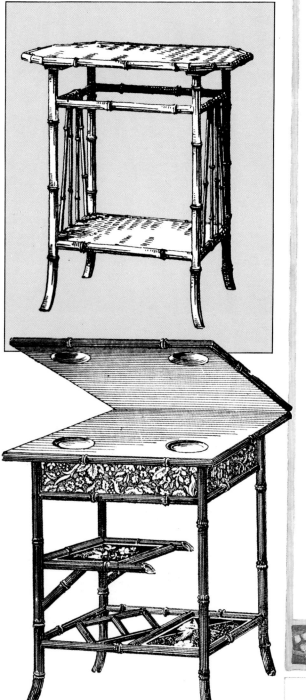

■

LEFT Small bamboo table covered with 'Old Gold' matting, produced by Liberty and Co.

BELOW LEFT Bamboo card table by Liberty and Co., mounted with gold-leather paper.

97

RIGHT Silver and enamel pendant by Omar Ramsden, c. 1900.

BELOW RIGHT 'Tudric' tea set designed for Liberty and Co. by Archibald Knox, 1904.

BELOW Worcester teapot in the form of an Aesthete, inspired by the operetta Patience.

RIGHT Poster for the operetta Patience *by H.M. Brock.*

'THE HIGH AESTHETIC LINE'

PATIENCE

D'OYLY
CARTE
OPERA
COMPANY

Patience provided a good entrée, albeit in satirical form, into the world and the pretensions of the aesthete and the way in which artistic sensibilities were perceived. Distinct from the bourgeois philistine, the 'super aesthetical ultra poetical' men and women who patronized Liberty's store saw art as a consuming passion that absorbed the senses, leaving no room for the mundane realities of life. As one of the operetta's characters observed:

There is a transcendentality in delirium – an acute accentuation of supremest ecstasy – which the earthly might easily mistake for indigestion.

The pretensions pilloried by Gilbert and Sullivan were evident in the literary and artistic figures lionized by fashionable society, notably Wilde and Whistler. Wilde had been educated at Trinity College, Dublin, and had come into contact with Ruskin, Matthew Arnold and Walter Pater at Oxford. In London society his flamboyant dress and manner – later to become an obligatory part of the Aesthete's uniform – attracted instant attention. Wilde's apparel was invariably eccentric consisting of velvet knee breeches and frockcoat, the latter garnished with a lily, which, together with the sunflower and peacock feather became the commonly recognized symbols of aestheticism.

In 1882 Oscar Wilde exported the Aesthetic creed to North America during an 18-month-long lecture tour taking in major cities in both Canada and the United States. The original purpose of the tour, according to Wilde, had been to offer culture to a wealthy, clever but not particularly cultivated nation. Wilde lectured on three basic themes: 'Art and the Handicraftsman', 'Interior Decoration' and the 'English Renaissance in Art'. The content of the lectures was often muddled and indiscriminately linked trends and styles that were quite distinct in origin. The beauty of machinery, Keats, Pre-Raphaelitism, Ruskin, Morris, the stylistic influences of Classical Greece and the Orient were just some of the themes touched upon in his lectures. One has only to consider the difference between two of his themes – 'Morris' and 'machinery' – to catch a glimpse of some of the inconsistencies that riddled his work. Despite these contradictions, Wilde appears to have been a great success in the United States. Several provincial newspapers took umbrage with his foppish and exclusive manner, but the vast majority of his audiences, particularly leisured society women, listened in awe to his pronouncements.

Although Oscar Wilde indiscriminately championed the cause of a variety of progressive but contradicting artistic styles, the Aesthetic cult with which he is associated had a credo of its own. Wilde's aristocratic and elitist posturing was, in fact, party to a well-defined artistic theory and one very different to the theories associated with the Arts and Crafts. The 19th-century French critic and writer Théophile Gautier had argued that art need have no purpose. He had indicated that the pursuit of beauty was a perfectly legitimate end in itself and that art need not be justified by moral or ethical concerns, principles that had hitherto preoccupied art and literature for

THE SIX-MARK TEA-POT.

Aesthetic Bridegroom. "It is quite consummate, is it not!"
Intense Bride. "It is, indeed! Oh, Algernon, let us live up to it!"

important to remember that in the mid-19th century such ideas were trying to displace a centuries-old academic tradition that maintained that timeless standards of beauty had been set by Classical antiquity and it was to these that artists and writers should always aspire.

Wilde betrayed a strong influence by Pater and wrote a popular account of Aesthetic conventions in the dialogue between two characters, Ernest and Gilbert, in *The Critic as Artist*, written in 1891. Their discussion showed the new role into which Wilde had cast literature, art and design. The Arts and Crafts tradition had stated that art could not only be taught, but that a germ of creativity could be found in all men and women. It had been beliefs such as these that had led Ruskin to celebrate some of the technical inadequacies of medieval craftsmen and had led C.R. Ashbee to recruit unskilled labour in the Guild and School of Handicraft. In contrast, Wilde promoted a characteristically exclusive view that anything worth knowing could not be taught. In the rarefied atmosphere of the 'artistic' society depicted in Wilde's *The Critic as Artist*, access into the arcane world of art is subject to an aesthetic grace that no amount of training or learning could induce. Art was useless and its qualities needed no explanation or justification. If prosaic souls did not have the sublime wherewithal to appreciate its merits there was little that artist or critic could do. For some late 19th-century painters, critics and poets, the arts were devoid of purpose and became increasingly self-obsessed. Painting became predominantly concerned with superficial form rather than with any story or idea. Poetry became equally self-obsessed, concentrating on metre and rhyme rather than subject matter. Music for this reason was seen as an appropriate Aesthetic medium: it had the unique capacity to touch the senses without any obvious material reference to the mundane everyday world.

Some impression of the insular way in which art was perceived was given by Wilde when he discussed the purpose of criticism. The purpose of the critic is not to act as a mediator between artist and public but rather to record impressions and feelings. Criticism has the capacity to be as sublime, or even more sublime, than the works on which it passes comment. Wilde wrote:

centuries. The theory that art could be made or written for its own sake appeared in England and gradually led to a schism between artists, writers and the public at large. Swinburne, writing in 1866, asked ' . . . whether or not the domestic circle is to be for all men and writers the outer limit and extreme horizon of their world of work'. The arena in which some poets and painters were increasingly operating did not require public interest or approval and at times deliberately sought to outrage bourgeois standards of taste and convention. Themes of sexual excess were often addressed by painters such as Beardsley and poets such as Baudelaire, Verlaine, Swinburne and Wilde, demonstrating the triumph of unfettered feeling over convention.

The notion that art need serve no particular purpose was partly developed by Wilde's mentor Walter Pater. Pater had insisted that the appreciation of art or nature was a largely personal issue and had declined to set an absolute standard to which artists or writers might aspire. By current standards Pater's ideas hardly seem remarkable, although it is

*LEFT Mahogany
cabinet by E.W.
Godwin and J.A.M.
Whistler, exhibited at
the 1878 Exposition
Universelle in Paris.*

... Who cares whether Mr. Ruskin's views on Turner are sound or not? What does it matter? That mighty and majestic prose of his so fervid and so fiery-coloured in its noble eloquence, so rich in its elaborate symphonic music, so sure and certain, at its best, in subtle choice of word and epithet, is at least as great a work of art as any of those wonderful sunsets that bleach or rot on their corrupted canvasses in England's Gallery ...

The decorative arts assumed particular significance for the Aesthete. Painting, even the avant-garde painting of the Impressionists, was on occasion considered too self-consciously intellectual in that it was a vehicle for ideas of one description or another. The applied or decorative arts, however, had none of the didactic qualities associated with painting, they simply existed in their own state of beauty, more sublime for the simple fact that they had no artistic pretensions whatsoever. They were empty vessels in which the refined spirit of the Aesthete could pour any amount of arcane and refined feeling. Wilde, or more accurately his character Gilbert, explained:

Still, the art that is frankly decorative is the art to live with. It is, of all visible arts, the one art that creates in both mood and temperament. Mere colour, unspoiled by meaning, and unallied with definite form, can speak to the soul in a thousand different ways ...

He continued:

By its deliberate rejection of Nature as the ideal of beauty, as well as of the imitative method of the ordinary painter, decorative art not merely prepares the soul for the reception of true imaginative work, but develops in it that sense of form which is the basis of creative no less than critical achievement.

George Du Maurier passed comment on the sublime qualities of the decorative arts in a *Punch* cartoon. An 'Intense' bride and her 'Aesthetic' groom, surrounded by suitably Aesthetic furniture, inspect a teapot. 'It is quite consummate, is it not?' asks the groom. 'It is indeed!' the bride replies. 'Oh Algernon, let us live up to it!'

Although the 'artistic' fabric and objects from Liberty's store, the pretensions of Wilde and the characters of Du Maurier's cartoons and W.S. Gilbert's libretti were muddled in the popular imagination with the work of the Arts and Crafts Movement, closer inspection shows that they were in fact very different in aims and temperament. The difference between the

Aesthetic tradition and that of the Arts and Crafts Movement was brought sharply into focus in 1877, in a famous dispute between the painter James Abbott McNeill Whistler and John Ruskin.

The dispute centred around the now famous libellous comment made by Ruskin in the July 1877 edition of the *Fors Clavigera* against a painting by Whistler, *Nocturne in Black and Gold*, painted in 1875 and exhibited at the Grosvenor Gallery two years later. With characteristic vitriol Ruskin stated:

For Mr Whistler's own sake, no less than for the protection of the purchaser, Sir Coutts Lindsay ought not to have admitted works into the Gallery in which the ill educated conceit of the artist so nearly approached the aspect of willful imposture. I have seen, and heard, much of cockney impudence before now; but never expected to hear a coxcomb ask two hundred guineas for flinging a pot of paint in the public's face.

Ruskin was too ill to attend court, although several painters inspired by the critic's work were called in his defence, among them Edward Burne-Jones. The cross-examination that followed concerned the degree of 'finish' in Whistler's painting. Burne-Jones expressed appreciation for the colour and atmosphere in *Nocturne*, but was unable to see any composition or detail in the painting to warrant the price asked in the Grosvenor Gallery. Burne-Jones stated to the court that he considered the work little more than a sketch. A painting of

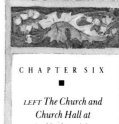
the Venetian Doge, Andre Gritti, believed to be by Titian, was brought into the court as an example of a work containing the finish Whistler's work so clearly lacked. The painting was, in essence, more overtly naturalistic; in Burne-Jones' words: 'It is a very perfect example of the highest finish of ancient art. The flesh is perfect, the modelling of the face is round and good . . . . [it] is an "arrangement in flesh and blood!"' Similar sentiments were expressed by one W.P. Frith, a Royal Academician, and by Tom Taylor, a contributor to the *Times* and the editor of *Punch*. Both men believed the colour in the painting to be pleasing enough, although neither could see any real attempt on Whistler's part to approach the standards demanded by Ruskin, namely, that painting should reproduce natural appearances. The preoccupation with finish was exacerbated both by the price Whistler demanded for his *Nocturne* and for the time it took him to paint it. Popular opinion maintained that the amount of effort and visible handiwork that went into a picture reflected to a large extent upon its artistic and ultimately its financial worth. Whistler would submit to none of these Ruskinian standards and argued that although the picture took only a day or two to paint it contained the 'knowledge of a lifetime'. The value of the painting, then, was characterized not as craftsmanship, its merit visible in handiwork, but rather as something quite elusive that defies definition.

Whistler's defence of his work makes interesting reading and demonstrates the extent to which the principles of Aestheticism differed from those of Ruskin and the Arts and Crafts Movement. Under cross-examination from Ruskin's counsel, Whistler ambiguously described his *Nocturne in Black and Gold*. It was, he stated, a night piece representing fireworks rather than a simple record of landscape, and, to the mirth of the court, he conceded that if it was called a view it would bring about nothing but disappointment. Whistler tellingly described the painting as an 'artistic arrangement', an abstract term that could apply to a number of his pictures given titles more appropriate to pieces of music than painting. The comparison with music is an interesting one. Although it is possible to demand a precise meaning from pictures – and this was certainly the view taken by Ruskin and his followers – it is harder to make similar demands upon music. Music can be evocative, as indeed can the paintings of Whistler, although it would be difficult to attribute to it any concrete and readily explicable meaning. Whistler had pointed out to Ruskin's overly literal counsel, desperate to read something concrete in his painting, that he could, in fact, impose anything he liked upon the picture. 'My whole scheme', Whistler explained, 'was only to bring about a certain harmony of colour'. Whistler thus emphasized the importance of the form of the picture at the expense of the content, a

ARTS & CRAFTS

■

BELOW RIGHT
The main
entrance to the
Glasgow School of Art
by C.R. Mackintosh.
Construction of the
school took place
between 1897 and
1899.

BELOW FAR RIGHT
The library
at the Glasgow School
of Art by Charles
Rennie Mackintosh.
Mackintosh's proposal
was the successful entry
in a competition to
design the school held
in 1896.

preoccupation evident in the ideas of writers associated with Aestheticism and also with some architects connected with the movement.

Whistler's ideas had mystified the court. It is important to recognize that the approbation of the public terrified the Aesthete. Wilde, in the guise of Gilbert, had stated unequivocally in *The Critic as Artist* that he lived in fear of 'not being misunderstood'. Whistler echoed something of this sentiment. He held that none but an artist could be a competent critic of his work, and was not disturbed to discover that his work mystified the general public. His position became even more extreme when he attacked not only the philistine but also the growing number of those who had expressed an interest in things artistic. In the *Ten O'Clock Lecture* of 1885, Whistler completely ridiculed the idea of an empathy between artists and their public. He maintained that artists had always been set apart from the public and that, following the Industrial Revolution, art had been relegated to an object of mere curiosity, becoming little more than a fad and the preserve of a public meddling in something about which they knew little.

Aesthetes, no matter how otherworldly, re-

quired a roof over their heads and Aestheticism extended into architecture and particularly into relatively modest town and suburban housing. In many instances, the architecture associated with the Aesthetic Movement differs little in appearance from that connected with the Arts and Crafts. Both depend heavily upon vernacular styles and traditions of building and consistent attempts are made to reconcile the design of the exterior with that of the interior and its contents. The principal distinction centres, again, upon the motive of architect. In general, the radical calling that inspired Arts and Crafts architecture is absent in that connected with Aestheticism.

One of the first building projects connected with the cult of Aestheticism was the suburban estate at Bedford Park. Jonathan T. Carr had bought the site in the suburbs of west London in 1875 and began to develop an entire village designed to appeal to an artistically aware middle-class clientele keen to leave the city for an idealized version of a small rural community. The project began in 1877 and included not only homes but also schools, an inn, a clubhouse, a church and an art school. A number of architects were contracted to work

on the project. E.W. Godwin was involved in the early stages of the development, although Bedford Park is principally associated with Richard Norman Shaw. The appearance of the houses – which William Morris disliked intensely – tends to differ, although most are variations on the 'Queen Anne' style that was to have such a resonant appeal in the United States. The houses were mostly constructed in red brick and often had hanging tiles, steeply pitched and gabled roofs, and leaded windows; they were fronted by gardens with sunflowers, the statutory symbol of Aestheticism. The style is only loosely associated with Queen Anne and the early 18th century. The buildings are, in fact, a blend of several styles and were generally intended to give the impression of an old English village rather than to reconstruct a community with any great architectural accuracy. Robert McLeod, in his study of recent English architecture, observed that the design of the houses is predominantly inspired by a concern for formal appearance and overall visual effect rather than practical utility. Many of the buildings show a marked feel for balancing architectural forms and motifs with less regard for the living conditions within. This interest in abstraction of form, colour and metre also occurred in the art and poetry associated with Aestheticism.

Bedford Park attracted a variety of middle-class residents, many of whom were in some sense artistically inclined or of radical sympathies. They included artists, actors, writers and architects. Voysey lived there for a short period, as did the Irish Nationalist John O'Leary. Membership of 'a high aesthetic band' was by no means obligatory. Bedford Park sustained enough families to supply a conventional church-school, different in persuasion to the more liberal, co-educational alternative preferred by the more radical residents. In the popular imagination, however, Bedford Park became inextricably associated with the pretensions of Aestheticism.

The 'elite' of Aestheticism were found not in the genteel avenues of Bedford Park but in Chelsea. Among the residents around Tite Street were Whistler, Sargent, Sickert, Wilde, his friend Frank Miles, and Carlo Pelligrini, together with a substantial band of now largely forgotten acolytes. E.W. Godwin designed a number of homes and studios in the district.

ABOVE *Design for a living room by M.H. Baillie-Scott, 1911.*

He had initially worked in the Gothic and Queen Anne styles, although he abandoned, or attempted to abandon, these in favour of a more aggressively formal style of building that anticipates the appearance of much 20th-century architecture. His designs for the White House, Whistler's studio, shed the surface decoration of Queen Anne and juxtaposed large areas of undecorated stuccoed wall and roof space, interrupted only by the inclusion of simple unadorned windows. The Metropolitan Board of Works so disliked the stark simplicity of the building that it insisted that some decoration in the form of relief sculpture be added to the exterior. Some compromises were made, although the sculptures were never included on the façade. The Board took even greater exception to another of Godwin's buildings, designed for Frank Miles at number 44 Tite Street. Again, the house was originally to be composed of interlocking geometric forms with virtually no surface decoration. The Board insisted that a Flemish-style gable be added and the balcony be altered to soften the aggressive appearance of the exterior.

A tendency toward novelty, and formal simplicity, was to become an increasingly important feature in the evolution of European architecture and design. Designers such as C.F.A. Voysey and Charles Rennie Mackintosh evolved a style of building that primarily exploited the creative possibilities of often stark architectural form. In addition, there was a tendency to abandon the example of history as a source of inspiration in building and develop new architectural forms and motifs. Mackay Hugh Baillie-Scott evolved a very individual style. His buildings followed the example of architects and designers of the Arts and Crafts Movement in that the interior and exterior are co-ordinated as one total design, yet his fanciful style is light years away from the practical designs of, say, Gimson or Stickley. Architecture, for Baillie-Scott, rather appeared as a 'charmed territory' in which to pursue adventures in colour, form and space with little regard for history or convention. The decorated organic designs for the interior and the furniture made in 1898 for the Grand Duke of Hesse at the Palace at Darmstadt give a clear insight into his latent romanticism. Simplicity and the absence of historical precedent are marked most notably in the works of the Glasgow Four, C.R. Mackintosh, Herbert MacNair, and Frances and Margaret MacDonald. Some examples of their work admit the odd historical detail. Mackintosh's School of Art at Glasgow grudgingly includes some Tudor motifs, although much of his work is very simple in design and decorated only with organic and geometric motifs devoid of any historical association. Hill House in Helensburgh, Scotland, is an excellent example of Mackintosh's formal purity.

This concern with form and with the pursuit of abstract and often obscure artistic ideals preoccupied many artists and designers in the early 20th century throughout Europe and the United States. The democratic ideal of the Arts and Crafts Movement, the notion that art could serve a purpose and be used as an object of social utility was, however, to be taken up again. In 20th-century Europe the most intelligent reading of the craft ideal occurs not specifically in England, but in Austria and particularly in Germany, with the foundation of the Deutscher Werkbund and the Weimar Bauhaus.

LEFT Hill House at Helensburgh, Scotland, by C.R. Mackintosh. The house was designed for the publisher William Blackie in 1900.

THE EUROPEAN CONTRIBUTION

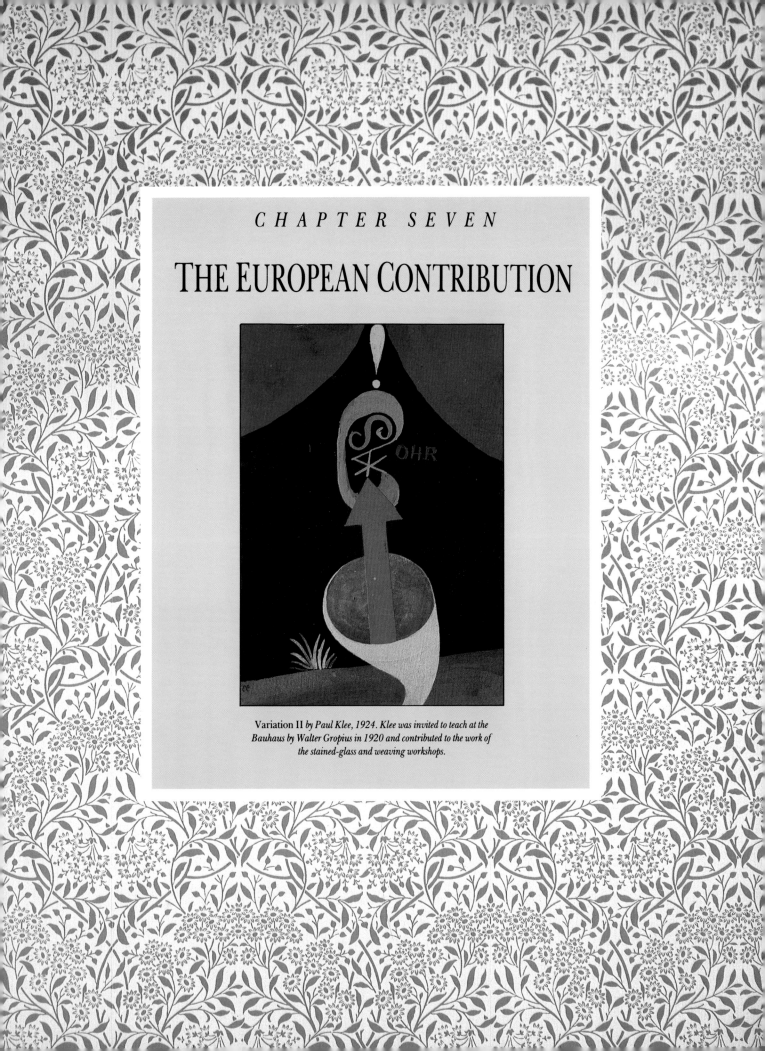

Variation II *by Paul Klee, 1924. Klee was invited to teach at the Bauhaus by Walter Gropius in 1920 and contributed to the work of the stained-glass and weaving workshops.*

Charles Robert Ashbee had said that the principles of the Arts and Crafts Movement were more consistently and logically developed in the United States and Europe than in Britain. The consistency of the American contribution to the movement has already been shown in some detail: architects and designers such as Gustav Stickley, Greene and Greene and Frank Lloyd Wright took on many of the problems of design, production, distribution and consumption that had haunted the Arts and Crafts Movement since its inception. With the assistance of machinery they were able to make significant amendments to the Arts and Crafts tradition and nurse the movement away from the well-intentioned but ultimately impractical phase of Utopian socialist craftsmanship, and some way toward the long-standing goal of making well-designed and good quality furniture for larger and less exclusive markets than those for which most British designers had worked.

A sense of consistency and logic is found not

only in the work of American artists and craftsmen but also in that of many European designers, notably those working in Germany during the first decades of this century. Not all British craftsmen and women, however, were adherents to a tradition preoccupied only with the pernicious effects of industrialism and a lost medieval ideal of handicrafts and labour. The architect William Richard Lethaby (1857-1931) had attempted to help design and industry coexist and had considered establishing an association, similar to the Werkbund in Germany, that would foster links between what, in English circles, had traditionally been regarded as bitter opponents.

Lethaby provided an interesting staging post between the romantic but impractical stage within the evolution of the Arts and Crafts Movement and the realistic integration of art and industry that was to occur with the Werkstätte, Werkbund and Bauhaus in Austria and Germany. Lethaby was born in Barnstaple in 1857 and was originally apprenticed to a local architect concerned primarily

LEFT Brockhampton Church (All Saints) in Herefordshire by William Richard Lethaby, 1901.

with the construction of practical farm buildings. At the age of 22 he became the chief clerk in Richard Norman Shaw's practice and worked intermittently for Morris and with Kenton and Co. At first glance Lethaby's ideas on art and architecture appear to be contradictory. On the one hand, he was acutely conscious of architectural tradition; he admired medieval building and was active within the Society for the Protection of Ancient Buildings. On the other hand he appeared to advocate something approaching a functionalist aesthetic. Lethaby constantly stressed the importance of efficiency of purpose, describing art as the 'well doing of what needs doing'. He was suspicious of artistic considerations in architecture and matters of taste. 'I would', he wrote, 'have buildings tested by such generally understandable ideas as fitness, soundness, economy, efficiency, reasonableness, intelligibility, carefulness, science and mastery . . . . There are two dozen words of this type which I should like to become the stock in trade of architectural critics.' Lethaby, in addition, was involved with the Design and Industries Association, a cooperative venture between artists, designers, producers, teachers and consumers that admitted the importance of mechanized industry to modern design.

The key that enables one to reconcile Lethaby's simultaneous admiration for both the architectural conventions of the past and the innovations of the present was his appreciation of the place of building within history. Building, for Lethaby, was an organic part of the cultural environment from which it sprang and, at its best, represented a tradition that need not be thought of in self-consciously artistic terms. It is interesting to note that Morris had spoken of medieval art in a similar context, finding within it an 'unconscious intelligence'.

For Lethaby, architecture need not be isolated and considered as some specialist refined realm of sensibility. A more healthy alternative, and one that Lethaby believed to have existed in the Middle Ages, was an environment where individual creativity was a commonplace human attribute, and sound building evolved out of spiritual and practical necessity of the period. Consequently, a medieval church, say, was built and decorated from local material with local skill, to fulfil an estab-

lished spiritual need. The same basic principle could be applied to any era. The appearance of building would necessarily change as needs within the community changed. However, the traditions of building and of practicality remained the same. It was this tradition of sound, practical and purposeful construction that, as far as architecture was concerned, historically linked the past with the present. Change should be written into sound architecture and design, and in this sense Lethaby was distinctly modern in his approach.

In his writing, however, Lethaby introduced a caveat to explain the process by which change should occur: sound building, he believed, should concentrate on the modification of traditional forms. His church at Brockhampton-by-Ross, in Herefordshire, is an impressive practical example of his approach. The simply designed church is constructed with massive piers made partly with coke-breeze concrete on a stone string course. The modern concrete, however, supports oak purlins which themselves carry a traditional thatched roof. Speaking of the way in which modern requirements are grafted on to tradition, Lethaby had stated that a well-designed 'table or chair or book has to be very well bred.' In this sense, then, Lethaby was dependent upon an historical tradition but unlike some members of the Arts and Crafts Movement he did not connect tradition with any particular style. History, for Lethaby, found form in a tradition of common-sense practicality that spanned the centuries.

Lethaby applied this blend of respect for the past and the practical recognition of the needs and demands of the present at the Central School of Art where, together with George Frampton, he was appointed co-principal. Halsey Ricardo, who taught architecture under Lethaby at the Central School, advised students that his classes were concerned with practical issues rather than style, and it was from this practicality, Ricardo stated, that beauty sprang. The school's programme focused primarily on the applied arts and actively sought to serve the needs of industry. The fine arts were only admitted into the curriculum as adjuncts to the more practical and useful disciplines.

The school's prime concerns fell in the categories of metalwork, the production of books,

*RIGHT The Sezession
Building, Vienna, by
Joseph Maria Olbrich,
1897–98.*

building, decoration, woodwork and cabinet-making, and carving. The bulk of the school's activities was concentrated in the evening, enabling both students and teachers to participate in industry. Unlike their contemporaries in more academic schools, they would, either as students or designers, have the practical day-to-day experience that was absent in more conventional art education.

Despite Lethaby's importance in the evolution of the Arts and Crafts Movement, the nettle of industrialism was grasped with far greater confidence not in England but in centres throughout Europe, particularly in German-speaking countries.

The Arts and Crafts had first been exported to Europe through a number of channels. The work of Ashbee and Baillie-Scott at Darmstadt attracted great attention in Germany and had a direct influence on the works of both German and Austrian architects. The work of the Guild and School of Handicraft was represented at exhibitions in Berlin and Vienna together with submissions from French, Belgian and Scottish designers. C.R. Mackintosh's aggressively modern designs were ecstatically received by Viennese architects who were labouring under the weight of parochial interpretations of bastardized classical and Gothic traditions. *The Studio*, a progressive magazine with accounts of the fine and applied arts from a number of European centres, was another important means of disseminating ideas.

Interest in the British Arts and Crafts Movement was not only limited to aesthetic concerns. Germany was rapidly emerging as a powerful industrial nation and was eager to learn from the example of British designers and architects. In fact, Hermann Muthesius, an attaché to the German Embassy in Britain, was despatched in 1896 to provide an account of British prowess in the fields of architecture and design. (He wrote the seminal study *Das Englische Haus* from his research.)

At the beginning of the century, progressive styles in British design and architecture were absorbed with little distinction between the often different attitudes of the architects concerned. In centres such as Vienna, modernity often appeared to have been far more important than the formation of a theoretically sound aesthetic doctrine. This interest in progressive styles devoid of an historical association was caused by a reaction toward a long tradition of support for conventional art and architecture based upon the constant repetition of past styles.

The Secession group, established in Vienna in 1897 by a number of avant-garde artists who had seceded from the conservative *Künstlerhaus*, had no hard and fast aesthetic party line. Its prime concern was that those in its ranks should avoid the oppressive example of history and begin to create anew; as the movement's declamatory maxim stated, 'To the Age its Art, to Art its Freedom'.

The Secession distinguished itself from the more conventional *Künstlerhaus* by a general desire to promote modern art, to avoid the trappings of commerce in art and to establish a direct relationship with the public. The movement also insisted that there should be no traditional division between the applied and fine arts, believing both to be of equal worth. The Secession's eighth exhibition (primarily of applied rather than fine arts) contained submissions from a number of avant-garde artists and designers throughout Europe who, in the main, had also attempted to reject the past and forge a novel and often radically simple style. Among the exhibits were the works of the French Maison Moderne and of the Belgian designer Henri Van de Velde. Ashbee was also represented, although it is doubtful whether the ideals of the Guild and School of Handicraft were fully appreciated by the Secession.

Of far more immediate interest to the Secessionist was the ascetic, geometric but still ultimately decorative style of Charles Rennie Mackintosh. Like the florid, organic Art Nouveau style that had blossomed in France, the Secession style also rejected the past and based its forms upon ahistorical motifs, but instead of employing forms from nature, it took geometry as its principal starting point. This decorative use of geometry, as distinct from the functional application it was given by contemporary architects such as Adolf Loos (1870–1933), is evident in much of the work of the Secession. It occurs in Joseph Maria Olbrich's (1867–1908) Secession building and appears in his designs for metalwork and in the glass designed by his contemporary Koloman Moser (1868–1918). In each case geometry is used as an aesthetic source rather than as an entrée into a rational design.

The Wiener Werkstätte never resolved the conflict between their admiration for the time-honoured principles of craftsmanship and their recognition of the inevitability of mechanized production. The Viennese architect and contemporary of Hoffmann, Adolf Loos, however, began to embrace the prospect of a purpose-built, machine-produced environment with greater confidence. Loos did not believe that architecture or design should be made to appear modern for its own sake, and in an essay written in 1908 he criticized some craft workshops for being self-consciously contemporary, for thrusting a 'podgy hand in the spinning wheel of time'. Loos' attitude to the historical development of design is similar to that of Lethaby. He wrote:

No man – nor any association – had to create our wardrobes, our cigarette boxes, our jewellery. Time created them for us. They change from year to year, from day to day, from hour to hour. For we ourselves change from hour to hour and with us our attitudes and habits. This is how our culture has changed . . . . We do not sit in a particular way because a carpenter has made a chair in such and such a manner. A carpenter makes a chair in a particular manner because that is how we wish to sit.

Loos advocated that the design of something should be determined by its function and in his essay on the historical pretensions of Viennese architecture, 'Potemkin's Town', he criticized Viennese architecture for its patently unrealistic aspirations. A series of apartments occupied by people of limited means should, he felt, be represented as modest dwellings rather than dressed in some wholly inappropriate Gothic or classical garb. There was no shame, he believed, in using inexpensive materials to build homes for ordinary people. Of greatest importance was the quality of the craftsmanship and, above all, honest design.

The idea that the appearance could be fashioned by utility was also taken up by Hermann Muthesius in *Das Englische Haus*. Muthesius was particularly taken with the humble bourgeois character of English building. The cultural identity of the middle classes in Germany was poorly established and bourgeois culture was often nothing other than a pale imitation of the culture of the aristocracy. In England, however, the middle classes had been long established as a cultural force, they had a clear cultural identity and

demonstrated a strong sense of practicality, independence and self-confidence in their style of living. Muthesius particularly admired the self-effacing style of British vernacular building and felt that its simple character was symptomatic of the way in which the British bourgeoisie felt no need to imitate the manners of their social superiors. Such buildings, he felt, evolved out of practical necessity; windows in English homes, for example, were placed where they were needed and not simply to satisfy the demands of architectural unity. The prime concern for the Englishman's home was comfort. Muthesius listed the 'Exemplary qualities in the English House'.

English houses, as we can see, are wisely reduced to essentials and adapted to given circumstances; the point, therefore, that is worth copying from them is the emphasis that is laid on purely objective requirements. The Englishman builds his house for himself alone. He feels no urge to impress, has no thought of festive occasions or banquets and the idea of shining in the eyes of the world through lavishness in and of his house simply does not occur to him. Indeed, he even avoids attracting attention to his house by means of striking design or architectonic extravagance, just as he would be loth to appear personally eccentric by wearing a fantastic

CHAPTER SEVEN
■

FAR LEFT *Annesley
Lodge, Platts Lane,
Hampstead, London,
by C.F.A. Voysey,
1895.*

LEFT *The Tristan
Tzara House, Paris, by
Adolf Loos, 1926–27.*

suit. In particular, the architectonic ostentation, the creation of 'architecture' and 'style' to which we in Germany are still so prone, is no longer to be found in England.

Muthesius exerted a strong influence on the German cultural establishment and in 1907 he was appointed to the Chair of Applied Arts in the Berlin Trade School. His polemical address to the school gave a damning account of the backward-looking attitudes of some contemporary German designers. So damning was the address that it led to a schism. Two factions were to emerge within the school. The first was reactionary and petitioned the Kaiser for Muthesius' resignation. This faction had a strong sentimental attachment to the German ideal of the pre-industrial craft guild, and the same ideal was later to have a strong appeal to the romantic nationalism of the National Socialists. The other faction defended the progressive ideals of Muthesius and were eventually to form part of the Deutscher Werkbund.

The Deutscher Werkbund, a confraternity of craftsmen, architects and industrialists, was formed in 1907 from a number of Werkstätte dedicated to the reform of the applied arts. Newly industrialized Germany had suffered a fate not dissimilar to that of mid-19th-century England. Mass-production had generally compromised the traditional standards of German craftsmanship and the Werkbund was seen as a society for reform. Yet it is important to state from the outset that 'reform' meant different things to different craftsmen. The Werkbund contained a broad spectrum of opinion, one significant strand of which centred very strongly upon Muthesius' influence and the reform of design with the aid of mechanized industry. Such reforms had already begun, or at least been considered, by the Dresden Werkstätte, one of the most influential within the Werkbund. Established in 1898 according to Ruskinian principles of un-alienated labour and creative fulfilment, its founder Karl Schmidt was nonetheless quite able to reconcile his concern for the well-being of his workforce to the use of machinery and even to standardized techniques of production. It is worth noting that mass-production was criticized in Germany, yet many designers and architects were able to see that in the right hands machinery could be re-directed to produce well-designed goods. British designers, by contrast, were on the whole more timorous and most, at best, only grudgingly compromised with machinery. Other workshops,

craftsmen and industrialists rallied to Muthesius' cause, among them the Austrians Hoffmann and Olbrich. Peter Behrens, who was attached to the electrical manufacturers AEG as a resident designer and architect, was also active in its foundation of the Werkbund, as were Bruno Paul, Richard Riemerschmid and Theodor Fischer. Industrialists in the field of glass manufacture, metalwork, weaving and publishing were also represented, motivated, in part, by the hope that a coalition between workers and benign industrialists might serve as an antidote to socialism and workers' control of industry.

The Werkbund, through the medium of an ever-growing number of provincial offices, hoped to establish a clear and unified direction for German art and industry. Sound design was applied not only to domestic goods but also to heavy industry. Conspicuously well-designed goods would, it was hoped, establish an unmistakably German identity in product design and increase its international standing among trade competitors. Naumann believed that Germany's economic health and reputation should be founded not on direct competition with its industrialized neighbours but on the development of expertise in specialized fields. Muthesius played upon such nationalistic tendencies by associating the patronage of Werkbund workshops and industries with a German sense of patriotism. The Werkbund undertook a programme to educate public

taste and attempts were made to wean consumers away from the twin evils of traditionalism and novelty. The evangelism of the Werkbund even spread abroad through displays of German design in various diplomatic missions. It is interesting to note that the Werkbund had emerged through the intervention of Muthesius from the Arts and Crafts tradition in England. The redemptive capacity of the English craft ideal was associated not with workers' emancipation and socialism but, in this instance, with the ambitions for German Nationhood. This was eventually to end in war and a significant adjustment of the craft ideal in Germany.

The Werkbund went from strength to strength with almost 2,000 members by the beginning of 1914. Its progress was, however, interrupted by the outbreak of the First World War. It was also distracted by an acrimonious debate between two factions at its exhibition, held only months before the eruption of hostilities. Those factions were represented by Muthesius on the one hand and Henri Van de Velde on the other, and the point of conflict centred around the degree of autonomy that should be afforded to the architect or designer. Muthesius had held that design should be standardized to accommodate mass-production and aspired to an almost transcendental logic, wherein the rational spirit of the age rose above the individual creative whim of the designer. Van de Velde, in contrast, upheld in-

dividualism and the creative autonomy of the designer. Prominent members of the Werkbund gravitated toward the two respective causes, although four years later the defeat of Germany had cast mechanization and mass-production in a less than favourable light: machines produced not only domestic goods but weapons in quantity and to disastrous effect. Walter Gropius, who had supported Van de Velde at the Werkbund and, incidentally, saw active service at the front, held that the uncritical admiration of machinery and technological progress was the source of Germany's undoing. It is perhaps significant that the early days of the Weimar Bauhaus were characterized by a marked return to an interest in handicrafts.

The Bauhaus served as one of the last significant staging posts of the Arts and Crafts tradition. It was established in 1919 under the direction of Walter Gropius (1883–1969) and had emerged from the amalgamated schools of fine and applied arts in Weimar with the proposed addition of a new school of architecture. The programme of the Bauhaus contained a number of ideals common to the Arts and Crafts tradition: Gropius had stated that the school aimed to reconcile the fine and applied arts, and to put them to the service of building. The prime point of departure for the Bauhaus curriculum was handicraft. Gropius maintained that there was no real difference between the work of the artist and that of the craftsman and that craft was the proper basis for all creative achievement. Teachers at the Bauhaus were classified as Masters of Form, and craftsmen as Technical Masters. The old academic and class distinctions between the fine and the applied arts, in principle at least, were forgotten. The guild ideal was extended in the relationship between staff and students. Teachers were known as 'masters' and students either as 'apprentices' or 'journeymen'. The curriculum was to consist of an initial six-month preliminary course, after which students would receive training under the direction of both Masters of Form and Technical Masters. Masters of Form taught theoretical issues under the categories of Observation, Representation and Composition, each of which had their own sub-divisions; and Technical Masters supervised teaching in craft workshops in the fields of stone, wood, metal,

ABOVE LEFT *The Allgemeine Elektricitäts Gesellschaft factory before its redesign.*

LEFT *The redesigned AEG factory by Peter Behrens, 1907–1908.*

BELOW LEFT *Electric kettle for AEG designed by Behrens, c. 1908.*

RIGHT Pewter tea service by Peter Behrens, 1904.

CENTRE RIGHT Universal Typeface designed by Herbert Bayer, 1925. Bayer ran the painting and typographic-design workshops at the Bauhaus.

clay, glass, colour and textiles. The Bauhaus was ill-equipped and was distracted not only by the explosive political climate in post-war Germany but also by internal dissent among members of staff from the old Academy of Fine Arts who were resentful of the Bauhaus' radical new programme. The school was also dogged by half-hearted support from the Weimar authorities and was eventually forced to leave the city for the politically more clement climate of Dessau.

The move to Dessau marked a period of re-organization that served to give the Bauhaus something of the unity of direction it had lacked in Weimar. The aims of the Dessau Bauhaus, as Gillian Naylor has observed, shifted from craft-based activities to the construction of industrial prototypes. The metal-work of Wilhelm Wagenfeld and tubular-steel furniture of Marcel Breuer are notable examples of this shift toward industrial concerns. Gropius also became increasingly interested in standardized design, thus echoing sentiments that had been presented by Muthesius a decade or so earlier. Among the first projects at Dessau was the building of the school itself, consisting of workshops, administrative buildings and accommodation for both staff and students in a style that was at once practical and studiedly contemporary. An estate consisting of inexpensive workers' housing was also undertaken in Dessau and it was around this period that the school became increasing interested in social and statistical theory as the logical point of departure for

architecture and design. The estate consisted of over 300 dwellings assembled from prefabricated materials and was to form an ideal modern housing community. Some contemporary observers, however, thought the houses thoroughly 'un-German'.

The Bauhaus was against academic convention and the divisions that traditionally separated art and craft, yet it never followed a one-party line alone. Gropius had championed Van de Velde in the dispute with Muthesius on the creative autonomy of the architect and designer and continued to allow students similar freedoms. Even at Dessau it becomes difficult to pin the school down to anything other than a number of articles of faith focusing on machine production, rational design and an awareness of living in a modern age. Marcel Breuer's much imitated tubular-steel pieces of furniture were not simply rational designs in a new material hitherto reserved for industry. Breuer spoke enigmatically about constructing furniture in space. A functionalist spirit is evident in much of the output from the Bauhaus, yet such abstract interest in artistic form often lurks nearby. Some members of the Bauhaus recognized a contradiction between the respective aims of art and functionalism and realized that what works well need not necessarily look artistic and vice versa. Intellectual consistency was imposed upon the school under the directorship of the left-wing architect Hannes Meyer.

Meyer was appointed as Gropius' successor in 1928 and attempted to inject undiluted

ABOVE LEFT Tea service in silver with wooden handles by Christian Deli, produced at the Bauhaus metal workshop, c. 1925.

LEFT Bauhaus building at Dessau, 1925–26 (from an aerial photograph of 1926).

BELOW LEFT Tubular metal chair. The prototypes for tubular furniture had been produced at the Bauhaus by Marcel Breuer about 1926–27. Chairs closely resembling Breuer's original designs are still in production today.

social utility into the Bauhaus curriculum, purging many of the distracting 'incestuous' artistic theories that had circulated in the school since its inception. Practical architecture became the dominant interest and theoretical studies revolved around town planning, economics and sociology, with the inclusion of classes in physical exercise as a counter balance to mental labour. Under Meyer's directorship the school even supported its own communist cell. Left-wing ideals found form in the emphasis given to the production of cheap, mass-produced items, to mass-housing pro-grammes and to collective rather than individual work on the part of students. Meyer was ousted from the Bauhaus when his contract was terminated in 1930. His high left-wing political profile was impractical in a political milieu that was steadily lurching to the right. Meyer's career at the Bauhaus marked the effective demise of the Arts and Crafts Movement. The link between Meyer and Morris is a tenuous one, yet aspects of Morris's work – his socialist convictions and his interest in a commonplace, logical, democratic art, often undertaken collectively rather than individually and serving the needs of the common man or woman found more than a passing similarity to the last days of the Bauhaus.

The final days of the school under the direction of Mies van der Rohe are depressing. Attacked by both the left and right wings and fraught with internal unrest, the Bauhaus eventually closed under pressure from the National Socialists in August 1933.

A GUIDE TO
ART NOUVEAU
STYLE
WILLIAM HARDY

●

RIGHT: *Embroidery by Hermann Obrist. Here is the purest expression of the Art Nouveau love of an undulating line. Obrist has taken his inspiration from plant life (roots, leaves and flowers all being discernable here) but has developed the forms into an elaborate "whiplash" pattern.*

 The essence of Art Nouveau is a line, a sinuous extended curve found in every design of this style. Art Nouveau rejected the order of straight line and right-angle in favour of a more natural movement Whether these lines were used in realistic depictions of natural forms or as abstracted shapes evoking an organic vitality, the emphasis was on decorative pattern and also flatness, a surface on which this concern for the linear, the line of Art Nouveau, could be developed. Solidity, mass, permanence, any connection with weight or stability and stillness ran counter to the Art Nouveau style. The insubstantiality of line was best exploited in light malleable materials, or those that could be fashioned to appear so. It was, in essence, a graphic style of decoration that was transferred onto a variety of solid objects. This curving, flowing line brought with it a feeling of airy lightness, grace and freedom.

Nature was the ultimate source book of the Art Nouveau artist, particularly the plant world, for many artists had a scientist's depth of knowledge of botany. Flowers, stems and leaves were chosen for their curving silhouettes. Naturally, lilies, irises and orchids were favoured, although any and every form, from palm fronds to seaweed, offered potential for development into an animated pattern. Insects and birds of colour and grace lent themselves to the same stylizing and refining process — dragonflies, peacocks, swallows, or creatures such as snakes or greyhounds. These decorative possibilities could also be developed from the curves of the female body, particularly when combined with long, loose, flowing hair which could be arranged into a fantasy of curls and waves. As the style developed, the quest for more novel forms grew.

Art Nouveau developed in the late 1880s and was at its creative height in the subsequent decade. By 1905 it had declined into being a much diluted ingredient in commercial design, soon to be replaced by an aesthetic felt to be more in keeping with the new century.

However, Art Nouveau itself owed much of its own popularity to its modernity, as reflected in the French term for the style which has since become universal.

The 19th century had seen enormous changes in society in both Europe and America, with the spread of industrialization resulting in the creation of great wealth concentrated on the new industrial and commercial cities. The mass-production methods of factories not only created a whole new class of workers but also a vast range of goods more widely available than ever before. Simultaneously, advances in technology — trains, steamships and the telegraph — were easing the problems of communication. The world had changed, yet there was no corresponding change in the styles employed to shape its appearance. In the design of everyday objects, just as in the design of buildings, the new age was offered continual revivals of old styles: Classical, Gothic, Renaissance, Baroque or Louis XV. Art Nouveau was the first style that did not seem to have its roots sunk deeply into European history. Instead it seemed to be the first truly new style of the century, despite the fact that it did not emerge until the closing decades. This helps to explain the fervour with which it was pursued and the rapidity of its spread.

The characteristic curving forms of Art Nouveau first appeared in England, yet they were to spread rapidly throughout Europe to a wide range of cities, each with a distinctive interpretation of the style: Paris and Nancy in France, Munich, Berlin and Darmstadt in Germany, Brussels, Barcelona, Glasgow and Vienna all become focal points for the style that was soon universal in Europe, and — with centres in New York and Chicago — equally influential in America. At the time, this range of regional styles resulted in some confusion as to terminology as well as sources. Often it was the theme of modernity that was to provide a name — 'Art Nouveau' and 'Modern Style' in France, 'Modernismo' in Spain and 'Moderne Stile' in Italy — or else a simple reference to place as with 'Belgische Stil' (Belgium Style) in Germany or 'Stile Inglese' in Italy. There was no clear idea as to a common origin, nor shared characteristics, until the style was in its decline. Only with hindsight has a more coherent view of the period been formed.

However, some contemporary terms for the style do throw light upon the way the style was disseminated, and serve to stress its internationalism. The term itself, 'Art Nouveau', derives from the Parisian shop of the same name run by a German emigré, Samuel Bing. Bing had been trading for ten years in Japanese art when, in 1895, he re-opened his premises as 'La Maison de l'Art Nouveau' and started to show the work of

LEFT: *New machinery at the 1851 Great Exhibition. Industrial technology had introduced the mass production of everyday artefacts and threatened the role of the craftsman. The iron beams and columns, and glass ceilings of the Crystal Palace were themselves revolutionary elements in 19th century architecture.*

contemporary designers as well as painters and sculptors. This mixture of gallery, shop and showroom became the Parisian base for the new style, encouraging Bing to commission works for the shop and to promote his artists and craftsmen abroad. Bing's reputation as the impressario of Art Nouveau was sufficient for him to be allotted an entire pavilion for his own designers at the Paris Exposition Universelle of 1900. Another Italian term for the style, 'Stile Liberty', was a tribute to the London department store of the same name that sold the designs of progressive British craftsmen.

This mixture of commerce and art, so suitable for the Art Nouveau interest in household artefacts, was not restricted to a few enlightened retailers, but is best seen in the way the style spread through the great international trade fairs of the era. These events were products of the great age of industrialization, for they were descended from the 1851 London Great Exhibition, housed in the Crystal Palace, which had been held to demonstrate the possible applications of new technology. These exhibitions soon became an increasingly important feature of international commerce, at which the new styles of decorative art could be displayed. Particularly important events in the development of Art Nouveau were the international exhibitions of 1889 and 1900 in Paris, and of 1902 in Turin, while that of 1905, held in Liège, marked the end of the style's importance. Emulating the success of these commercial exhibitions were a number of international Fairs specifically devoted to the arts, such as

those of 1897 in Munich and Dresden, and a second Dresden show in 1899. Supporting these large events were innumerable smaller exhibitions of craft guilds and progressive groups of artists in Europe and America which reflected a widespread interest in new styles in every art form.

The depth of interest among the public in the new fashions in art, and particularly the decorative arts, was also reflected in the huge numbers of new magazines and periodicals devoted to these trends which appeared in the Art Nouveau era. The German version of the style, 'Jugendstil', even derived its name from the influential Munich-based journal *Jugend* (youth), while also sometimes being called 'Studiostil' after the widely read English, and later American, periodical *The Studio*. Equivalent publications were *Pan* from Berlin and *Ver Sacrum* from Vienna. The German language periodicals also included contemporary literature, poetry and criticism, but as in all such journals of the time the main coverage of the new style came not in specific articles but in the actual design of the publication itself. The title-page, typeface and illustrations were all the work of Art Nouveau graphic artists. Such periodicals had a wide circulation beyond the limited circle of craftsmen, but there existed too journals such as the influential *Art et Décoration* from Paris which concentrated more exclusively on the decorative arts, and included many photographs. Through exhibitions, shops, galleries and magazines the Art Nouveau style spread rapidly throughout Europe and America, both feeding off and stimulating the public's interest.

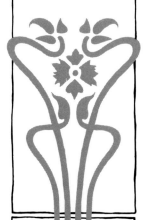

ORIGINS

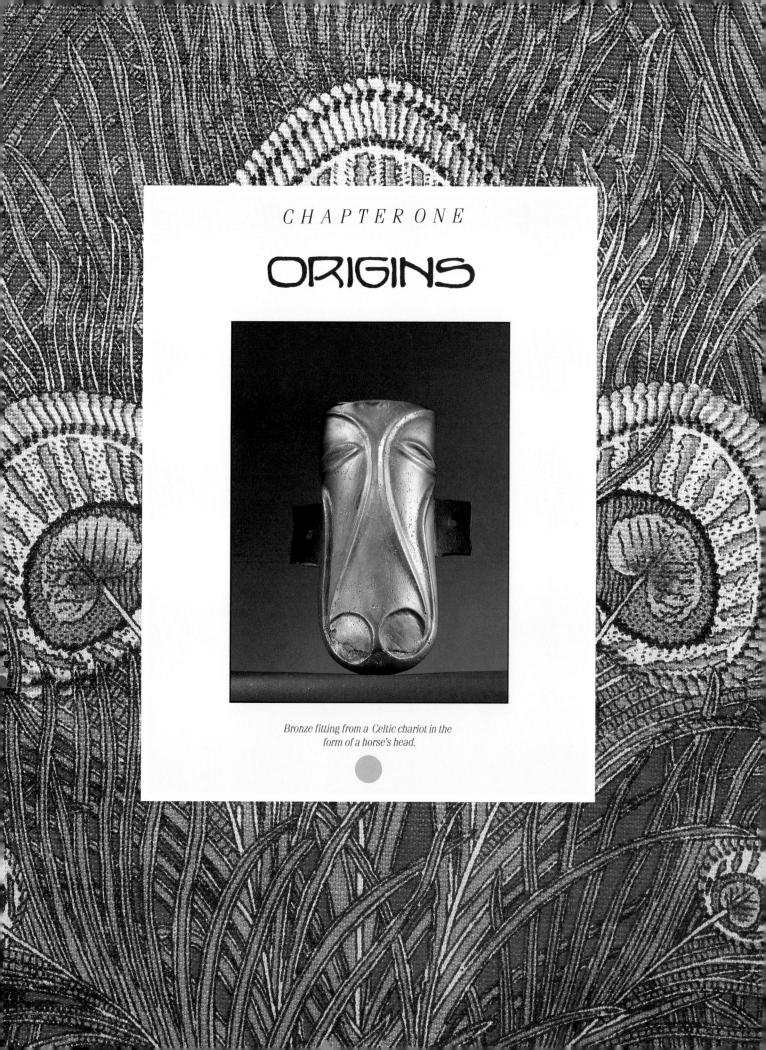

*Bronze fitting from a Celtic chariot in the
form of a horse's head.*

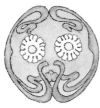

i once a king and chief · now am the tree-barks thief :

eftr twixt trunk and leaf · chasing the prey ·

The origins of the Art Nouveau style are to be found in Victorian England. Here one discovers not only the sinuous decorative line that was to characterize the appearance of the style, but also the ideas that were to become its theoretical base. The Great Exhibition of 1851 had been held, not only to advertise new technology and promote trade, but also to advertise what were held to be examples of well designed objects. Some of the profits from the event went into the foundation of the Victoria and Albert Museum in London, whose purpose was to encourage a further interest in the decorative arts by means of its exemplary displays. A general climate of interest in the subject had been created, but the standards of the Exhibition were harshly criticized by the influential writer on art, John Ruskin.

Ruskin abhorred the products of mass-production and called for a return to craftsmanship inspired by a romantic view of the Middle Ages. He rejected as artificial the division that had arisen between the so-called fine arts and the decorative arts, pointing out that Michelangelo's great Sistine Chapel ceiling had in fact been primarily a work of decoration. By revitalizing the crafts, Ruskin hoped to develop an alternative to what he saw as the horror of factory labour, as well as improving the aesthetic quality of everday objects.

FAR LEFT
A Morris tapestry of 1885. Morris' inspiration lay partly in the natural world, and his depictions of plants, animals and birds are all well-observed but simplified and integrated into the overall design.

LEFT: *The Strawberry Thief, a Morris textile design of 1883. Curving natural shapes are symetrically ordered, unlike the more abandoned developments of Art Nouveau.*

CENTRE LEFT: *William Morris in 1877 when the Arts & Crafts movement that he had created was beginning to revolutionize English design.*

He advised craftsmen and architects to return to nature for their forms, rejecting the historicism of Victorian revivalism and anticipating the work of the Art Nouveau architects Horta, Guimard and Gaudí.

Ruskin's ideas were taken up by his disciple, the craftsman, poet, pamphleteer, printer, erstwhile painter and architect, William Morris. Ruskin's friends were the painters of the Pre-Raphaelite group and Morris began his career, firstly as a painter, as a follower of the group's dreamy interpretation of the medieval past. However, Morris had a more practical view of that period when it came to his attempt to recreate its idyll of painters, architects and craftsmen working together, often on the same tasks: in 1861 he founded a company to produce the type of objects he wanted to see in every home — this became Morris & Co. Morris was able to effect a genuine bridging of the divide between artists and craftsmen by employing his friends among the Pre-Raphaelite painters to decorate cabinets and bureau, and to design tapestries, fabrics and chairs. Morris' company was able to produce a complete range of goods to furnish the home, in a uniform style, to achieve an overall harmony of effect. In this, he anticipated the versatility of the Art Nouveau artist/craftsman.

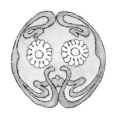

RIGHT: *Title page for Mackmurdo's* Wren's City Churches

FAR RIGHT: *Morris painted glass from Wightwick Manor. The central figure of Chaucer emphasizes the medieval inspiration for Arts & Crafts stained glass.*

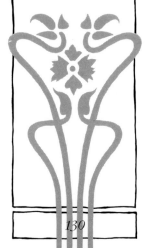

The actual appearance of these goods was often reminiscent of medieval models, particularly in furniture, but in fabrics, carpets, wallpaper and decoration the Morris style derived largely from natural sources, inspired by plant, bird and animal forms. The use of hand-crafted, natural materials made these goods too expensive for ordinary people, yet despite this Morris still hoped that his products would become widespread enough to improve the quality of the lives of as many people as possible. Like Ruskin, he hoped to free the working man from the drudgery of factory labour and, through craftsmanship, enable him to gain pleasure from his work. Morris' ideals became polarized into socialism, which he espoused with increasing vigour toward the end of his life. In 1888 he established the Arts and Crafts Exhibition Society through which his work and that of his associates was displayed.

The example of the Morris Company encouraged other similar enterprises in Britain, usually referred to under the general term 'Arts and Crafts Movement'. Chief among these was the Century Guild, formed in

1884 by Arthur Mackmurdo. Influenced by the flowing, natural forms of Morris, Mackmurdo developed these shapes into elongated, increasingly elegant patterns and was the first to produce the characteristic vocabulary of Art Nouveau. The breakthrough is seen to be Mackmurdo's illustration for the title page of his book, *Wren's City Churches*. Here the flowers used by Morris, and roosters at either side framing the design, are drawn up into an artificial, stylized slenderness. The stems of the flowers undulate in an asymmetrical, rippling pattern like underwater plants animated by unseen currents. As early as 1883 Mackmurdo had created the sinuous, flame-like shapes that were to be the hallmark of Art Nouveau for the next 20 years.

Mackmurdo was undoubtedly the originator of a new direction, and the theme was rapidly developed in the work of the Century Guild and a similar pioneering body, the Art Workers' Guild, created by Walter Crane and Lewis Day in 1882. Through the Arts and Crafts Exhibition Society and the increasing output of Morris' followers, the work of the Arts and Crafts movement began to gain international recognition and the

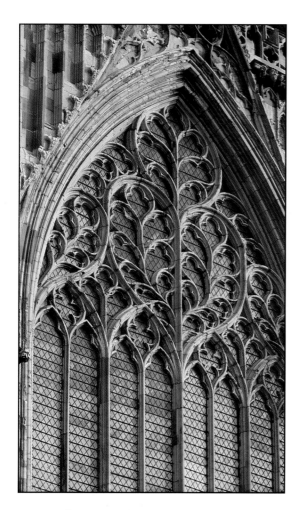

medieval art of the mid-nineteenth century had emphasized the value of curving, organically inspired shapes seen in the architecture, sculpture and stained glass of the Middle Ages as a contrast to the rectilinear severity of classicism. Both Ruskin and Morris had turned to the medieval artists' study of nature as their inspiration and their interest was reflected in that of their contemporaries, the Pre-Raphaelite painters.

Dante Gabriel Rossetti and Edward Burne-Jones, leading Pre-Raphaelites, both designed and painted furniture for Morris as well as including specific details of dress and armour in their paintings. As this kind of historical appreciation of Gothic grew, so too did the awareness that this term encompassed a num-

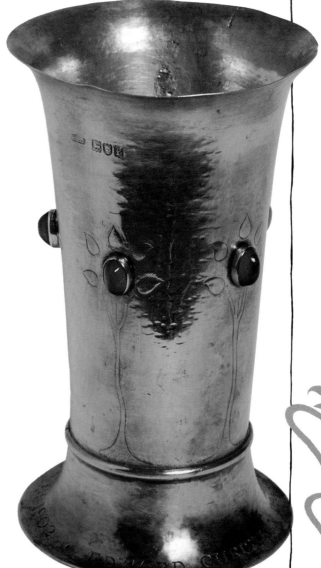

forms of Art Nouveau started to emerge to be developed elsewhere. However, it was not only a stylistic influence that was apparent but perhaps, more importantly, the ideals of Ruskin and Morris that acted as an inspiration to painters and architects to extend their activities into the decorative arts, to become craftsmen, and to revitalize society as a whole. Art Nouveau, as a style embracing all the arts, therefore owed its ultimate origin to the earlier English Crafts revival, with its concern for a unity of the arts allied to rather Utopian ideas of social renewal through handicrafts.

The first examples of the flowing forms of Art Nouveau occurred in the work of Mackmurdo's Century Guild. Not all stylistic features can be traced so easily to one source, nor, despite the apparent modernity of the movement, are they devoid of historical links. Despite the anti-revivalist, novel qualities of Art Nouveau, some of the strands of its complicated and extensive root structure were grounded in the revival of past styles. The Gothic revival served in some ways as an inspiration, for the fervent examination of

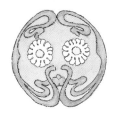

●

RIGHT: *The mirror room in the Amalienburg pavillion of the Schloss Nymphenburg, Munich for which French craftsmen produced a perfect expression of the rococo in 18th century Germany. The light, capricious elegance of the restless rococo line influenced Art Nouveau designers.*

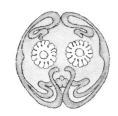

ber of different styles, from the chaste, plain lines of its early period to the flamboyant fantasy of later medieval art. It was this form of the style that was to inspire the Art Nouveau. Stained glass, too, immediately reminiscent of the Middle Ages and revived by the Arts and Crafts workers, was also to play an important part in Art Nouveau design. The late Gothic style was plundered not to afford pedantic historical details, but as a sourcebook for new ideas.

Viollet-le-Duc differed from Ruskin in his acceptance of new industrially-produced materials in art, particularly the use of iron in architecture. Another Frenchman offers a striking parallel to both Ruskin and Morris: Léon de Laborde, the organizer of the French entry in the 1851 Great Exhibition. Laborde's report on the Exhibition criticized the gap that had been created between the arts and mechanically-produced artefacts. To correct this, he advised artists to concern themselves in future less with reviving the trappings of past styles and more with the design of everyday objects. These very Morris-like ideas were echoed by Viollet-le-Duc in his teaching at the Parisian Ecole-des Beaux-Arts, where he recommended far closer collaboration between all the arts, focusing on architecture, to produce a stylistically harmonious whole. With these two men, French Art Nouveau could look to its own theorists and writers for inspiration.

If flamboyant, late Gothic provided an example of the creative use of the past by the Art Nouveau, then so too did the inspired re-examination of the 18th century rococo style in France. This style had become one of the many open to the revivalists of the next century, but rather than resurrect it completely Art Nouveau observed its forms and characteristics with an independent eye. Rococo had been more broadly associated with use of a capriciously cavorting, light and delicate line as an ornament in all the decorative arts. This was very close to the line of Art Nouveau, and the connection became clear when, in France, the designers of the regional Nancy school began to incorporate references to rococo in their work. The common source of natural forms of plant and wave in both Art Nouveau and rococo made the blend harmonious. The rococo preference for light, high-keyed colour in interiors was also pursued by Art Nouveau, in reaction to the heaviness and solemnity of sombre Victorian interiors. While it was strongest in France, Munich had also been an important outpost of rococo in the 18th century, and it is no coincidence to find that the lightest, wittiest and most fanciful forms of Jugendstil were later to be found in that city in the work of Hermann Obrist (1863-1927) or August Endell(1871-1925).

LEFT: *A detail from the Amalienburg revealing the curling leaf forms of rococo.*

BELOW LEFT: *Viollet-le-Duc's interest in the Gothic combines with a fascination for the use of iron in this design for vaulting. The elaborately-moulded brackets supporting the iron columns, and the openness of the interior made possible by the new materials, both anticipate subsequent developments in Art Nouveau.*

BELOW: *Iron is used here not only as a decorative element on the balconies but also as a structural framework, as can be seen from the buttresses dividing the shop windows, in this illustration to Viollet-le-Duc's* Entretiens.

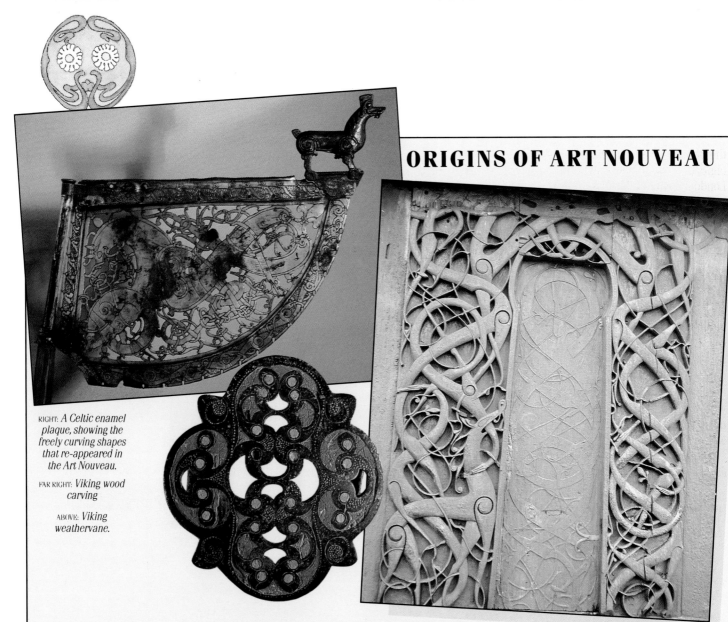

RIGHT: *A Celtic enamel plaque, showing the freely curving shapes that re-appeared in the Art Nouveau.*

FAR RIGHT: *Viking wood carving*

ABOVE: *Viking weathervane.*

Some stylistic revivals of the 19th century were partly inspired by the growing nationalism of the time, which was tinged, as ever, by a romantic idea of the past. Some of these revivals of national artistic consciousness also percolated into Art Nouveau, and helped to form its many regional variations. The revival of interest in early Celtic art became an important influence on the Glasgow school, and its most renowned figure, Charles Rennie Mackintosh. Celtic jewellery and the ancient gospel books of Durrow, Lindisfarne and Kells revealed precisely their elaborately curving and twisting decoration, the combination of stylization and

natural inspiration that typified Art Nouveau itself. More particularly, the use of lavish ornament confined within strict limits and contrasted with more open areas had strong parallels with the work of the Glasgow designers in all media. Interest in Celtic art was matched by enthusiasm for the similar ancient Irish and Anglo-Saxon styles, all evident in an example such as Liberty's 1900 range of jewellery, mysteriously named 'Cymric'.

An interest in early Nordic art in the Scandinavian countries emphasized their revived artistic vitality, and the intricate curves and spirals of this tradition found their way into the

local form of Art Nouveau, as in the designs of the Norwegian Henrick Bull. It was even occasionally termed the Dragon style in deference to its Viking source. Morris himself had also toyed with this style after several trips to Iceland, as well as translating the Viking sagas of that country.

Clearly Art Nouveau, although drawing from previous centuries, was far-removed from the rather naive and concentrated revivalism that had preceded it. With its capricious use of past and peculiar mixture of styles, Art Nouveau could not be anything other than a uniquely novel style. Its eclecticism extended to its strong roots in oriental art, and in particular

that of Japan. Japan was a relatively new discovery for the West, having been opened up to Western trade by the American Commander Perry in 1853. Perry stimulated the creation of a formal trade agreement in the following year, and the quantity of Japanese goods available in Europe and America steadily grew, as too did public interest in the highly sophisticated work of Japanese artists and craftsmen. Wood-cut prints became popular among the avant-garde artists, particularly in France, who discovered in them exciting new solutions to problems of composition and use of colour. Some of the leading figures of Art Nouveau began their involvement in

the decorative arts as champions of the new Japanese style. In London, Arthur Liberty set up business in a small shop trading in oriental goods before expanding his premises into the great turn-of-the-century department store, Liberty & Co. Before opening 'l'Art Nouveau', Bing had been one of the leading oriental dealers in Paris, and had formed an impressive personal collection. So to had one of his most important collaborators, the American designer and decorator Louis Comfort Tiffany, who later became one of the most prominent artists of Art Nouveau glassware.

The formal links between Japanese prints and Art Nouveau are strong. The emphasis on decorative line, creating flat, patterned work was immediately found to be sympathetic. Nor did the Japanese artists overburden their work with excessive ornamentation. Instead, they maintained a refined interplay between decoration and background, setting a light and elegant design against plain ground. The curving, flowing Japanese line was drawn from observation of nature, filtered through a developed design sense to create more abstracted forms and patterns with the precise degree of artificiality that the Art Nouveau artists found so pleasing. These features combined to create a sense of delicacy, refinement and sheer stylishness that was the aim of every Art Nouveau craftsman.

The art of Japan became by far the greatest single oriental influence on Europe at the time, but 19th century interest in the exotic, parallel to the infatuation for the romance of the past, had also stimulated a renewed interest in other cultures.

Java was one of the Dutch colonies at this time, and as Holland became a centre of Art Nouveau, Javanese art became a noticeable influence upon the Dutch form of the style. Javanese batik work, a form of textile printing using wax, was the most transportable art form and one whose exotic, flat patterns was of particular interest. The influential Dutch painter, Jan Toorop, made use of such patterns as well as of the distinctive insect-like stick puppets of Java. His 'Three Brides' is a highly stylized work that owes much of its disturbing elegance to this source, largely unknown thoughout the rest of Europe. Besides Japan and Java, Art Nouveau craftsmen also studied art of the Muslim world which had a similar tendency toward the abstraction of natural shapes and the creation of flat, rhythmic patterns. Art from Persia, Turkey and North Africa occured as occasional exotic influences.

ABOVE RIGHT: *Wind-blown waves by the master Japanese print maker Hiroshige whose ability to create an effective composition through flowing expressive line and a combination of simple flat shapes inspired the painters and designers of late 19th century Europe.*

BELOW FAR RIGHT: *An Indonesian stick puppet used in shadow theatre. The Dutch painter and designer, Jan Toorop, used the attenuated forms of these figures in his art.*

ABOVE FAR RIGHT: *The intricate, curving pattern of these Thai figures also supplied European artists with decorative ideas.*

BELOW RIGHT: *A medieval Persian flask whose twisted handles and irridescent surface are typical of the features that fascinated the exponents of Art Nouveau.*

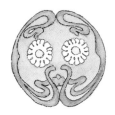

BELOW RIGHT: *J. McNeil Whistler's Peacock room including his own painting* La Princesse du Pays du Porcelaine *over the fireplace. Whistler based himself in late 19th century London but was familiar with artistic and literary life in Britain and France. An eminent dandy in the manner of Oscar Wilde, he also used his paintings to evoke moods in a manner comparable to the work of Symbolist poets. Here his concern is to create a complete environment, designing all the elements himself. Of particular interest are the peacocks on the gold-painted window shutters whose extravagant plumage is treated with Art Nouveau sweeping linearity.*

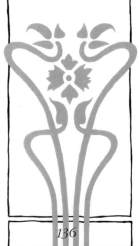

While Art Nouveau drew stylistic inspiration from the orient, and to some degree from the past, it was also firmly embedded in its own time. Socially, economically and intellectually, it was created by the needs of the age. Europe was at its wealthiest before the disasters of the two world wars; the upper and middle classes in every country were prepared to spend surplus income on expensively-produced objects for the home which made their owners feel themselves to be discerning and stylish.

The techniques and materials employed in the production of these goods were very often the result of 19th century technological progress. This applied not only to the more dramatic products of industrialization, such as the use of iron architecture, but to new firing and glazing processes in ceramics and glassware, electroplating in metalwork and the use of the electric light. The technological aspects of process or material might not be stressed by the Art Nouveau designer as he wrapped metallic ivy around an electric lamp or turned his ironwork gate into a medievally-inspired dragon, but, despite a nostalgia for craftsmanship, designers nevertheless placed the products of the style firmly in the industrialized age.

There was a strong connection between the decorative arts and literature throughout Europe. All the arts were retreating from the aggressive realism of the previous decades into a more creative and imaginative response to nature. In painting, this took the form of a reaction to the truthful rendering of the visual sensation of the Impressionists, in literature a reaction to the social realism of Zola or Dickens. Instead, there was a new emphasis on subjective inspiration.

Music as a non-descriptive art form was a common inspiration, but visual artists also turned to writers in order to explore a world of feelings and moods. More artists began to illustrate works of literature or refer to them in their work. This applied to Art Nouveau craftsmen too. Emile Gallé inscribed furniture and glassware with favourite quotations from contemporary poets, pieces of pottery or jewellery were given semi-literary titles, mythological themes were alluded to, all in an attempt to endow the work with extra significance.

The Symbolist school of literature placed greater emphasis on evocation of moods or emotions, often intangible and mysterious, rather than factual description. The Art Nouveau artist pursued a similar path when he abstracted forms from nature, intending to communicate the essence of a flower by its gentle lines and fresh colour, rather than by minute description. Poets such as Mallarmé also stressed the artificiality of their work and its aesthetic qualities, and tried to emulate the ornament and decoration of the artist by intricate language and the use of unusual words.

For the self-styled decadents, the pursuit of excellence in art was the most important thing in life, for beauty was more important than morality. Everything might be sacrificed in order to attain a beautiful result. This extreme aestheticism reached its peak in the figure of Oscar Wilde, whose libel action and subsequent trial in 1895 for homosexuality discredited the fashion for decadence in England.

In France, the most extreme dandy of this type was Count Robert de Montesquiou, a great patron of Art Nouveau craftsmen, whose every possession had to be of the most exquisite beauty and quality. This was a strange, ironic mutation of Morris' theory that the homes and lives of poorer people could be improved by the better quality of their possessions. Montesquiou was immortalized as the decadent aristocrat, Des Esseintes, in the novel by Huysmans *A Rebors*, which consists of lengthy descriptions of the beautiful objects which surrounded the hero. This degree of luxury and aesthetic commitment to the quality of the

smallest possession sustained the resurgence of the decorative arts during the Art Nouveau era.

The relationship between Art Nouveau and contemporary painting was more ambiguous and complex. Although the flat, flowing shapes of Art Nouveau are first discernable in Mackmurdo's work in England, they also appear independently in French painting of the time. Reacting to Impressionism, Paul Gauguin began to develop his own form of symbolist painting, concentrating on large, flat, interlocking areas of colour strongly outlined by emphatic, curling contours. In this he was as much influenced by Japanese woodcuts as subsequent Art Nouveau artists were to be. The strongest example of this, the *Vision After the Sermon* of 1888, was heralded by him as the beginning of the cloissonist or enamel style, paying tribute to an influence from the decorative arts; for enamel work, like stained glass, consists of flat areas of strongly-outlined colour.

Gauguin's style was well-known to those Art Nouveau craftsmen who began as painters, but Gauguin himself cannot be described as an Art Nouveau artist. Although there are similarities in style, Gauguin's personality was strong and he used these stylistic features to communicate a personal view rather than as a purely decorative feature. However, the followers of Gauguin, who in 1893 formed themselves into a group called the Nabis, seized upon the flat, decorative aspects of his style.

The Nabis knowingly blurred the distinction between fine and decorative arts. One of their number, Maurice Denis, made the famous statement that a picture 'is essentially a flat surface covered with colours assembled in a certain order'. Denis' paintings of this period do indeed appear like Art Nouveau designs, with their flat shapes, broad flowing curves and subject matter that is merely charming and decorative rather than interesting in its own right. It bears a close similarity to the embroidery of the Art Nouveau designer Henry Van de Velde, essentially a piece of decorative craft work. With a newfound Catholic faith to fire his painting, Denis later repudiated his flirtation with the principles of graphic art and Art Nouveau, but his work and those of his fellows Nabis reveal the closeness of the fine and decorative arts in the 1890's.

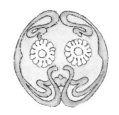

●

BELOW LEFT: The Kiss, *by Gustav Klimt. The figures, and consequently the subject of the piece, become overwhelmed by his interest in pattern.*

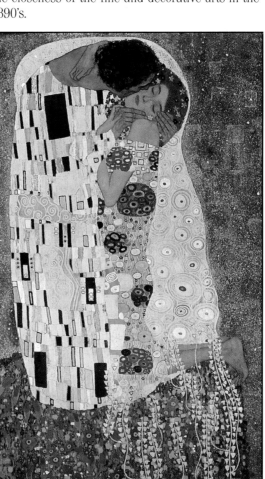

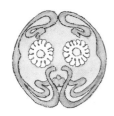

RIGHT: Le Divan Japonais, *poster by Henri de Toulouse-Lautrec. Working on a poster, Lautrec became a master of Art Nouveau design, whilst maintaining a more personal style in his paintings.*

FAR RIGHT: Emile Flöge *by Gustav Klimt. Here Klimt incorporates decorative elements into what is still a painterly work.*

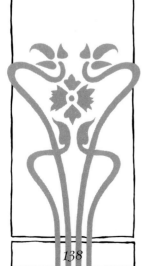

Painters who did not pursue Gauguin's style also explored similar areas. Pierre Puvis de Chavannes built a successful career on large mural paintings with a strong decorative element, consisting of muted colours and generalized, rather flat shapes of figures in landscape. Georges Seurat, who in many ways continued the exploration of the light effects and brushwork of the Impressionists, also became interested in the expressive possibilities of pure line, exploiting, in his later works, an equivalent of the whiplash contour of Art Nouveau decorators. The poster artist, Chéret, who also influenced Henri de Toulouse-Lautrec was a strong influence on Seurat at this time. Although Toulouse-Lautrec was also inspired by the impressionist Raoul Dégas, and painted similar cabaret and brothel scenes, he too was inclined to flatten shapes out and concentrate upon an expressive, meandering line. Toulouse-Lautrec also produced many successful posters which, with their curvilinear stylizations, simplifications and flowing, active lettering, deserve to be treated as masterpieces of Art Nouveau graphic art.

In some ways, the traditional view of painters being the serious experimenters and innovators whose creations inspire those of their colleagues in the minor decorative arts, can be seen to be true in the case of Art Nouveau, particularly in its relationship with Gauguin. However, the converse is also true, that the vitality and inventiveness of Art Nouveau designers inspired painters. Certainly many painters, sculptors and architects deserted their own specialities to work in the sphere of general design, which they felt to be both more lively and socially useful. Art Nouveau crafts were rapidly accepted as arts and displayed on an equal footing with painting, as in the pioneering exhibitions of the Vingt group in Brussels which influenced the development of Horta and Van de Velde.

It is easier to discuss a painter in terms of Art Nouveau influence, or of certain common characteristics shared with Art Nouveau, than it is to discuss an Art Nouveau painting. Since Art Nouveau is a term most accurately applied to the decorative arts, it implies some degree of judgement of a painter's subject matter if one classes his work as Art Nouveau. The example of Gustav Klimt typifies the dilemma. Klimt was an Austrian painter who had very close associations with Viennese designers and architects. As his style progressed, he became more influenced by their work, and by mosaics, until his figures became very flat and set into a background consisting of a purely decorative frieze of gold and abstract patterns. Klimt's subject matter retains its concentrated eroticism, which is the theme of his work as a whole, but he comes as near as a painter can to painting in Art Nouveau style.

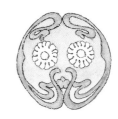

CHAPTER TWO

ARCHITECTURE

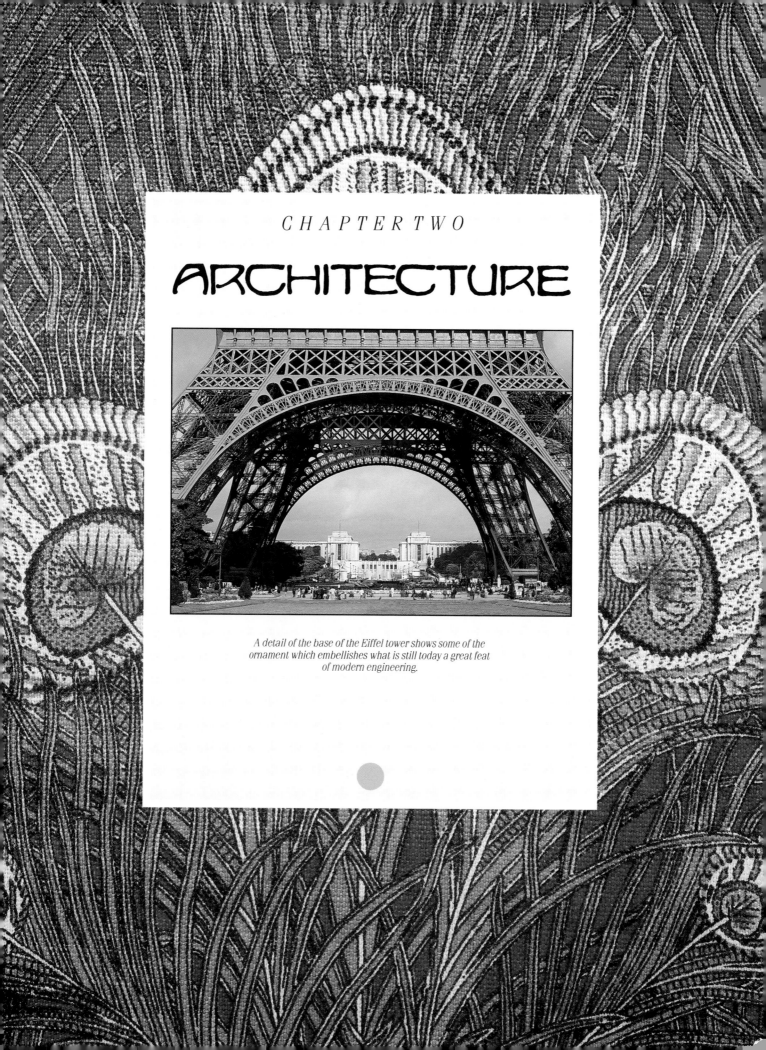

*A detail of the base of the Eiffel tower shows some of the
ornament which embellishes what is still today a great feat
of modern engineering.*

ABOVE RIGHT: *The iron and glass vaulting of Brighton Station typifies the use made of these materials by railway engineers before they entered the mainstream of Art Nouveau architecture.*

BELOW RIGHT: *The curling iron work of Victor Horta's Tassel House in Brussels.*

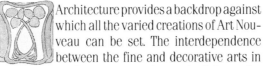

Architecture provides a backdrop against which all the varied creations of Art Nouveau can be set. The interdependence between the fine and decorative arts in Art Nouveau is best seen via the work of the major architects of the time, who required fittings in keeping with their domestic architecture while their fellow craftsmen needed the appropriate setting to display their work. From among the fine arts it is architecture that has the strongest technical, craft base, and when the conventional crafts were on the decline in the face of industrialization architects were at the forefront of their revival. William Morris, his colleague Philip Webb, and Arthur Mackmurdo were all trained architects. Many of the leaders of Art Nouveau were also architects: Horta, Guimard, Van de Velde, Behrens, Mackintosh, Gaudí, Gaillard and Grasset.

The architects of the Arts and Crafts movement looked back to a nostalgic pre-industrial era of simple brick and stone country dwellings, inspired by the rich tradition of English architecture, but the architecture of Art Nouveau began from an opposing premise. Instead of a reactionary rejection of the industrially-produced material of iron and glass, now more readily available and so dramatically demonstrated in the 1851 Great Exhibition in London, Art Nouveau architects eagerly embraced the possibilities these suggested. Art Nouveau architecture became an important basis for twentieth century developments, and opened the way to the modernist style.

The use of iron to provide strong and comparatively light frames for buildings was first developed in the architecture of the railways and other related industries. It was clear that its strength would inevitably lead to its use in more traditional architecture too, but in England, where iron had been most dramatically used, the development was tentative. Ruskin's distaste for industrial materials was a strong influence, and when iron was used its structural role was hidden as much as possible by the more conventional brick and stone. However, in France, Viollet-le-Duc had no qualms in recommending the open use of iron in his writings, realizing its suitability for the light, high vaults of his favoured Gothic style and, very significantly, suggesting ways in which it could be shaped to create foliage patterns to embellish its role as a structural element. This exploitation of the initial malleability of iron to create naturalistic ornament was to be of the greatest significance for Art Nouveau architects. In complete contrast to Ruskin, Viollet-le-Duc was excited by the industrial architecture he saw. The Chocolat Menier factory built outside Paris in 1871 prompted him to speculate in his *Entretiens sur l'ar-*

chitecture on the further uses of iron and to produce a design for the combination of iron and stained glass (again with recourse to Gothic), a combination whose lightness and colour recommended it to the proponents of Art Nouveau.

The great engineer, Gustave Eiffel, also carried the influence of English engineering to France. Eiffel was

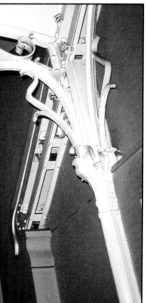

ARCHITECTURE

●

LEFT: *The Solvay house façade, gently curving with large windows. The ironwork of the balconies and window mullions provides the decoration.*

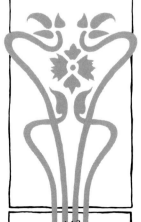

increasingly involved in the design of pavilions at the numerous international exhibitions, allowing more and more of the supporting metal frame to be revealed. It was for the Paris Exhibition of 1889 that his most famous and daring creation, the Eiffel Tower, was produced. When this was allowed to remain after the dismantling of the Exhibition it became an important, if controversial, monument to the possibilities of the new medium. In the manner of Viollet-le-Duc, Eiffel had also attempted to embellish his engineering masterpiece with some decorative flourishes in iron. The result is a compromise between English rectilinearity and the Belgian and Spanish Art Nouveau extravagance.

The work of Viollet-le-Duc and Eiffel was in some ways carried on by the highly influential first Art Nouveau architect, the Belgian Victor Horta. That such architecture emerged in Brussels before Paris is a tribute to the highly-developed artistic climate of the Belgian capital. The foundation of the exhibiting Société des Vingt in 1884 had given Brussels a place among the main centres of Symbolist painting. In 1892, when les Vingt began including decorative art in their exhibitions, it was as a recognition of the change in emphasis in the arts associated with Art Nouveau. The same year, Horta began his Tassel House at 6 Rue Paul-Emile, and Art Nouveau architecture had begun in Brussels.

Horta's early work had been with his employer, the academically classical architect Alphonse Balat, who had built the imposing Musée Royal des Beaux-Arts. The Tassel House could not contrast more strongly with this ponderous official architecture. In the interior, Horta exposed the iron columns in the hall and stairwell that carried much of the building's weight, refusing to conceal them with brick or plaster. These slender forms were then given a treatment entirely Art Nouveau in character. Rather than mould them into a conventional Gothic or classical column, as had been done before in similar circumstances in industrial architecture, Horta shaped these supports to resemble the stems of some fantastic vegetation. At the capital level of the column he attached numerous twisting and turning metal fronds, as if the main column had sprouted fresh growths that were tender and malleable. The design of the metal was emphasized by wall-and-ceiling paintings of similar loosely-flowing tendrils, which were repeated in the mosaic pattern of the floor. These features and the pale colour scheme gave the building an air of freshness, vitality and movement. Horta even managed to give the walls of the main floor characteristics of their own by using moulded and shaped partitions. The less striking exterior of the Tassel House confirms the importance of the interior for Art Nouveau, where the artist could exert a more complete control, and it is the stairwell rather than the façade that is of most importance.

The fully-fledged Art Nouveau of the Tassel House had an immediate impact, and Horta began to develop his style through a number of commissions. The Hotel Solvay in Brussels, originally designed as a

VICTOR HORTA

OPPOSITE ABOVE FAR LEFT: *Horta's own letterbox.*

OPPOSITE BELOW FAR LEFT: *A light fitting, hanging like a creeper from the ceiling of the Horta House.*

OPPOSITE RIGHT: *Glass ceilings and delicate iron columns enabled Horta to create open, airy interiors in his own house*

FAR LEFT: *The Van Eetvelde house interior, designed by Horta.*

THIRD FROM LEFT: *Horta's concern for the design of every aspect of his environment is seen here in the Horta House.*

SECOND FROM LEFT: *In the Van Eetvelde House, the forms of iron brackets are echoed on the ceiling decoration.*

LEFT: *Metal fitting from the Van Eetvelde House.*

private residence, is the most successful of his surviving façades, in essence a gentle curve between two framing bays supported by iron columns and almost entirely glazed. Horta was eager to lighten the effect of his architecture as much as possible with large windows, wide doorways and open stairwells giving an impression of open, airy space to his interiors. Now that these devices have become more commonplace it is easy to overlook the refreshing effect these rooms must have had after the cluttered gloom of a Victorian interior. There is little decoration on the stonework of the Hotel Solvay exterior; char-acteristically it is the ironwork of the balconies that embellish it. The curving effect is contin-ued in the panels of the main door and in the interior with banisters, handles and light fit-tings, all designed by Horta. The latter are particularly success-ful, falling from the ceiling like inverted creepers whose flow-ers are the shades for the elec-tric light bulbs. Horta's attention to detail is such that all the fit-tings in the house, down to the furniture and the locks, continue the curvilinear theme. Not sur-prisingly, considering the degree of control over his envi-ronment which he exerted, Horta designed his own house, which is now the Musée Horta in Brussels.

Horta's most ambitious work of this period was the Maison du Peuple, a vast social centre, since demolished. In the large auditorium of this building Horta supported his structure upon a metal frame that was entirely exposed, a daringly modern device typically coun-terbalanced by the reassuringly smooth curves of the iron ribs, beams and balconies. The exte-rior, built almost entirely of metal and glass, again used a mixture of modern materials, with the more typically Art Nou-veau curving façade and a cer-tain fussiness of massed win-dow and balcony features. The Maison du Peuple, as a cultural and social centre for the work-ing classes, reveals Horta's involvement with socialism, appearing superficially at odds with the kind of refined elegance characteristic of his art and the influence of Morris' ideals. His use of English wallpaper in the Tassel House also emphasizes his debt to the Arts and Crafts movement and underlines the impetus from England that set Art Nouveau on its course in the early 1890s.

ABOVE RIGHT: *Detail of the Castel Béranger shows Guimard's fluid handling of metalwork. Note too the abstract forms of the stonework behind.*

BELOW RIGHT: *The entrance to Guimard's Castel Béranger where stone is carved to create the impression of a malleable material.*

Horta's influence was soon felt in Paris, where the leading French architect of Art Nouveau, Hector Guimard, acknowledged Horta as one of the originators of the new style, coupled modestly with his own name. While Horta limited his plant-like decoration mostly to interiors, and even there treated it with a certain coolness, Guimard allowed fantasy to dominate his work. At times, as in his furniture designs, he seemed to be deliberately challenging the accepted limitations of his medium, whether it was iron, wood, or stone. This kind of wilfulness finds its extreme form in the Spaniard Gaudí, but Guimard's roots are very French, based on the ideas of Viollet-le-Duc but without using any form of overtly Gothic style. The nearest Guimard came to this was in the rather self-consciously rustic chalets he produced, such as the Castel Henriette, with quaint, pitched roofs and a restless sense of movement in the forms of gables, doors and windows. The greater informality of out-of-town architecture is also well demonstrated in the Villa Henry Sauvage built for the designer Louis Majorelle, outside Nancy. The house, with its high gables, assertive asymmetry and details of chimney pots and balconies, approaches a fairytale whimsy. Only hinted at here, the verticality of Gothic was often very near the surface of French Art Nouveau architecture, as in the work of Charles Plumet who liked to use steeply-roofed dormer windows and pointed arches, or in the town house that the jewellery designer René Lalique created for himself by adapting the vocabulary of French châteaux architecture.

If Guimard's country villas had a sort of quaintness, then his Parisian work is more forceful. In building his own house on the Avenue Mozart he carved the stonework into the most dramatic forms, no longer simply just natural in origin, suggesting trees and plants, but exaggerated into a more artificial fantasy and elegance. Guimard's concern for detail was equal to that of Horta. In this house as well as in his major apartment block, the Castel Béranger, his designs in metalwork and stained glass are particularly notable. In these he created purely abstract forms, emphasized by the terracotta panels decorating the entrance of the building, which ooze and flow across the walls as if they were still molten.

However, it was Guimard's work for the Paris Métro that gave him most public prominence, and even resulted in a local variation, the style Métro, one of the many different names used to describe Art Nouveau. While the overhead structures of the Métro in the suburbs had been given a conventional treatment, incidently earning a decoration for their architect, Guimard was commissioned to produce shelters and

confronts one of the strangest variations of Art Nouveau, so firmly embedded in the peculiar local conditions that it is almost possible to see it as a purely local style. Yet, paradoxically, one of the strongest features of Art Nouveau was its very diversity. The remarkably different set of characters, linked by common Art Nouveau traits, sets the short-lived movement apart from the homogeneity of previous styles, arid and easily-transferred from master to pupil. The blossoming of Art Nouveau in Brussels, Barcelona, Glasgow, Munich, New York and so many other centres was a unanimous rejection of excessive uniformity.

Catalonia in particular had its own traditions. It was the wealthiest and most modern part of Spain, with its own industries and the thriving port of Barcelona, and was immensely proud of its trading history. These were vital to the Catalan identity at a time when the central government in Madrid was attempting to integrate the region more completely into Spain, partly by discouraging the use of the native Catalan language. In this context of spirited Catalan patriotism, Gaudí began his architectural career as a Gothic revivalist, but more specifically as a revivalist of the local Gothic style. This had its own element of fantasy, which Gaudí managed to emphasize through his study of the Moorish architecture of southern Spain and North Africa. To this, Gaudí added a knowledge of Viollet-le-Duc's work and the light, almost tent-like, forms of his iron-supported Gothic vaults, and of Ruskin, with his ideals of the unity of the arts and of architecture making use of colour and carving more for its effects.

Gaudí was fortunate enough to have an outstanding patron for much of his work in the local shipping magnate Don Eusebio Güell, whose wealth allowed for very ambitious schemes. Gaudí's development was slow at first, and his 1880s city mansion for Güell is largely inspired by Catalan Gothic, but for the two massive parabolic arches of the portals, swelling up to be filled by some of the most free-flowing ironwork decoration seen before Horta and Guimard. Perhaps inspired by the flowering of Art Nouveau in the rest of Europe, Gaudí's work of the 1890s began to develop into something unique, much more than just the sum of his early influences. Equally liberating must have been the scale on which he was invited to work by Güell. A development of workers' housing did not get very far but the centrepiece of a parallel scheme for a middle class neighbourhood, the Park Güell, exists today as a municipal park.

The Park Güell could be seen to be a rare opportunity for the Art Nouveau artist to display his art against its source. Since this was a landscaping commission,

archways for the entrances to the underground sections. These were so startlingly Art Nouveau in their design that they provoked considerable controversy.

In keeping with the modernity of the new underground railway, Guimard restricted himself to the use of iron, enamelled steel and glass. The iron elements were produced in a large number of standard parts, making their assembly into a huge variety of differing arches and pavilions a tribute to Guimard's inventiveness and versatility. The treatment of the ironwork was typically curvilinear with barely a straight line to be seen in the whole design. Lamps sprouted from metal branches and the word 'Metropolitain' itself was carefully composed into harmonious Art Nouveau forms. Some of these ironwork shapes, although organic in feel, had an angular tension strangely reminiscent of bones and lacked the fluid grace of much of Guimard's interior designs, and of French Art Nouveau as a whole.

A typical Art Nouveau blend of rather esoteric revivalism and startling novelty is to be found in the work of Spaniard, Antonio Gaudí. In Gaudí's work one

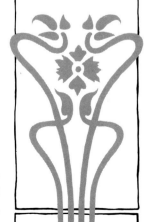

RIGHT: *The interior of Gaudí's mansion for Don Eusebio Güell shows the architect's early interest in the ornate Gothic style.*

RIGHT: *Details of the polychromatic decoration including the Güell monogram and coronet.*

Gaudí was able to employ the stylized, sinuous forms of Art Nouveau against the very natural shapes of the trees and flowers that had, in part, inspired them. Serpentine paths did, indeed, weave through the park, but the centrepiece was a vast covered market roofed in under a forest of massive columns. On the plateau created above this area, Gaudí placed benches, arranged in an almost continuous, undulating line from which the view could be enjoyed. The backs of the benches were decorated with a mosaic of broken tiles arranged, either in patterns or haphazardly, to create a dazzlingly colourful display. The same theme was continued on the roofs of the pavilions within the park below. With further grottoes and concrete buttresses seemingly in the form of petrified treetrunks, the overall effect of the park is that of a strange mixture of the subterranean and maritime, perhaps appropriate for a city set between the mountains and the sea. The forms used within this fantastic realm have been justly likened to enormously magnified versions of the Art Nouveau creations of Horta and Guimard, amplifying the air of strange, in this case oversized, biological mutations. An interest in polychromatic effects gained through a combination of media, as in the Park Güell, was a frequent concern of Art Nouveau with characteristic ensembles of wood, metal and stained glass, and it was pursued by Gaudí in his Casa Battló

apartment block of 1905-7. This commission involved remodelling an existing block and the emphasis was inevitably on the façade. Gaudí had to contend with rectangular windows, already a part of the building and totally at odds with the shapes of Art Nouveau. In order to distract attention from them as well as exploit the shimmering light of a coastal city, coloured tiles were again used to create a flowing pattern throughout the façade, which was finished with a steep roof of tiles coloured orange to blue-green. These brilliant colour effects enabled Gaudí to move away from the more symmetrically-composed façades of the neighbouring houses. By means of a rather exotic turret and the fabric-like folds of the roof, the Casa Battló also managed to rise above its companions in the street. Gaudí reworked the base by using a stone cladding, whose flowing lines and softly-modelled protuberances seemed closer to underwater life than architecture. Some of the remaining windows of the upper storeys received bizarrely shaped iron balconies, somewhat resembling fish skeletons. While the Casa Battló was concerned with a rather two-dimensional presentation, the Casa Milá apartments, completely designed by Gaudí, received a much more plastic, virtually sculptural, treatment. Rapidly named La Pedrera, the quarry, by the locals, Casa Milá seems to allude to many natural sources. Like a cliff face or a

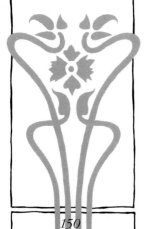

●

LEFT: *For the housing development around the Güell Park. Gaudí designed the church of Santa Coloma de Cervello, whose perilously leaning interior columns create an uneasy sense of movement. Equally distinctive is Gaudí's furniture. The insect-like forms of wood and iron intensify the impression of restlessness, furthered by the broken light from the stained-glass windows.*

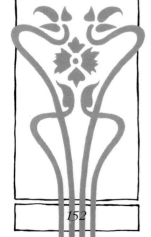

rock outcrop eroded by wind into a collection of grottoes and tunnels, it seems to have been converted to human habitation only at some late stage in its history. Even in plan it appears like some cellular organism rather than the work of an architect, and the internal structure, was indeed, only arrived at at a late stage by the use of partitions. As Gaudí's career developed, it is probable that he increasingly abandoned architectural drawings and worked at first hand with his craftsman, like a latter-day William Morris. Certainly he became was much less reliant on iron and glass than Horta or Guimard as seen in the Casa Milá. Instead, the effect of erosion is produced by careful carving of each block of the stone façade. In total contrast to this softness is the ironwork of the balconies which is moulded into intricately-twisted plant forms, like seaweed hanging from the cliff face before the next wave breaks upon it. Such marine analogies seem most applicable when one is faced by this huge block which

seems to flow around the street corner, softening the grid plan of the streets in this part of the city. However, there are no natural parallels for the forms of the chimney pots that crown the building. These spiralling shapes seem more like giant works of confectionery, and are the epitome of the free cuau carried into massive, spiralling, three dimensions.

Gaudí's great Barcelona church, the still-unfinished Sagrada Familia, occupied him for his entire career and, like the Casa Milá, is an example of extreme Art Nouveau fantasy enlarged into monumental three dimensions. It, too, is that typical combination of the reactionary and the revolutionary, stemming from Gaudí's extremely devout, rather anachronistic Roman Catholicism, here given a form of unique novelty: Gothic seen through the Art Nouveau eyes of the late nineteenth century. Like the Casa Milá, it invites comparison with natural rock forms. It has been suggested that one of the most important

LEFT: *The Casa Battló interiors reveal more of Gaudí's inventiveness. In the hall, a fireside alcove is scooped out from the wall whilst above it, wall and ceiling merge in an undulating contour.*

CENTRE ABOVE LEFT: *The arches of the Casa Battló dining room recall Gaudí's earlier involvement with Gothic style.*

CENTRE BELOW LEFT: *The roof of Gaudí's Casa Battló whose fantastic forms are in sharp contrast to the conservative lines of the neighbouring building.*

FAR LEFT: *Casa Battló: the sinuous curves continued in the stairwell. The sense of natural forms is increased by the bizarre vertebrae silhouette of the staircase.*

images that impressed itself on Gaudí was that of Montserrat, the mountain behind Barcelona, on which stands a Benedictine monastery dedicated to the Virgin Mary as well as being the legendary resting place of the Holy Grail. Perhaps the completed Sagrada Familia has elements of a holy mountain and a gothicized natural rock formation. Certainly the finished church would have been on a grand scale, what is left today is merely the façade of one transept. In the Sagrada Familia and its encrustations of sculpture, mosaic and glass, one sees Gaudí's obsession, the project that epitomizes all that is unique in his art, and thus a building that defies inclusion in any category whose construction continued long after Art Nouveau had died as a style.

If, in Barcelona, Gaudí provided examples of liberated fantasy at one end of the Art Nouveau spectrum, then at the opposite end of Europe, in Glasgow, Charles Rennie Mackintosh was establishing a style of greater restraint in which free-flowing forms were more carefully controlled. Mackintosh and his wife constituted one half of the Scottish group of designers, 'The Four', who were themselves part of a larger crafts group in Glasgow with strong Art Nouveau connections. However his work as an architect necessarily set him slightly apart from the intricacies of purely decorative art. This more austere art can best be seen in Mackintosh's Glasgow School of Art, which launched his career as an independent architect in 1897. The asymmetry and the hint of turrets evident in the front entrance refer to Mackintosh's early enthusiasm for the Gothic revival. In the starkly-mullioned great windows of the north-facing studies and the apparent simplicity of the whole, there is evidence of the influence of the uniquely British Arts and Crafts architects with their Tudor references. Yet Mackintosh is a figure of European significance for the Art Nouveau, and like Gaudí, his importance extends

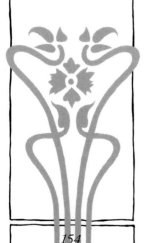

beyond the local. Thus, in the curving stonework in the centre of the main façade and the stylized elongation of the windows of the west front display is the refinement of Art Nouveau and the connection becomes stronger in the details of the building. The carving over the entrance has the curving, Celtic lines of Art Nouveau graphics and metalwork of the Glasgow school, and the ironwork indulges in more abstract curves. This is used to contrast with the harder lines of the stone background in a way reminiscent of Horta's Hotel Solvay. The ironwork, resembling buttresses against the main studio window, is rounded off in intricate, loosely-bound knots of metalwork, almost like enlarged pieces of jewellery. The strange decorations on the railings at street level, and the bundles of arrow shapes supporting patterned dishes, derive from Japanese heraldry, stressing the internationalism of Mackintosh's references and his affinity with the orientally-inspired refinements of Art Nouveau.

The simplicity and elegance of Japan are again recalled in the interior of the school's library, designed throughout by Mackintosh. He was reluctant to experiment with structural ironwork, so wood is used throughout to support the galleries. Mackintosh's fascination with beams and joints was a typically eclectic Art Nouveau fusion of his Japanese and Gothic interests, and is seen again in the open rafters elsewhere in the building. The use of dark, stained wood also gives the library interior an oriental sobriety. By opening out a continuous central space, Mackintosh created a slender, vertical beams, echoed in the delicate light fittings, while creating a variation of one of the great themes of Art Nouveau architicture, the open, light and spacious interior, in this case lit by the long, triple bay windows of the west façade.

Mackintosh was a very influential figure in late European Art Nouveau at the beginning of the twentieth century, yet his architectural career is limited largely to the Glasgow School of Art and some houses for private Scottish patrons. His career suffered after a move to England; in order to see the architecture of those who appreciated his work it is necessary to turn to the Austrian Art Nouveau of Vienna.

The Viennese Secession group of artists and architects had been formed in 1897, both as a reaction to the tired revivalism of academic artists and as a celebration of modernity. It was therefore almost inevitable that the work of its members should directly reflect the influence of the Art Nouveau style which by then was fully-developed in Western Europe. The Secession Style, as it was known in Vienna, began as something of a local variant on Art Nouveau. This late flowering of the style was to prove to be a turning point

LEFT: *The Casa Milá, with its wrought iron balconies, that recall tangled seaweed.*

between Art Nouveau opulence and 20th century austerity. Even in their earlier works, the Austrian architects preferred a framework of straighter lines to set off the opulent curves of Art Nouveau. They were particularly appreciative of these qualities in Mackintosh's style, which helped to form their own, and of the English Arts and Crafts architects who, by this stage, were opposing the sensuality of Art Nouveau. The master of the older generation was Otto Wagner (1841-1918). An influential writer and theorist, Wagner's architectural career had not brought him a great deal of public success; the Secession supported his pupils, Josef Maria Olbrich and Josef Hoffmann, who were founding members. In 1899, Wagner became a full member of the Secession and severed his connections with his own generation.

The year before, Wagner had publicly shown his allegiance to the Secession style by his treatment of the façade of an apartment block he had designed, aptly dubbed the Majolikahaus. In essence, this consisted of a completely regular grid of windows, devoid of any architectural or sculptural decoration. However, to counteract this austerity Wagner decorated

the whole façade with brightly-coloured majolica, floral-patterned tiles that seemed to grow up from the second floor, gradually enveloping the whole building in the light, sinuous lines of Viennese Art Nouveau. It has been suggested that it was his pupil, Olbrich, who was principally responsible for the temporary conversion of Wagner to a local variant of Art Nouveau. Certainly Olbrich's own sympathies were with the more exotic strains that were then in vogue. He was also interested in the contemporary revival of crafts, having travelled to England to study developments there. Olbrich and Hoffmann were later to found the Austrian equivalent of Morris & Co or the Century Guild, the *Wiener Werkstätte* (Vienna Workshop).

Before the establishment of the Secession group, Olbrich was working as Wagner's assistant when the latter was appointed architect to the new Viennese underground and suburban railway, the Stadtbahn. The design of the Stadtbahn stations immediately invite comparison with Guimard's work for the Paris Métro. They lack the free-flowing fantasy of Guimard, yet they have a rather Roccoco grace and lightness, with abundant floral detailing, which is the closest point in Austrian architecture to the French style of Art Nouveau. Olbrich's own contribution to the Secession was designing the group's exhibition building, reputedly inspired by a rough sketch by Gustav Klimt. The central feature of the Secession Building is a hollow dome, framed by four towers, and entirely constructed of metal leaves. This almost matched Gaudí in fantastic invention, but it is telling that the shape of this crowning foliage is a perfect hemisphere, a poised form of rest rather than a restless growth. The details continue the theme of the dome around the main entrance and at either side but the carved foliage, although intricately woven, is restrained by being framed within rectangular panels from which only the occasional, suspended stem is allowed to escape. Like much of the Secession's work in all art forms, the effect is achieved through well-controlled contrast rather

•

LEFT: *The Karlsplatz Station of the Vienna Stadtbahn (subway train) by Wagner.*

CENTRE ABOVE LEFT: *Otto Wagner's Majolica House, showing the combination of severity and ornament typical of the Viennese secession movement.*

CENTRE BELOW LEFT: *Otto Wagner's Post Office Savings Bank, Vienna, a transitional design between Art Nouveau and Art Deco, well in advance of its time.*

FAR LEFT: *Josef Maria Olbrich's Secession building, Vienna whose strong lines are enlivened by the foliage and writhing snakes over the entrance.*

ABOVE RIGHT: *In structure, Sullivan's Carson, Pirie Scott department store in Chicago, Illinois anticipates much of 20th century architecture.*

BELOW: *The decorative metalwork over the Carson, Pirie Scott store recalls the florid exuberance of Art Nouveau.*

In America, the same contrast between lush ornament and more rigid structure was being explored by Louis Sullivan, the leader of an innovative group of architects based in the booming city of Chicago. Sullivan's importance as a pioneer of twentieth century architecture extends beyond the isolated decade or so of Art Nouveau. He led the movement toward exploitation of the new steel-framed structures, which, with the development of the elevator, enabled him to produce the most successful early skyscrapers. His architecture is more concerned with expressing the structural skeleton of the building, by allowing a very plain grid form to appear as the basic design and by hollowing out the ground floor until it rests on just a few reinforced columns. These innovations of Sul-

LEFT: *Louis Sullivan's Auditorium Building, whose austere façade contrasts with the lavishness of some of the interior decoration.*

in his attitude toward the embellishment of his buildings. His theories on the subject were highly developed and he saw the contrast between the rectilinear and curvilinear as parallel to the division beween intellect and emotion, and throughout his architecture he tried to maintain a balance between the two. The actual form of his ornament was often reminiscent of oriental abstractions from nature, but just as frequently he used more overt natural forms of intertwining leaves and branches which became very much a Chicago version of Art Nouveau, home-grown but with very strong formal links with the style as it had developed within Europe. The bar interior of the great Auditorium Building, a complex of opera house, hotel and offices, shows an opulence of detail and the involvement of the architect in every small feature, which is wholly characteristic of Art Nouveau. Nor was Sullivan adverse to turning his bare exposed vertical beams, part of his grid façade, into rather exotic tree forms by a flourish of foliage at the top, as in the façade of the Gage Building of South Michigan Avenue, Chicago. More frequently, Sullivan preferred to contain very lush and flowing natural ornament within quite rigid limits, as in the Wainwright Building in St Louis, where it serves to articulate the horizontal beams set against the plain verticals, and to embellish a very ornate cornice which caps the whole composition. The natural forms of Sullivan's decoration not only recalled those of French Art Nouveau, but also had symbolic importance for him. The energy of organic growth was what Sullivan was attempting to evoke, and in particular its application to the rapidly developing cities of America. Just as Art Nouveau was self-consciously the modern style, so Sullivan was attempting to create a powerful, growing architecture.

His Guaranty Building in Buffalo, New York, extends this Art Nouveau concern for growth beyond the decoration itself, into the structure as a whole. Linked by arches at their peak, the great verticals of the building seem to be enormous stems pushing up to the cornice which curls over in a gentle curve reminiscent of growing form. In this case, the ornament makes the analogies more explicit. Sullivan's last great work, the then Carson, Pirie & Scott department store in Chicago, seems for the main area of its façade to be too plain for any reference to Art Nouveau to be made, yet in the first two storeys, and particularly around the corner entrance, there is reliefwork of Gaudí-like extravagance even, in this unlikly context, recalling the Sagrada Familia. This seems largely based on an elaborate Gothic fantasy, yet its tense spider's web lines and twisting foliage can ultimately only be seen as a personal Art Nouveau composition.

livan's were eventually to become commonplace in modern architecture throughout the world.

Yet Sullivan remained very much a man of his time than an unbridled release of free-flowing form. This is a development of the 'classic' Art Nouveau style into something new, and it was to be the theme of early 20th century architecture, which eventually discarded all non architectural ornament. This is largely true even of Wagner's later work, though his design for the Postsparkasse (Post Office Savings Bank) in Vienna (1904), the openness of the interior, the attention to every detail of furniture and fitting, the light, glass roof and particularly the elegantly tapering piers supporting the gently curved vault, all suggest the remaining echoes of Art Nouveau.

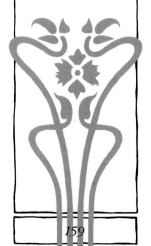

CHAPTER THREE

FURNITURE

*A desk and chair in Louis Majorelles's later style, showing a
more restrained use of curving forms.*

Art Nouveau furniture bears all the variety of the regional styles of the movement. True to the spirit of Art Nouveau, few craftsmen specialized exclusively in furniture, and most had been trained in other arts or crafts. Most Art Nouveau furniture makers had been, or remained, architects, concerned to extend their control into the interior of their buildings. The same tensions between ornament and structure, form and function were evident in furniture making as they were in architecture.

Through the range of Art Nouveau furniture it is possible to see designs stripped down to the most elegant bare curves, as well as those which are adorned with carving, brass, gilt or ivory. A similar contrast exists between designs that are obviously designed for comfort and utility, and those that come close to sacrificing both these concerns for the sake of effect. What gives coherence to this variety are the irrepressible curves and sense of idiosyncratic inventiveness. Occasionally these had to be curbed especially when designs were intended for mass production. The attention to detail and the manipulation of the materials generally meant that Art Nouveau furniture was unsuited to any mode of production other than that of the individual craftsman. As in the Arts and Crafts movement in England, the Art Nouveau designer was forced to accept the fact that his work was primarily an expensive luxury for an élite, despite whatever Morris-like Utopian ideals of art for everyone he might hold. Factory-produced Art Nouveau furniture inevitably lost much of its natural vitality and was a coars-

ened version of the hand-worked equivalent. Art Nouveau architects might have been eager to embrace the new materials of iron and steel, but when they turned to designing furniture their style was fundamentally unsuited to modern production techniques.

Much of the vitality of Art Nouveau derived from various provincial centres. In France, the decorative arts were not confined to Paris, but also flourished in the city of Nancy in Lorraine. Nancy was historically the home of the glass-making industry. The leader of the Art Nouveau revival of Nancy's main industry was Emil Gallé (1846-1904),heir to a small ceramic and glassware business. Gallé travelled to England in the 1870s and had been caught up in the growing enthusiasm for the decorative arts. He also studied the oriental art collection of the Victoria and Albert Museum in London and, with his new found knowledge of Chinese and Japanese techniques, he returned to Nancy to revitalize his father's workshop. Gallé was not only an enthusiastic orientalist but also possessed a specialist's knowledge of botany and entomology, his other amateur passions. He was equipped with a very detailed first-hand knowledge of leaf, flower and insect forms, which, when combined with the decorative, abstract tendency of the Japanese, combined to form the Art Nouveau blend. A third ingredient, rococo, was already evident in Nancy, which had many fine houses and decorations in that style.

In 1884, after some years of working in glass and ceramics, Gallé started designing and producing furniture. At first his designs were somewhat ponderous though but invariably enlivened with vivid natural details. Success came at the 1889 Paris International Exhibition, where Gallé was acknowledged as an innovator, creating a new style in reaction to the unimaginative revivalism of contemporary French furniture. Gallé's work became increasingly lighter and more ornate. Natural forms were not restricted to detail; whole arms, legs and backs were carved in plant or insect forms, curving and twisting to animate the whole and seeming to defy the nature of the wood itself. Although stylized, those graceful shapes were always clearly identifiable plants of a species known to Gallé. His favourites were local plants including cow-parsley, water lilies, orchids and irises though he also used exotics, such as bamboo.

Gallé preferred soft woods, of which he had a very thorough knowledge, to facilitate the creation of his effects, which included his remarkable revival of the art of marquetry. Most of the surfaces of Gallé's furniture became fields for the most intricate inlays featuring plants, insects or landscapes in what could

LEFT: *On this buffet table, Gallé uses his marquetry skills to create astonishing landscapes.*

BELOW RIGHT: *Mantelpiece by Eugène Vallin. The designer worked with a greater feeling for sculptural form than his master, Gallé.*

become an overloading of effects. So fine was the craftsmanship, though, that Gallé's own willowy signature could be reproduced on his pieces.

Gallé's mastery of marquetry opened the way to the expression of poetry and literary themes in his furniture. He liked to include suitable quotations and, as a mark of the fusion of arts and crafts in Art Nouveau, he gave some pieces names in the manner of paintings or music. A console he created became *Les Parfums d'Autrefois* (Perfumes of the Past) and his last masterpiece, the bed he designed while dying of leukemia, *Aube et Crépuscule* (Dawn and Dusk). This latter piece is evidence of Gallé's increasing restraint in his late style, simplifying forms and eradicating much of the over-intricacy of his earlier work, as well as being a tour-de-force of marquetry. The dark shadows of dusk are enveloped in the drooping wings of a fantastic insect on the headboard, while at the foot of the bed the rising wings of another huge insect are depicted in lighter woods and mother-of-pearl.

Gallé was the inspiration behind a couple of craftsmen, termed the Nancy School, who became a loosely formal group in 1901 with the foundation of the Alliance Provinciale des Industries d'Art (1859-1926). Second to Gallé was Louis Majorelle who trained as a painter but then concentrated on running his family's furniture business in Nancy. Majorelle began designing in an 18th-century style until persuaded by Gallé to inject a more vital naturalism into his work His pieces are, nevertheless, rather more solid than Gallé's, partly because he favoured the use of harder, more exotic woods. The more sculptural elements in Majorelle's pieces come in the ornamentation, which, still partly inspired by the baroque and rococo, he added in gilt, copper or bronze. Majorelle equalled Gallé in the quality of his marquetry, but generally his

style differs in its smoother lines. Majorelle was consequently able to make a successful transition to the simpler style of the 1920s.

Other cabinetmakers in Nancy worked for either Majorelle or Gallé, and occasionally both. Victor Prouvé (1858-1943) specialized in marquetry work for both masters as well as designing his own pieces. Eugène Vallin (1856-1925) worked for Gallé and produced pieces of a far greater weight than those of his master. Vallin's work eschews intricate natural detail and instead concentrates on broad, swaying, linear rhythms anticipating the end of his career when he took up architecture and used cast concrete for his effects. Jacques Gruber produced designs for Majorelle and was also Professor of Decorative Arts at the Ecole des Beaux-Arts in Nancy. His furniture shares the same flowing forms as that of Vallin, and is removed from Gallé's roccoco touches.

FURNITURE

•

BELOW LEFT: Aube et Crépuscule, *Gallé's last great work that sums up his concern to capture a poetic mood through the craft of marquetry.*

ABOVE LEFT: *A cabinet by Louis Majorelle, including characteristic bronze fittings.*

RIGHT: *Room setting of furniture by the Parisian designer Georges Hoentschel. Furniture, as any product of Art Nouveau, was designed to be seen as part of a unified environment.*

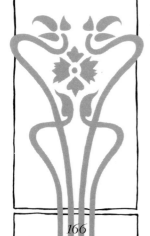

In Paris, Samuel Bing's 'Galerie de l'Art Nouveau' was the principal showcase for Art Nouveau furniture, as for other crafts. Reflecting the nationalism fashionable in time in France at the time, Bing encouraged the craftsmen who worked for him to study the great French tradition of 'grace, elegance, purity and sound logic', and principally the refined poise of 18th-century work. The Parisian Art Nouveau designers tended to avoid the more overtly floral detailing of Nancy and concentrated instead on a purity of light, flowing line. Bing showed a great range of work, but he favoured a nucleus of three furniture makers: Eugène Gaillard, Georges de Feure and Edward Colonna.

Gaillard represents the functional side of Art Nouveau furniture; he studied the problem of function in design and produced designs of an increasingly light, almost classic, simplicity. His chairs were concerned with comfort, had moulded backs, sometimes padding at the shoulder, and leather or fabric-covered coil-sprung, upholstered seats. Georges de Feure, a painter

and poet, was something of a dandy. He was a keeper of greyhounds, which he admired for their fine Art Nouveau lines. He brought more colour and decoration to his furniture, with gilding and coloured lacqueur, as well as the kind of carved detail rare in Gaillard's work. The third, Edward Eugène Colonna, had emigrated from Cologne to America where he worked under Tiffany, before returning to Europe to continue his carrer in Paris, Colonna's furniture, like de Feure's was part of a larger output including procelain and fabrics, and had a delicate, attenuated elegance also close to de Feure's style. When Bing was honoured with his own pavilion devoted to Art Nouveau at the 1900 Paris World's Fair, these three designers were given the task of decorating and furnishing it.

In England, the major crafts began to veer away from the Art Nouveau style at the beginning of the twentieth century. This was paradoxical as Mackmurdo and his Century Guild had virtually created it in the 1880s. At that time Mackmurdo had produced

LEFT: *Office suite, consisting of a desk, matching chair and sideboard by Eugène Vallin, in the exaggerated Art Nouveau style, known in France as* Style Liberty.

BELOW LEFT: *Chair by Gaillard. The leather upholstery and simple lines show a concern for function above uncontrolled fantasy.*

some furniture with carving that used the unmistakable swirling forms of his frontispiece to *Wren's City Churches*, but by the time the style was common elsewhere, English designers had retreated to harder rectilinear forms or the simplicity of cottage styles. The same was largely true in the United States, where the influence of the English Arts and Crafts work, and a national preference for a simple Gothic style, was strong. However, the exception was the American designer Charles Rohlfs, who was very successful. Rohlfs retired from an acting career to concentrate upon crafts, and managed to skillfully combine the swirling forms of European Art Nouveau with the native influence of the Baroque-inspired Mission style, giving his furniture a cosmopolitan aura flavoured with an individually native touch. Rohlfs exhibited at Turin in 1902 and was successful enough to open eight showrooms in the United States, with headquarters in Buffalo.

ABOVE LEFT: *The Art Nouveau curve of the legs of this table by Edward Colonna is underplayed in its refinement, and emphasizes the stylistic differences between Bing's Parisian designers and the more exaberant work of their counterparts in Nancy.*

BELOW LEFT: *Occasional table by Hector Guimard, showing the same rather taught, sinuous shapes as his entrances for the Paris Métro.*

OPPOSITE ABOVE LEFT: *American furniture by Solomon Karpen Bros of Chicago. Curves, natural ornament and the long-tressed Art Nouveau maiden are all prominent, but a stolid heaviness still prevails.*

OPPOSITE CENTRE LEFT: *An elegant screen by de Feure.*

OPPOSITE BELOW LEFT: *Chair by Josef Hoffman, leader of the Viennese Secession.*

CENTRE: *A console table by Georges de Feure. The forms are pure Art Nouveau but the gilding reveals 18th century inspiration.*

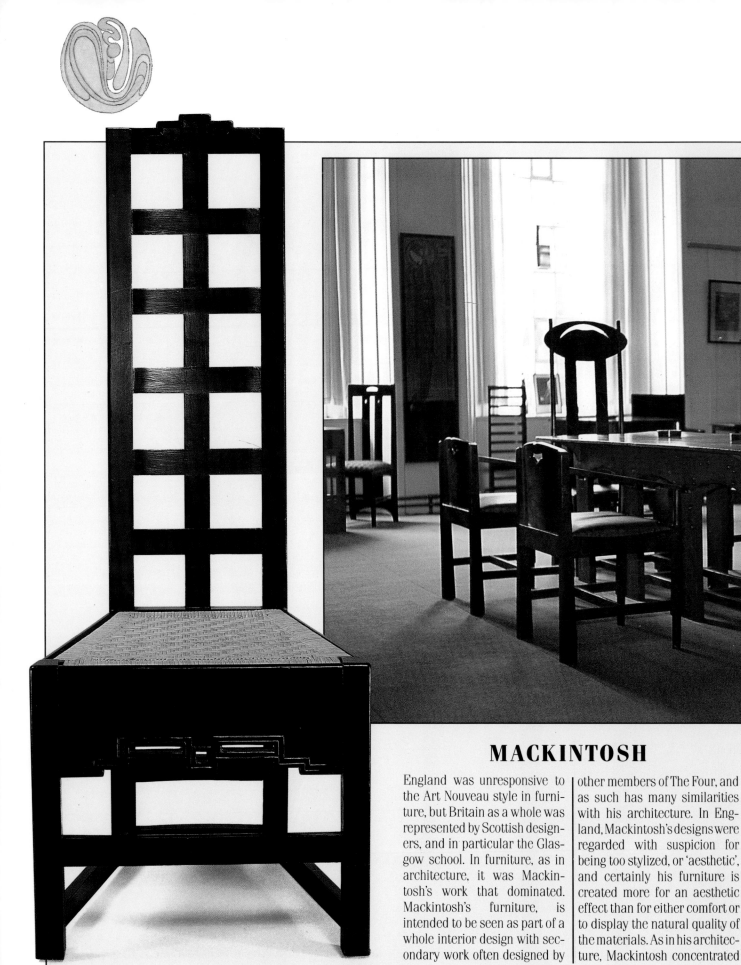

MACKINTOSH

England was unresponsive to the Art Nouveau style in furniture, but Britain as a whole was represented by Scottish designers, and in particular the Glasgow school. In furniture, as in architecture, it was Mackintosh's work that dominated. Mackintosh's furniture, is intended to be seen as part of a whole interior design with secondary work often designed by other members of The Four, and as such has many similarities with his architecture. In England, Mackintosh's designs were regarded with suspicion for being too stylized, or 'aesthetic', and certainly his furniture is created more for an aesthetic effect than for either comfort or to display the natural quality of the materials. As in his architecture, Mackintosh concentrated

upon extremely elegant, exaggerated verticals, particularly in the backs of his chairs which could be exceptionally tall and slender. These were cut into ovals, grids or ladderbacks that descended down to the floor. Curves might occur, but with Mackintosh they were primarily used to stress the rigidity of verticals. A Japanese simplicity reveals itself occasionally, as in the domino table for the Ingram Street Tea Room, where sections seem almost to be slotted together by simple joinery. Mackintosh felt uncomfortable with the natural grain of the wood and attempted to minimalize it by deep, dark staining and eventually by lacquering or ebonizing it into matt black. He explored a converse neutrality by painting other pieces white to act as a suitable background for lilac and silver harmonies. On lighter furniture, Mackintosh stencilled stylized designs.

●

ABOVE RIGHT:
*Chairs by Koloman
Moser of the Viennese
Secession movement,
showing the great
restraint of the style
partly inspired by
Mackintosh.*

BELOW RIGHT: *Cabinet
and chair by the
Viennese Secessionist
Josef Maria Olbrich.*

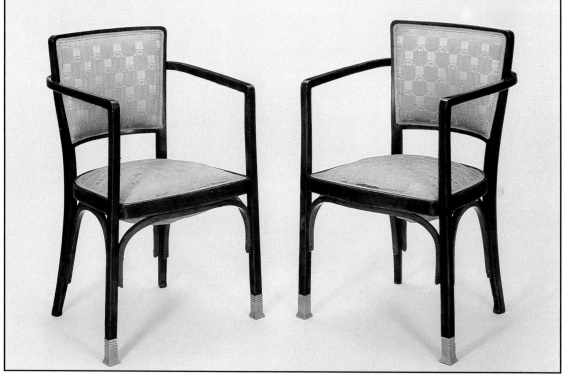

Mackintosh's influence emerged most strongly in
Vienna with the artists of the Secession movement. In
1903, the Secession moved into crafts, including furniture designs with the foundation of the Wiener
Werkstätte, a Viennese arts and crafts guild, headed
by the architect Josef Hoffmann and the painter Koloman Moser. Wiener Werkstätte furniture has the luxury of materials — rich veneers, marquetry and gilding — associated with Art Nouveau and the Secession
Style (*Secezionstil*), but is rigid angularity is a continu-
ation of Mackintosh's style that places it in the con-
cluding chapter of a discussion of Art Nouveau. Similarly elusive of categorization is the furniture of the
extraordinary Italian designer, Carlo Bugatti, which
was the sensation and *cause célèbre* of the Turin
Exhibition in 1902. Bugatti represents the culmina-
tion of the nineteenth-century fascination for the
exotic, in his case a Moorish, Egyptian and Byzantine
fantasy. Almost every material was used to enhance
these references in his furniture: carved and painted
wood, polished brass and copper, painted vellum and
rich silks. The overall effect is certainly powerful. To
some it was magnificently theatrical, to others pom-
pous and coarse. The ornateness, the unity of theme,
and the use of broad, sweeping arcs all relate Bugatti
to Art Nouveau, but there is much, too, that sets him
apart from all contemporaries and places him as a
pioneer of Art Deco and Hollywood glamour.

CHAPTER FOUR

METALWORK

*Teaset by Archibald Knox for Liberty & Co, part of the Tudric
range he designed continuing the Celtic theme.*

Wrought-iron has already been seen as a significant part of Art Nouveau architecture, both structurally and decoratively. Victor Horta had made its structural use clear in his work in Brussels and he had also used it decoratively, exploiting its relative malleability to provide lighter patterns in contrast to the weightiness of stone. In Art Nouveau architecture, metalwork serves as a link between the building itself and the style of its contents, often the product of the same designer. From exterior balconies, gates and window mullions it continues to the interior in columns, beams, bannisters and door handles, and even to embellishments on furniture, With metalwork, the versatility of use and range of metals available meant that almost every Art Nouveau interior designer turned his hand to metalwork at some stage. Like many another Art Nouveau medium, it is important to visualize metalwork as part of its context in the interior. It could appear in the form of candlesticks, candelabra, cutlery, clocks, light fittings, mirrors, tableware, caskets or combs.

Guimard's Métro entrances emphasize the versatility of the medium as they can be seen as architecture as well as architectural sculpture or even enormous decorative pieces. They use the same forms as his great iron gates for the Castel Béranger apartments as well as the bannisters within. Horta carried the same continuity of form from the iron balconies to the bannisters for the staircase, the main architectural and sculptural feature of the interior of his magnificent home in the Rue Americaine in Brussels, as well

as in the other homes he designed. Comparable in function, although more fantastic in form, were the balconies of Gaudí's Casa Milá, modelled like tangled masses of seaweed. It is easier to separate Gaudí the metalworker from Gaudí the architect, since he executed metalwork at times independent of his buildings and as a composition in its own right. Gaudí's father had been a coppersmith, and he must have been profoundly influenced by seeing this malleable material being worked at heat. Certainly Gaudí treated wrought iron as if it were as tractable, particularly in the form of grilles and gates. In his early work for the Casa Vicens he achieved the effect of palm fronds with the spikes cut at the top bent in every direction as if they were drooping leaves. His entrance gate to the Güell Estate in Pedralbes is even more oustanding, for almost the entire piece is given the form of a writhing dragon whose gaping jaws reach out for the visitor as he grasps the handle. Such a bizarre fantasy is more easily absorbed in the small-scale medium of jewellery; to see it on such a large scale is shocking. The gate was produced in 1885 and reveals that Gaudí had already reached the peak of Art Nouveau sinuous form and fantasy in metalwork when his architecture was still in the Gothic style.

Work in the more traditional precious metals, particularly silver, had sunk to a low level of design and workmanship through industrialization until it was revived by the English Arts and Crafts movement. These craftsmen stressed the virtues of hand-made objects, and even occasionally chose to stress the method of production with obviously hand-produced hammered dents left on the surface. Less precious metals were often also used for cutlery (flatware) which was normally associated with silver. Knives, forks and spoons might be made of bronze, brass, tin, pewter or copper, which were often easier to use for more daring designers. As well as having fewer of the historical associations of the more traditional materials, they could be more readily associated with a new style linked to political convictions and beliefs. Art Nouveau crftsmen liked to work across the complete range of metals, at times mixing them with enamel, ivory, wood or anything other material required to create the appropriate effect.

A typical Art Nouveau duality appeared with regards to the means of production. Some designers, following in the Arts and Crafts wake, produced hand-made and therefore very exclusive items, while others tailored their designs to large-scale production and found themselves more in tune with the future course of design. The work of The Four, the Glasgow group around Mackintosh, falls into the former category.

LEFT: *The elaborately-treated iron balconies and columns on the façade of Horta's house.*

ABOVE RIGHT: *Silver biscuit (cookie) box by Archibald Knox with decorations deriving from Celtic and Nordic interlacing patterns.*

BELOW RIGHT: *Another Knox teaset for Liberty and Co. with echoes of Art Nouveau in the elongated forms and asymetrical settings of the enamel ornament.*

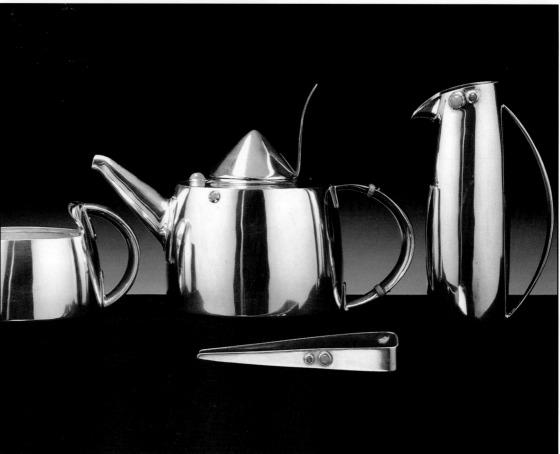

Half of the Four, the sisters Margaret and Frances Macdonald (the former being Mrs Mackintosh), produced together and singly much relief work, either of beaten tin or silver, as mounts for objects such as mirrors or as decorative objects in their own right. The pale coolness of these pieces perfectly complement the Mackintosh interior and add a figurative and floral dimension to the Glasgow style. Elongated, undulating maidens derived from Toorop are a common feature, as well as rather spikey growths whose long tendrils weave themselves into Celtic patterns or droop into Art Nouveau curves. A hand-crafted impression is created by the frequent use of a rough ground to offset the more polished figures.

A similar mood is created in the metalwork of Alexander Knox, the principal designer for the Liberty department store in London, who had actually studied Celtic design in the appropriate setting of Douglas School of Art on the Isle of Man. Knox worked more exclusively with silver, often setting it with semi-precious stones to produce exquisitely-designed work decorated with sparsely-applied Celtic-style relief. These works were produced in some quantity for the store, as were the designs of Christopher Dresser.

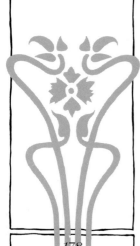

JESSIE KERRIE

●

ABOVE RIGHT: *Copper wall sconce by the Glasgow designer Marian Wilson, which combines a smoothly-finished motif with an obviously handworked ground.*

BELOW RIGHT: *Teaset of oriental refinement by Christopher Dresser.*

Dresser was one of the few craftsmen of the time to have visited Japan, as evidenced by the restrained purity of line in his work. Only rarely does a sweeping curve of Art Nouveau appear, since Dresser was more concerned with function and economy to simplify the mass-production process. In Germany, factories had managed to a surprising degree to combine large-scale production with some of the most extravagant Art Nouveau pieces of tableware. This was particularly true of the products of the Württembürgische Metallwarenfabrik (WMF) works at Geislingen, although the Metallenfabrik Eduard Hueck at Ludenschied also produced designs by such leading figures as Behrens and Olbrich.

In France the Nancy school concentrated more on furniture, glass and ceramics, although Louis Majorelle, who had used gilt trimmings on his furniture, produced some gates and bannisters as did Victor Prouvé. More metalwork was produced by the Parisian craftsmen working for Bing and Meier-Graefe. The elegant Georges de Feure was one of the most versatile of these and designed objects, from candelabra to cane handles, based on stylized, fluid, plant forms. Others, like Colonna or Selmersheim turned to metalwork for a complete room setting, designing table-lamps, or chandeliers in the form of drooping plants whose flowers were the glass shades. Lucien Gaillard, who took over the family metalwork business in 1892, produced work of outright fantasy with intricate high relief detailing of grasshoppers, stag-beetles or vines. This sort of very naturalistic detail, surrealistically clustering on an everyday object, suggests the role of jewellery on a dress. In 1900, encouraged by René Lalique, Gaillard explored the possibilities of

LEFT: *A teaset designed by Josef Hoffman, in typical* Wiener Werkstätte *style. The forms are more traditional than most Art Nouveau ceramics.*

copper and bronze, as did Guimard, in a number of vases whose necks are twisted into an intertwining, restless abstract surface of strands.

The use of the human figure in Art Nouveau metalwork clearly draws it closer to sculpture. The bronze reliefs by Alexandre Charpentier of nude women in undulating poses set against the background of their impossibly long, flowing hair, seem to straddle the gap between art and craft, only the inconsequentiality of their subject matter drawing them back toward the latter. French sculpture at the time was dominated by the ageing giant, Auguste Rodin, whose work, principally in bronze, had exploited to the full that medium's possibilities for active poses and shimmering light. Rodin's work is too involved with symbolist and literary overtones to be described as decorative, yet his frequently twisting poses and erotic subjects recall some aspects of Art Nouveau. Certainly the flowing

relief of his *Gates of Hell* recalls the forms of subsequent, decorative Art Nouveau reliefs, such as the abstract patterning of Guimard's vestibule to the Castel Béranger. Similar, yet tiny, flowing groups of figures appear carved from ivory on a vase and a brooch by Lalique and have been attributed to Rodin.

The British sculptor Sir Alfred Gilbert, the creator of the Shaftesbury Memorial fountain at Piccadilly Circus in London (better known as 'Eros'), was a sculptor in bronze who made the transition to working on a smaller scale with precious and semi-precious materials. Even in the detailing of his larger public work Gilbert was fascinated by the intricate, grotesque curving and twisting forms, often tinged with elements of marine mythology taken from the 16th and 17th centuries.

Elements later explored in Art Nouveau metalwork had therefore made an earlier appearance in fine art

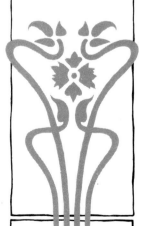

sculpture. The link was maintained by the Art Nouveau vogue for decorative bronze or gilt bronze statuettes, which, like Charpentier's reliefs, were on the borderline between sculpture and jewellery. Many Art Nouveau designers had been trained as sculptors so the connection is clear, yet many of these figures retain a functional side, often as lamps, or, less frequently, as card holders or vases. This was principally a French-inspired fashion pursued by such figures as Eugène Feuillâtre, Raoul Larche, Théodore Rivière and Rupert Carabin, who produced figures of a Gallic gaiety and charm. They were all nude or lightly-draped female figures, often dancers, creating sinuous Art Nouveau arabesques with their flowing hair or drapery. Occasionally, they attempted a more poetic mood in allegorical figures, nymphs, or the typically Art Nouveau hybrid figures of plant-women, metamorphizing into stems and flowers. A more thoughtful note was often struck by busts of maidens with downcast eyes. A regional variant of this genre was pioneered in Belgium by the jeweller Philippe Wolfers, who, in 1904 devoted himself entirely to this form of decorative sculpture. His mixed media figures were characterized by the use of ivory for the flesh. The ivory came from the recently-acquired Belgian Congo, and, for economic reasons, its use was sufficiently encouraged by King Leopold II to provoke a small school of artists following Wolfers in this type of work.

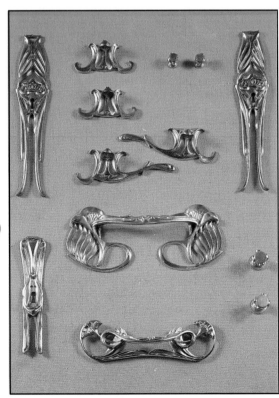

LEFT: *A coatstand by the Belgian designer Gustave Serurier-Borry marks the transitional phase of late Art Nouveau when its elongated forms become straighter and less ornate.*

ABOVE RIGHT: *Coffee set by Josef Hoffmann, showing the use of scalloped forms and a more typically 18th century mood.*

BELOW RIGHT: *The sinuous, long-haired, lightly-draped Art Nouveau female as she appears on a range of factory produced items.*

BELOW RIGHT: *Sinuous Art Nouveau plants in a silver bowl by C.R. Ashbee of the Guild of Handicrafts. Despite his Arts & Crafts background, Ashbee indulges in a magnificent Art Nouveau flourish in the handles of this piece.*

OPPOSITE LEFT: *A silver bowl by C.R. Ashbee of the Guild of Handicrafts*

OPPOSITE FAR RIGHT: *Comedy and Tragedy by Sir Alfred Gilbert. The fluid grace of the figure connects it with the decorative elements of Art Nouveau.*

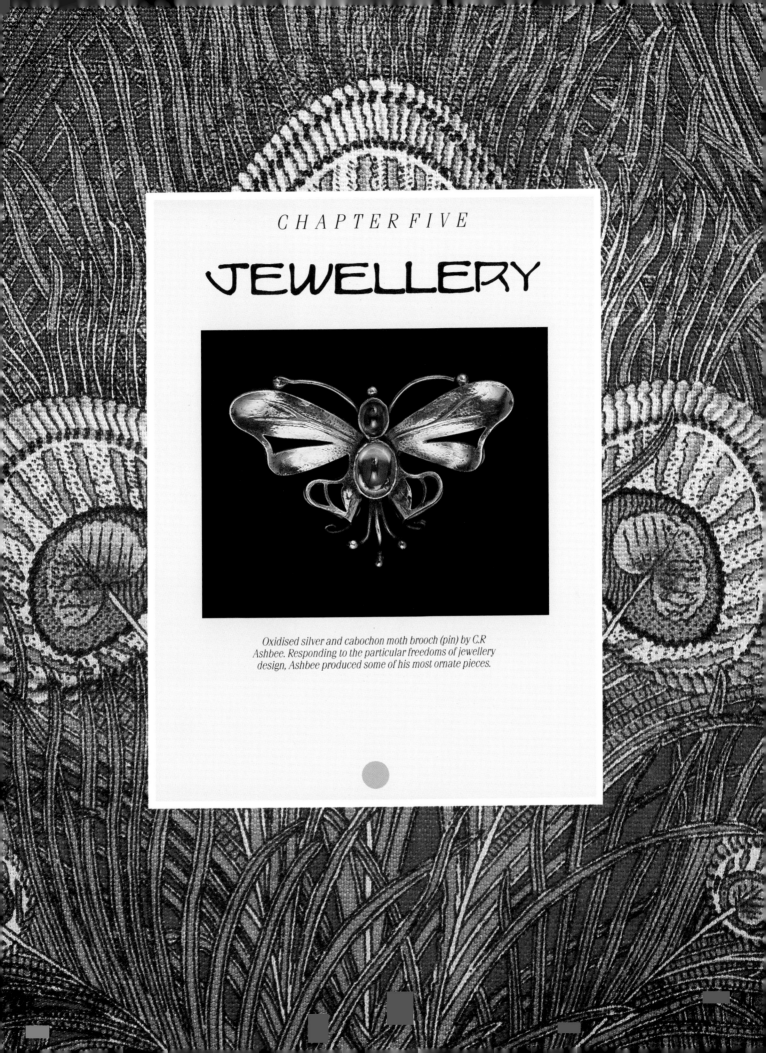

CHAPTER FIVE

JEWELLERY

*Oxidised silver and cabochon moth brooch (pin) by C.R
Ashbee. Responding to the particular freedoms of jewellery
design, Ashbee produced some of his most ornate pieces.*

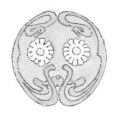

A Lalique clasp in gold-and-enamel, based on a pattern of pine cones and needles.

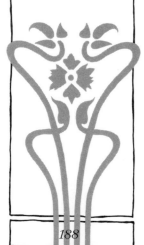

The great revolutionary designer of Art Nouveau jewellery was the Frenchman René Lalique. Lalique's background was a perfect mixture of art and craft, for on the death of his father he became an apprentice to a goldsmith at the age of 16 while simultaneously studying at the Ecole des Beaux-Arts. He freelanced as a jewellery designer for the Cartier house before becoming an employee of Déstape. In 1886 Déstape handed over the control of his workshop to Lalique in recognition of a unique talent. Lalique's jewellery was first exhibited at the Paris Salon in 1894, and three years later he was awarded the Legion of Honour for his work.

Before Lalique's début, French jewellery was as much concerned with displaying wealth as with art. Precious stones, particularly the cutting and setting of diamonds, had been the focus of the craftsman's skill. There was, in effect, a hierarchy of possible materials that could be used which corresponded entirely to their value and rarity. Strings of glittering stones were undoubtedly prestigious for their wearers but provided little opportunity for the jeweller to stretch his creative powers. Lalique's jewellery was completely uninhibited by such social conventions, and broke with all the traditional rules of design. The result was pieces that were conceived as independent works of art rather than mere ornaments, and Lalique was willing to use any sort of material that was needed to produce his effect. He used semi-precious stones, not as cheap substitutes, but for the sake of their colour, veins or surface. However, in Lalique's work the stones are only a part of the composition as a whole. All types of metal are used as well as onyx, crystal, enamel, glass, mother-of-pearl, amber, ivory and even horn, the latter carved for the first time in jewellery by Lalique. With this far wider range of materials Lalique was able to produce work of an enormous variety of shape and colour, virtually anything that his fantasy suggested. Although the cost of the materials varied the extraordinarily high standard of craftsmanship did not and these extremely intricate creations were thus prized as much for their originality, wit and inventiveness as for their intrinsic value. Some of Lalique's pieces, and those of his comtemporaries, were exotic and striking enough to present a challenge to their wearer's personality. Art Nouveau jewellery was less popular with the middle-classes than with the aristocrats and with actresses. The leading actress of the day was Sarah Bernhardt, who frequently indulged her passion for jewellery by commissioning a piece from Lalique, often for a specific stage role. Apart from aristocrats, actresses and many demi-

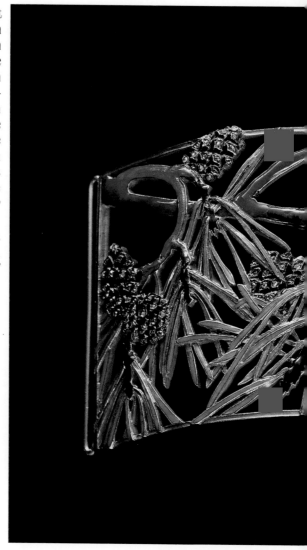

mondaines, Lalique's work was particularly prized by aesthetes, such as the great dandy the Count de Montesquiou. In his vocabulary of natural forms — butterflies, dragonflies, hornets, peacocks, snakes, lilies, orchids and so on — Lalique was the epitome of the Art Nouveau craftsman in any medium, but his eye for anecdote, and particularly his increasing taste for the grotesque and bizarre, brought him closer than many of his contemporaries to the style and concerns of the writers of the day. This was commonly acknowledged by the time of the 1900 Exposition Universelle when Lalique displayed work concerned more than ever with fantastic, even mythological; some, like Medusa, were recognizably literary in their source. Lalique was an excellent draughtsman and conceived his designs as graphic creations; in some ways his jewellery is allied to contemporary illustration. The anecdotal, even narrative, nature of the jewellery was further

emphasized by Lalique's use of the human figure; neglected by jewellers since the Renaissance, it was resurrected in the Art Nouveau nymph or femme fatale with her long flowing hair and voluptuous figure. The nymph was favoured by the great poets Baudelaire and Mallarmé, whose love of the sinister and erotic also found parallels in Lalique's work. Indeed it has often been remarked that the literary style of the fin-de-siècle 'decadents' strove to emulate jewellery in its fantasy, intricacy, hardness of surface and glittering ornaments.

Lalique's inventiveness, use of materials and supremely high level of craftsmanship made jewellery one of the leading media of Art Nouveau. His work revealed the great potential of jewellery as an art form and inspired a school of imitators in turn-of-the-century Paris. Some were Bing's versatile designers exploring a new form — Colonna and Grasset — yet

more were specialists. The Vever brothers, Paul and Henri, turned their family business over to the Lalique style, and specialized in enamel work, as too did Eugène Feuillâtre, who had been trained by Lalique, particularly in three-dimensional enamel work. In 1900, Lalique persuaded his friend, the metalworker Lucien Gaillard, to concentrate his fantasies into the smaller scale of jewellery. Other well-established firms began employing Art Nouveau designers: Lucien Lévy-Dhurmer worked for André Falize, Lucien Bonvallet for Ernest Cardeilhac, while Georges Fouquet employed the great Czech poster designer, Alphonse Mucha, to supply him with designs that rivalled Lalique's for bizarre inventiveness. Mucha was another great favourite of Sarah Bernhardt's, and he designed the posters for her productions as well as supplying her with stage jewellery.

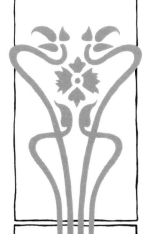

RIGHT: *A selection of Art Nouveau jewellery set against a School of Nancy marquetry landscape. The two larger pieces to the left — a hairslide and a parure de corsage — are by Lalique. Evident throughout is the range of colours and materials taking the form of plants or insects.*

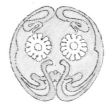

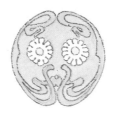

RIGHT: *A trio including a
ring by Archibald Knox
and below a
gilt-and-lustre Lalique
brooch (pin). The bat,
with its curving,
intricate wings was
almost as popular as
the dragonfly in Art
Nouveau.*

The work of the Parisian jewellers set the fashion for the rest of Europe. In Belgium, Philippe Wolfers produced work in a similar vein until he turned to decorative sculpture in 1904. In America, too, Lalique's influence was felt. Louis Tiffany of Tiffany & Co, already producing Art Nouveau silver, glass and ceramics, set up a jewellery department, under the supervision of the designer, Julia Munson. Even in England, where the Arts and Crafts movement generally shunned what was seen as the florid excess of French Art Nouveau, one of its leading figures, Charles Robert Ashbee, a founder of the Guild of Handicrafts, was seemingly seduced from the simplicity of his style by the decorative possibilities of jewellery. The Arts and Crafts movement and Art Nouveau are at their closest in Ashbee's jewellery which has a flowing, rather Celtic, line. Art Nouveau influence is evident, although Ashbee's materials do not match Lalique's for colour and texture. Characteristic of Ashbee is the use of decorative open wirework, a feature also evident, although reinterpreted in style, in the jewellery of the Glasgow Four. This plainer, more austere, English style can be seen in some of the work of the Belgian van de Velde and the Austro-German school, particularly among the Anglophile craftsmen of the Wiener Werkstätte.

RIGHT: *A delicately-
enamelled dragonfly
hairpiece by Lalique
set against a pendant
by Philippe Wolfers.*

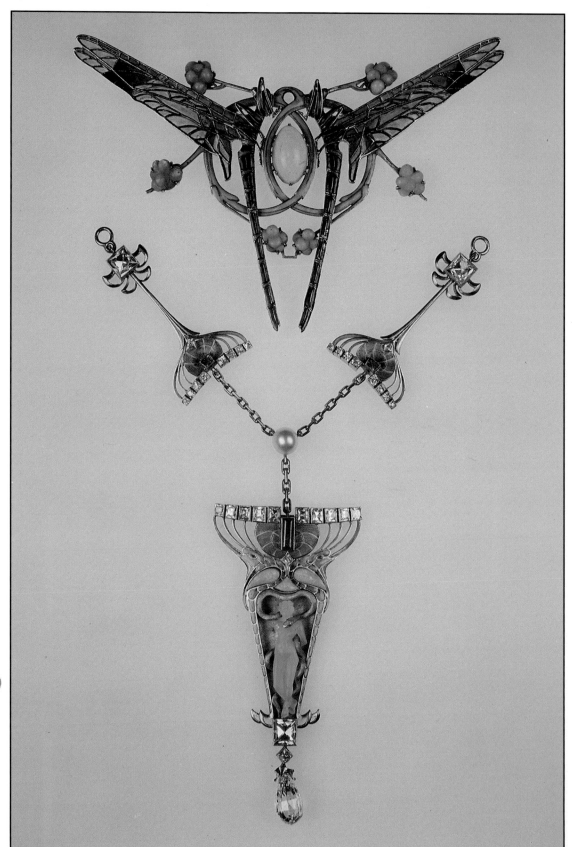

●

LEFT: *Horn and gold hair comb by Georges Fouquet.*

BELOW:
Silver, opal and mother-of-pearl peacock brooch (pin), by C.R. Ashbee.

CHAPTER SIX

GLASS

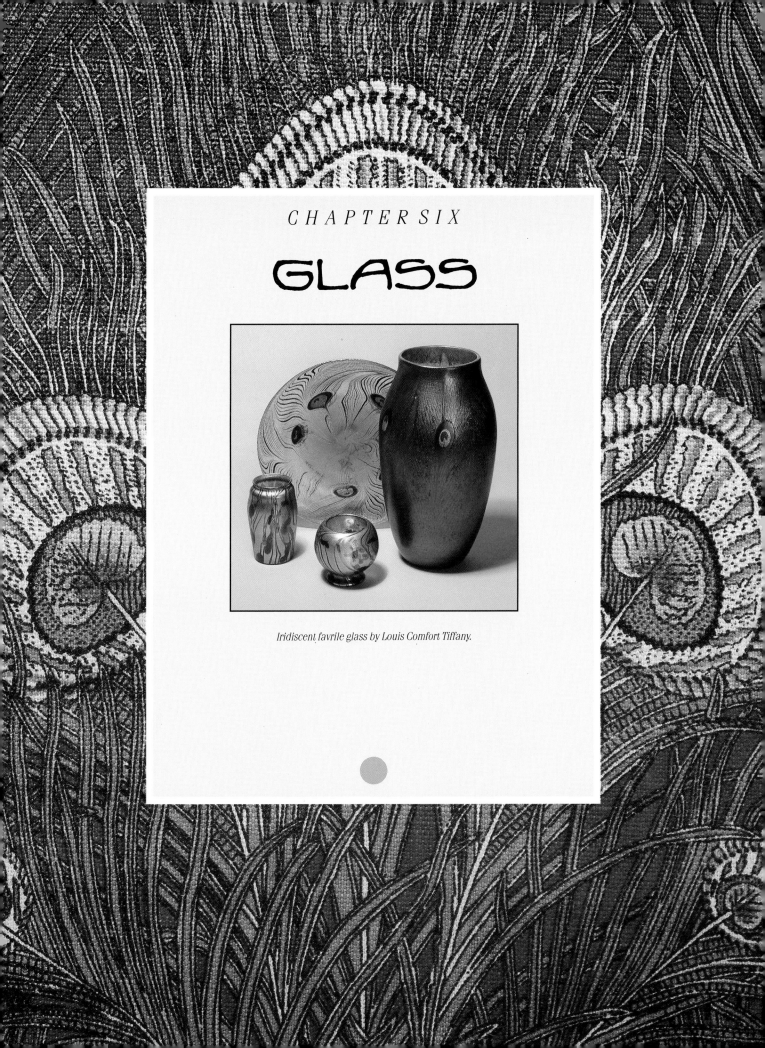

Iridiscent favrile glass by Louis Comfort Tiffany.

●

RIGHT: *Vases by Christopher Dresser. He experimented not only with translucency and pattern but with the forms of the vessels themselves.*

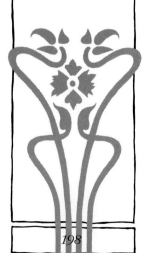

For the Art Nouveau craftsman, glass was, in its own way, as malleable and tractable as metal. The fluid contour of Art Nouveau could be as well expressed in the silhouette of a glass vase as in one of silver or bronze, but the translucency of glass was particularly suited to a style that was largely concerned with lightness and delicacy. The Art Nouveau interior presented a theme of openness and airiness, uncluttered and full of light. Glassware continued this theme, for it was the lightest and least substantial medium for the craftsman. Moreover, like stained glass, it could control the tonality and hue of the whole interior if it were set into a window, or the corner of a room if it were used as a lampshade. The designer could paint an interior with the delicacy of a watercolourist through his skill in manipulating the colour effects of glass.

As with the other crafts revitalized by the Art Nouveau, the history of glassware in the earlier 19th century was the story of technical advances, resulting in an impressively consistent quality of mechanical production. This was achieved largely at the expense of the aesthetic distinction created by the hand of the individual craftsman. In England, Morris and his followers had been the first to redress this imbalance in most of the crafts, but glassware was not one of them. To the Arts and Crafts movement glass meant, above all, the stained glass of their neo-medieval church windows. It was not until the 1890s, when Christopher Dresser began designing for the Clutha range of James Couper & Sons of Glasgow, that distinguished contemporary glassware was seen in Britain.

Dresser's electroplate and silverware is strictly and plainly functional in its design, but his work in glass is more flowing and graceful, with an Art Nouveau sense of line and colour.

The great innovators of Art Nouveau glass were French and American. The first was Joseph Brocard who studied Islamic art and restored Arab artefacts in order to learn more about the way they had been made. He was particularly interested in the colour effects that the Islamic craftsmen brought to their glassware through their use of coloured enamel finishes. Brocard's line of thought was followed and developed to its utmost by a series of brilliant technical innovations by Emile Gallé, the greatest master of Art Nouveau glassware.

Although producing furniture, ceramics, metalwork and textiles the Nancy School and Gallé as its chief designer, based its reputation upon the production of Art Nouveau glassware, glass being the traditional industry of the city. Gallé inherited his father's glass decorating workshop and, apart from his botanic and literary studies, his education included a year at the Meisenthal glassworks (now in Germany) which encouraged him to open his own glassworks in 1874. The inspiration for Gallé's work as a designer came partly from his great knowledge of botany and natural history, and, partly from his study of oriental glass and china, which began in London. Although the motto over his workshop door was 'My roots are deep in the woods', it was his study of the techniques of Japanese and Chinese glassmaking that helped him to give form to his delicate and tender vision of the natural world. Two of his great innovations were unveiled at the Parisian World Exhibitions of 1878 and 1889. Both his 'clair de lune' glass with its delicate sapphire tinge, and his relief moulded cameo glass were ultimately based on oriental techniques, Japanese and Chinese respectively.

Gallé increasing came to realize the full potential of glass as a medium. He began to explore the possibilities of colour, at first translucent, as in the 'clair de lune' work and then, in 1889, opaque colour, which made a greater range possible. Degrees of colour and translucency could be controlled by varying the process employed, and beautifully subtle light effects could be produced, evoking water or the atmosphere. Many more surface effects could be obtained by experimenting with the oxidation of the piece by acid baths, or using acid in the engraving process.

Gallé began to achieve relief effects by moulding the glass, adding further coatings or by using acid to strip down layers. Combined with effects of colour and translucence, this could provide marvellous effects of

●

LEFT: *Clutha glass by Christopher Dresser.*

BELOW RIGHT: *An early ewer by Gallé, influenced by the rococo, and a later bowl. The latter shows a more highly developed sense of relief, and more active form.*

BELOW FAR RIGHT: *A Gallé vase that reproduces the green and blue tints of underwater plant life beneath a relief detail of the plants themselves.*

underwater creatures against drifting waterweed, beetles crawling through the long grass or a butterfly alighting on a high branch. Gallé could also experiment by embedding further elements within the glass itself, such as metal leaf, gold dust or enamel, similar to the way in which an oil painter builds up his painting through the accumulation of subtly tinted, translucent layers of paint. The control of every technical detail of temperature and chemical mixtures had to be precise for a successful result. Gallé's mastery was such that he could exploit the production process to enhance the appearance of the piece, as in the careful creation of deliberate crazing in quartz to produce delicate, coloured veins as a feature, rather than a flaw. A combination of different ingredients might also be used, as in the *champlevé* technique in which cavities created in the glass were lined with gilt before being filled in by layers of translucent enamel whose glow would be enhanced by their backing. The use of enamel combined with glass gave Gallé the scope for deeper and more diverse colour, while the technique of *marquetrie-sur-verre*, the blending of semi-molten layers of glass on a semi-molten body, gave him a sculptor's control of form.

Glass was Gallé's natural medium. That which might appear florid and overwrought in his furniture became delicate and ethereal in his glassware. Gallé's nature studies were at their best in glasses, beakers and vases, since they allowed him to create a micro-cosm of the real world, where an insect's wing or a petal could be the largest form of the composition. Gallé's creation of beauty, mystery and surprise from what in natural or botanic terms was often mundane, was truly poetic. In the best Art Nouveau tradition, his glassware was prized far more as an artistic creation than for its functional design, and it was collected by writers and aesthetes. The admiration was mutual, for Gallé found much inspiration in poetry's celebration of exquisite sensation. He created his *verreries parlantes*- talking glassware — as a tribute to literature. Glassware inscribed with quotes from his favourite writers — Mallarmé, Rimbaud, Verlaine, Baudelaire, Hugo et al — tended to enhance the sensation on which he was concentrating. In Gallé's work, as in symbolist poetry, the evocation of a nuance of feeling or sensation was more important than practical purpose.

Most of Gallé's effect was gained through the surface, either through engraving, colour, etching with acid or inlaying other materials. However, the plasticity of his *marquetrie-sur-verre* encouraged a more three-dimensional approach to glassware. With the encrustation of relief, his vases gained a more animated silhouette. In his later work he began the final stage of experimenting with the actual shape of the glassware itself, rather than just the surface, so that whole new Art Nouveau forms were created.

Gallé's great success as a designer created its own

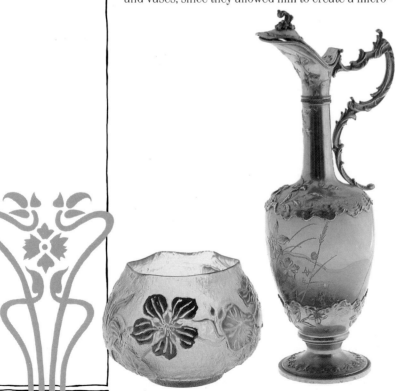

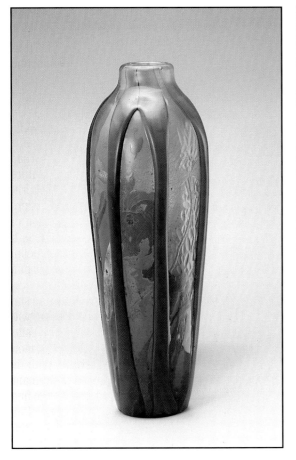

ABOVE LEFT: *Daum vase with poppy relief.*

ABOVE FAR LEFT: *Gallé here applies poured marquetrie-de-verre to a translucent vase engraved with irises, a favourite flower.*

difficulties in production as his career progressed. His reputation rested upon a limited production of works on which an enormous number of man hours had been concentrated. With increased demand, Gallé was persuaded to increase the capacity of his works by developing larger scale production, while simultaneously retaining a more exclusive hand-crafted output. The more numerous workshop designs inevitably lacked the degree of finish of his earlier work, but with a larger enterprise Gallé was able to expand his market, opening showrooms in London and Frankfurt, and ending his career as an employer of three hundred workers.

Gallé led a great renaissance of the glass industry in Nancy. The brothers Auguste and Antonin Daum, like Gallé, had taken over their father's workshop and begun to experiment with the new techniques to produce work in the Art Nouveau style. The Daum brothers were able to employ some of the talented designers working at Nancy, such as the versatile Jacques Gruber, and produced work very much in the Gallé manner. They too were concerned with opacity, colour and relief, using acid to eat away layers of glass to reveal hidden colour beneath and create delicately-modu-

lated backgrounds for relief work, or powdered enamel fused onto the surface in the furnace to create a glowing, opaque finish in a variety of colours.

The Daum brothers were also involved with the development of glassware produced by the more lengthy process of using pre-manufactured ground-down glass as an ingredient. By this means, and by the manipulation of oxidation to add the desired colour, an opaque form of glass, pâte-de-verre, could be produced, similar in appearance to alabaster. The technique had been known to the ancient Greeks and Romans, but was subsequently lost. Its rediscoverer, Henri Cros, used pâte-de-verre as a sort of mock marble, executing reliefs and free-standing pieces on a small scale, in a vaguely classical style. After Cros's rediscovery in the mid 1880s, pâte-de-verre began to interest Art Nouveau designers. The Conches craftsman, François Emile Décorchement, became the greatest specialist, but the Daum workshop also produced some designs by one of its employees, Alméric Walter. Walter perfected his pâte-de-verre technique at Daum before setting himself up producing statuettes in the medium.

Gallé's most important French contemporary in

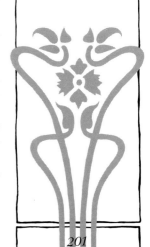

•

ABOVE RIGHT: *A Daum vase continuing the light and relief effects begun by Gallé.*

BELOW RIGHT: *Daum nightlight. The combination of glassware and artificial light was irresistible to the Art Nouveau.*

terms of experimentation and innovation was Eugène Rousseau, who began his career as an art dealer before starting up as a craftsman himself. The same year that Gallé exhibited his 'clair de lune' glass, Rousseau created an equivalent sensation with his Japanese-style glassware. He went on to become a technical pioneer; like Gallé, he used reliefs, inscriptions, tracery crazing in the glass, gold leaf and flecks. His most original work was using glass to imitate the texture and colour of gemstones. These appeared to be set into the glass vessel, but were themselves also made of glass. This work was continued by Ernest Léveillé.

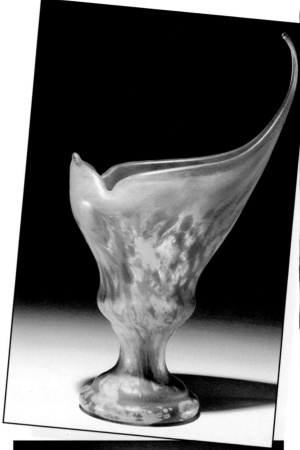

CENTRE: *Gallé lamp and orchid vase with (right) inscribed vase by Rollinant.*

ABOVE LEFT: *Daum glass chalice.*

BELOW LEFT: *Gallé lamp with overlay of butterfly and sycamores.*

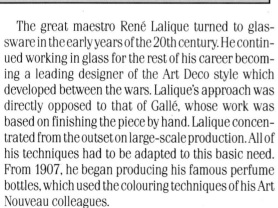

The great maestro René Lalique turned to glassware in the early years of the 20th century. He continued working in glass for the rest of his career becoming a leading designer of the Art Deco style which developed between the wars. Lalique's approach was directly opposed to that of Gallé, whose work was based on finishing the piece by hand. Lalique concentrated from the outset on large-scale production. All of his techniques had to be adapted to this basic need. From 1907, he began producing his famous perfume bottles, which used the colouring techniques of his Art Nouveau colleagues.

TIFFANY

RIGHT: *'Goose-necked' vase by Louis Comfort Tiffany, inspired by a Persian perfume flask.*

CENTRE: *Tiffany lamp combining mosaic, bronze and coloured leaded glass.*

OPPOSITE ABOVE: *Glass plate by Louis Comfort Tiffany, again using the favourite peacock feather theme.*

OPPOSITE BELOW: *Tall Tiffany favrile glass, using the peacock feather motif, a favourite Art Nouveau device.*

Louis Comfort Tiffany was the American designer who rivalled Gallé as a craftsman in glass. Tiffany came from a family of goldsmiths and jewellers and produced work in both these media, but after a study trip to Paris he began concentrating upon glassware. The Tiffany Glass & Decoration Company, founded in 1879, rapidly became a very successful enterprise, its most prestigious commission being the decoration of rooms in the White House. With the opening of a new glassworks at Corona, Tiffany began producing what he called Favrile, or hand-made glass goods. These exploited the use of chemical soaks or vapours to create different surface textures from matt to a burnished glow, and a variety of rich colours. Tiffany's glass rarely has the modelled plasticity of Gallé or Daum; its decoration, more abstract in its depiction of natural forms, rarely rises out in relief but appears to be more of an applied surface pattern. The silhouette of a Tiffany vase thus remains simple and elegant, although to complement the simplified decoration the vase shapes themselves are more adventurous, often stretched up on impossibly slender, plant-like stems or with twisting serpentine necks inspired by the works of the ancient Persian craftsmen. Unlike the Nancy School, Tiffany's glass never attempts to imitate gems, water, petals or any of other natural objects. Like Gallé, Tiffany's success encouraged a crop of imitators, chief among whom were the Quezal Art Glass & Decorating Company of Brooklyn, and Handel & Company of Connecticut.

The development of the incandescent electric lamp by Thomas Edison in the 1880s posed a new challenge for designers. Tiffany was one of the first to realize the potential of electricity for the Art Nouveau style, and soon his name became synonomous with a style of lamp which used coloured, glass set into leaded panels exactly like a conventional stained glass window. The glass shades were either designed as flowers in a conventional shape, or, as in the Wisteria Lamp, each fragment of glass was a leaf in the foliage of a tree-shaped lamp whose trunk and roots were formed by the moulded metal of the stem and base. The opportunity for mixed media work in metal, ceramic and glass gave the electric lamp an instant appeal for the Art Nouveau, quite apart from the bright, even light that could be harnessed as part of the composition. It is typical of a tendency in Art Nouveau that the modernity of the electric light, its startlingly technological aspect heralding a new age, was ignored by many designers. Instead, filtered by coloured glass, its light became a gentle glow, a part of the idyll of lilies, swans and butterflies that kept the fantasy of an Art Nouveau interior unsullied by brutish technology. The treatment of the electric lamp in the hands of Tiffany or Gallé is exactly parallel to the use of wrought iron in the architecture of Horta or Guimard: it is used willingly but, although playing a major part in the whole, is masked by its conversion, against its very manufactured nature, into the organic world of Art Nouveau.

Both Gallé and Daum produced lamps of a very similar style to their other glassware. Glass figured as both base, neck and shade, and, typically, the form of a mushroom was quickly used as the most analagous form in nature. Other table, bracket and standing lamps used more metalwork, but the plant form naturally remained. In designs by Majorelle, Guimard, Gallé or Vallin, sinuous metal plants or saplings are created which flower into electric bulbs. The electric light is used in the same manner as the precious stone in a piece of Art Nouveau jewellery: the whole setting, whether it is a vine, thistle, a sprig of mistletoe or a lily, constitutes the bulk of the work, while the electric globes are scattered around the metalwork as highlights. While the majority of Art Nouveau lamps feature glowing flowers, the bronze or gilt statuettes of nymph-like figures produced by many craftsmen could also be adapted to carrying an electric light, providing rather a coy interplay between ornamentation and function. These lightly-draped females supporting desk lamps are perhaps an indication of Art Nouveau's retreat from the challenge of a new medium. They have an escapist charm, but to the eyes of a future generation of designers they would show only a

retreat into impractical fantasy, at odds with the nature of the artefact itself. From the range of Art Nouveau craftsmen and designers only Henry van de Velde, commissioned by Bing, produced an electric lamp that took as its starting point the practical and scientific nature of the medium.

A more traditional part of glass design was that of stained glass. A huge revival of interest in the design and manufacture of stained glass had accompanied the Gothic revival, and it continued to be an important art form with the medievally-inspired English Arts and Crafts movement. The Art Nouveau treatment of stained glass grew from this revival and profited by the growing decorative similarities between stained glass, embroidery and painting. The first two crafts, by their very nature, were concerned with two-dimensionality, and, taking a cue from the crafts, painters of the 1890s in France were also concentrating on the

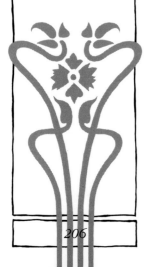

flat, decorative arrangement of colour in their works. Thus for Art Nouveau, stained glass was not so much a revivalist anachronism but a medium that was perfectly suited to the flatness, linearity and love of light and colour that were common to all the contemporary decorative arts. Also, a designer often wanted to control the light cast on his interior by making it harmonize with the flowing plant forms of the furniture, wallpaper and table ornaments. Tiffany even saw a useful social role in stained glass. In an age when many city dwellers were looking out onto a bare blank wall, a stained glass window could shield its owner from such a brutal sight and go some way to provide him with an idyllic world of flowers, birds and butterflies to gaze into instead.

Stained glass was widely manufactured and used to some degree in every wealthy home of the period, yet most Art Nouveau stained glass was not represen-tative of a high level of craftsmanship, but consisted of regularly shaped, painted or enamelled panes, easy to produce and assemble. Only in the best quality designs was the traditional method of production retained, in which each motif was carefully outlined in lead, using panels of differing shapes and sizes. In Nancy, Jacques Gruber produced his stained glass of exquisitely-observed plants, flowers and birds in this way, as did Guimard in Paris. Guimard's stained glass, like his ironwork was designed as part of an architectural whole, and one sees in his windows the same abstract arches, bows and ripples as can be seen in the ironwork of his gates. The Swiss Eugène Grasset, who was also based in Paris, produced stained glass designs which were more traditional in subject matter than Guimard's, being very strongly related to contemporary graphic art, with Art Nouveau maidens idling in beautiful summer landscapes.

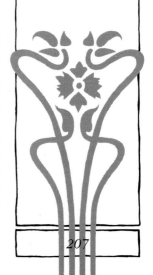

•

RIGHT: *Jacques Gruber
window from the
medical school at
Nancy*

ABOVE LEFT: *Austrian Art Nouveau glassware by (left to right) Zasche, Powlony and von Harrach.*

BELOW FAR LEFT *Irridescent glassware c.1902 by the famous Austrian glass designer Richard Bakalowits of Austria, using intricate metal settings.*

BELOW LEFT *Window by Georges de Feure. The elegant and alluring female derives from the work of Aubrey Beardsley and relates strongly to de Feure's graphic work.*

CHAPTER SEVEN

CERAMICS

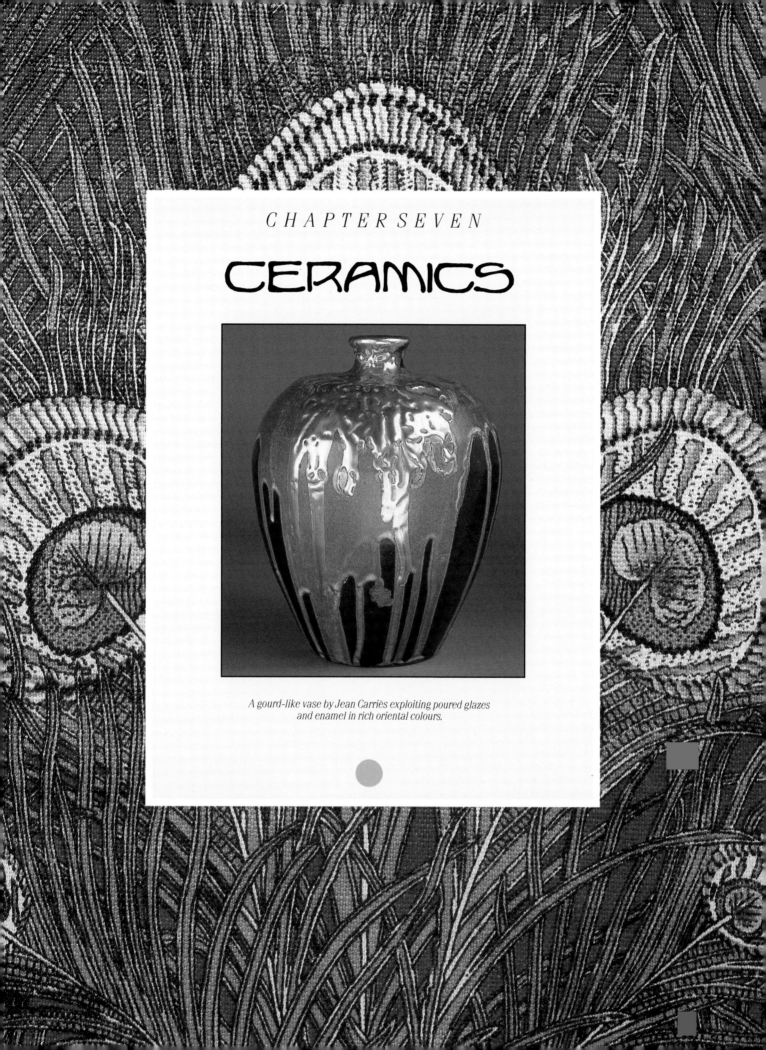

*A gourd-like vase by Jean Carriès exploiting poured glazes
and enamel in rich oriental colours.*

The divide between favouring individually-produced pieces and the volume production of factories was as great for the Art Nouveau ceramicist as it was for the glass craftsman. The two crafts were closely linked in both style and technique. Much the same kind of ware was produced in each medium and in both crafts the innovations of Art Nouveau increased the colour range and the possibilities for relief decoration, as well as changing the actual shape of the piece itself. However, whereas glassworks and metalworks tended always to be located in existing industrial centres because of the type of materials needed and processes involved, a pottery was a much smaller-scale establishment and in effect more 'portable'. The potter is only really concerned with a suitable clay, which can be obtained in a variety of locations. Pottery, at one level a commonplace and inexpensive necessity, had been produced in many small centres in both Europe and America. The craft tradition, on which the Art Nouveau revival was built, was widely spread, and a very large amount of ceramic wares were produced at many scattered provincial, and often rustic, centres.

This was particularly true of France, which was the centre of Art Nouveau ceramics. While their fellow craftsmen were concentrated mostly in the major centres of Paris and Nancy, and therefore had strong links with an entire cultural milieu, the Art Nouveau ceramicist often worked in isolation, in modest circumstances, and was therefore closest to the humble tradition of the potter. Gallé, de Feure, Colonna and others worked in ceramics too, but often their work was more closely linked with the major porcelain factories. These factories had acquired impressive new technology, but in terms of design creativity they had become stagnant. The new generation of artist-craftsmen turned their backs on fine porcelain almost entirely. Instead, they concentrated upon the production of more coarsely-grained traditional stoneware which was the subject of an enormous revival in the Art Nouveau period. The link between these innovators and their medium was strong enough in the public mind for their work to be simply and almost universally referred to as 'Art Pottery', neatly summarizing the designers, their medium and clientele. The artistic revival of stoneware created, throughout Europe and America, a whole new or revived tradition quite separate from that of porcelain production, and one that is still thriving today. The choice of a more 'democratic' medium was naturally not unselfconscious. It was very much influenced by the socially-conscious side of the Arts and Crafts movement that preferred plainer, cheaper materials that were free of associa-

tion with wealth and social aspiration. The exploration of stoneware had begun before the style of Art Nouveau was fully formed, yet it was primarily those working in the Art Nouveau manner that were responsible for developing the full potential of the medium. The same increased range of materials, exploring those that were hitherto seen as somehow inferior, has been noted in Art Nouveau metalwork and jewellery. The stress on aesthetic, rather than economic, criteria is entirely characteristic of Art Nouveau.

Despite its social implications, it is arguable whether the revival of stoneware would have been so significant if it had not been for the example of oriental, particularly Japanese, ceramics. The stylization, elegance and technical virtuosity of the oriental craftsman was once again an inspiration to their Art Nouveau cousins. Chinese porcelain had a very major impact on the west from the 18th century onward, and among aesthetes, such as Whistler and Wilde, there was a reverential enthusiasm for blue-and-white porcelain, although working craftsmen were more excited by the greater range of technical possibilities explored in oriental stoneware. Warm, rich colours

were possible, as were a variety of lustres, chance effects of liquid clay and glaze and a great range of textures, from porous roughness to cold, smooth glazes. All these areas were explored by Art Nouveau craftsmen. Art Nouveau's ambivalent, but important, relationship with scientific developments was also of significance for ceramicists. Advanced technical equipment and knowledge made new artistic effects possible in the crafts. An Art Nouveau variation of the artist-craftsman was the scientist-artist-craftsman typified in England by Dresser, in France by Gallé, Grasset, and Guimard's ceramicist-collaborator Alexandre Bigot, who was a professor of physics.

The Haviland workshop supported the works of pioneering French ceramicists. Originally established at Auteuil, it moved to the centre of Paris in 1881, where it was managed by Ernest Chaplet. Chaplet had been an apprentice at the state-owned Sèvres porcelain factory, While running the Haviland workshop, he rediscovered the technique for producing the much-envied *sang-de-boeuf* (oxblood) glaze of Chinese stoneware, which was as it name implies, deep red in colour. The secret of this process was something that Chaplet never divulged, but versions were developed by contemporaries, such as Adrien-Pierre Dalpayrat, the inventor of the similar, copper-based 'rouge Dalpayrat'. In 1887, Chaplet sold Haviland, moving to Choisy-le-Roi to continue his research. Here he developed a greater range of finishes — pitted, veined, dappled or polished. Chaplet's pupil and collaborator was Albert Dammouse who trained as a sculptor before devoting himself to ceramics. He was involved with Chaplet's innovations and also developed his own distinctive translucent paste. As one of the most talented of the new generation of ceramicists Dammouse was invited to use a studio for his experiments at the Sèvres works in 1892, because the directors, realised the need for some stylistic innovation in their rather conservative output. Ownership of Haviland passed from Chaplet to Auguste Delaherche. Delaherche developed one of the most distinctive motifs of Art Nouveau ceramics, the use of a drip glaze poured over the object. This was

A selection of vases and bowls by Ernest Chaplet, showing the range of finishes and forms he pioneered.

●

ABOVE RIGHT: *English Minton tiles with an Art Nouveau motif. Ceramic tile design had been revitalised by Morris & Co, and the Art Nouveau tiles were popular as a way of introducing further colour into the interior.*

ABOVE FAR RIGHT *Minton tile with stylized floral decoration, c.1880-1900.*

BELOW RIGHT: *Stoneware vessel by Christopher Dresser. The use of a sea urchin is typical of the interest in the more unusual natural forms.*

used by almost every ceramicist of the period and was a technique, once again, derived from the orient. The long, flowing curves of the poured glaze, its sense of vitality and almost organic growth, made it an enormously attractive technique for the Art Nouveau.

Although both Chaplet and Delaherche came from artisan backgrounds, a great painter was equally responsible for the development of an Art Nouveau style in ceramics. This was Paul Gauguin, whose influence over the whole area of decorative arts at the time was enormous. Gauguin experimented with ceramics at Haviland under both Chaplet and Delaherche, producing work free from the conventions that seem natural to the specialist but foreign to an artist from another discipline. Gauguin's ceramics appear rather crudely produced in comparison to the later, sleeker works of the Art Nouveau, but a certain primitive

coarseness was exactly the aim of his art at this time. Moreover, Gauguin's lack of inhibition in handling the clay resulted in haphazard budding, swelling and flowing forms with gnarled and twisted handles, and relief work taking the form of branches or some other less well-defined growth. These works, few in number, were produced in the late 1880s, both before and after Gauguin's trip to Martinique, and predate the development of the Art Nouveau proper of the 1890s. The Haviland workshop is of great significance for the development of Art Nouveau ceramics, technically through the innovations of Chaplet and Delaherche, and stylistically through Gauguin's experiments.

A parallel centre for stoneware production developed at Saint-Armand-en-Puisaye in the Nivernais region. The School of Saint-Armand focused on the charismatic and short-lived figure of Jean Carriès, who died at the age of 39. Jean Carriès discovered oriental stoneware in the collection of his friend Paul Jeanneney, who was to follow him to Saint-Armand and start producing orientalist ceramics. Carriès established himself in the local manor house and began exploring the range of coloured glazes for stoneware and the chance effects of poured enamel. His most distinctive work relies more on his training as a sculptor, for he also produced small figures and reliefs of grotesque faces and animals reminiscent of the extraordinary fantasies of the 16th-century Mannerists. These rather bizarre creations are some of the best examples of the fanciful and almost surreal side to much of the Art Nouveau borrowings from nature. Like metalwork, ceramics shares some common ground with sculpture, and the production of figurines or busts of the Art Nouveau nymph were as common in terracotta as they were in bronze. High-relief ceramic tiles, depicting aquatic creatures, mermaids, insects or birds, were also common as both interior and exterior decoration, as, for instance, those produced by Bigot for Guimard.

After Carriès death, his manor house was taken over by Georges Hoentschel, a versatile and successful designer who managed his own company. Inspired by Carriès, Hoentschel had moved to Saint-Armand in order to concentrate upon ceramics, and he continued to produce simple yet elegant ware enliven by the flowing lines of dripped glaze. Hoentschel also incorporated a great deal of floral detail into his vases. As in Art Nouveau glassware, this had the effect of breaking up the austerity of the silhouette by creating a more active contour. Hoentschel also used ormolu mounts for some of his pieces, immediately evoking roccoco precedents and emphasizing the sophistication of his work. In this respect Hoentschel's work is closer to

CERAMICS

●

BELOW LEFT *Three vases and two plates by Auguste Delaherche. Delaherche's range was considerable, involving drip glazes, incisions and relief work.*

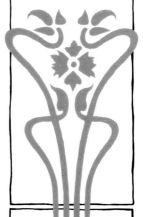

RIGHT: *Auguste Delaherche vase with a blue drip glaze and the almost ubiquitious peacock feather motif.*

FAR RIGHT: *Vase by Adelaide Robineau. The form and decoration of Art Nouveau continues here into a piece of stoneware from 1921.*

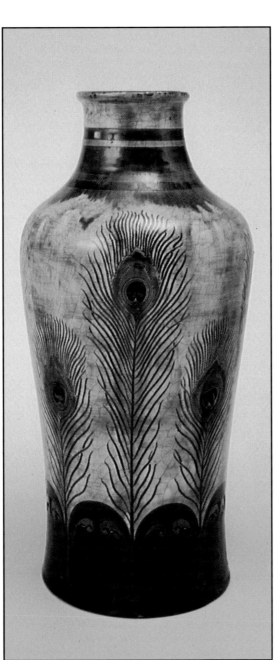

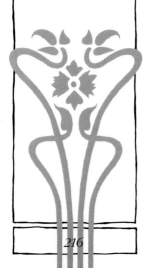

that of the Nancy school, such as Gallé and Majorelle, whose own work combines the glazes of the oriental style with the natural detail and intricate relief of the Nancy style as a whole. Gallé's work in particular, has a characteristically opulent air to it in contrast to the humble associations of stoneware. Insects or flowers might be picked out in gold and the colours were the brighter hues of faïence.

Somewhere between the rugged texture of stoneware and the bland finish of porcelain was the shimmering warmth of lustreware. The rich glow of lustreware glazes have an affinity with glassware, either the

matt finish of Tiffany's favrile vases or the opaque sheen of *pâte-de-verre*, emphasizing the closeness of the two media. The Messier workshop was the main producer of French lustreware, designed by the artistic director of the works, the noted Art Nouveau painter Levy-Dhurmer.

Stimulated by improving standards and increasing popularity, the two great state-controlled porcelain factories of Sèvres and Limoges forged links with established Art Nouveau designers. Apart from encouraging Edouard Dammouse's work, the Sèvres factory commissioned work from other designers

LEFT: *A selection of pierced stoneware vases by Auguste Delaherche.*

BELOW RIGHT *Sèvres vase showing a tentative response by the State French porcelain manufacturer to the natural detailing and elongated forms of Art Nouveau.*

BELOW FAR RIGHT *Vase by Taxile Doat, probably produced before his departure for America.*

independent of the company, including Guimard. Guimard's ceramic designs were well suited to porcelain for, rather than focusing on a natural warmth, texture and colour indentifiable with stoneware, they were essentially hard-lined, abstract, linear creations carried onto three dimensions, in which the rising curve of the vase's silhouette is incorporated into the composition. Georges de Feure and Edward Colonna designed for Limoges, an apt combination since both were sophisticates well versed in the eighteenth century style, which had been a strong influence upon the elegance of their interiors for Bing.

Taxile Doat was a ceramicist who made his name

working at Sèvres while continuing an independent production of his own. Doat treated porcelain to the techniques of the stoneware innovators using dripped glazes and even the vegetable shapes of gourds, marrows (squash) and pears, which had been used at Saint-Armand. He also varied the texture of his work by having *pâte-sur-pâte* medallions, like ancient cameos, applied to the surface, which proved to be popular. Doat increased his reputation by the publication of *Grand Feu Ceramics*, a treatise on the new techniques of firing and glazing. The book was read with interest in the United States, in particular by the entrepreneur Edgar Gardner Lewis. Lewis was a dynamic

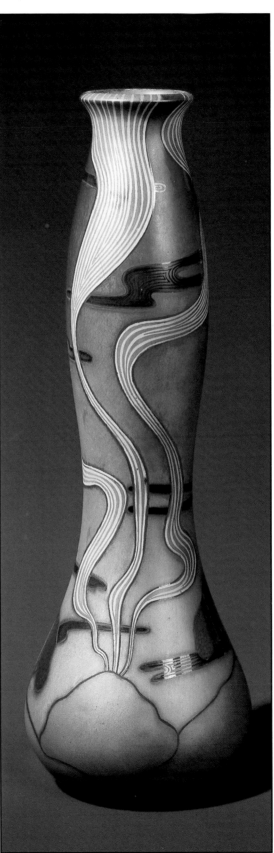

LEFT: *Stoneware vase by Joseph Rippl-Ronai for Zsolnay of Hungary. Maintaining the essentially fluid style of Art Nouveau, the Hungarian variation introduced a distinctively central European element to forms and colour.*

FAR LEFT *Ceramic bust by Gustave Obiols. The dreamy Art Nouveau maiden returns, this time in clay.*

figure, instrumental in founding the Women's League and the Art Institute of the People's University of University City, Missouri. Offered a fine supply of clay and the enthusiastic backing of the amateur potter Lewis, Doat left Sèvres in 1909 to work at the University City Pottery.During his five-year stay, Missouri stoneware gained an international reputation.

An enormous number of potteries opened up in America between the Philadelphia Centennial Exhibition, which introduced Arts and Crafts ideas in 1876, and the Chicago World's Fair of 1893. The development of American ceramics ran parallel to experimentation with the use of exotic glazes on simple stoneware shapes that occurred in France. The Robertson family of the Chelsea Keramic Art Works developed slip glaze decoration and an American version of the *sang-de-boeuf* glaze. In Cincinnati, Mary Louise McLaughlin, a gifted amateur, produced similarly pioneering work as did the commercial Rockwood Pottery in the same city. The Art Nouveau style was seen to some degree in the elegant, elongated vase forms and curving plant-like handles, but more particularly in the inlay of sinuous lilies, orchids and other Art Nouveau favourites. Newcomb College Pottery of Tulane University, New Orleans provided fine examples of this approach to ceramic design.

CHAPTER EIGHT

GRAPHICS

Tropon *by Henry van de Velde, The most influential
theoretician of the Art Nouveau.*

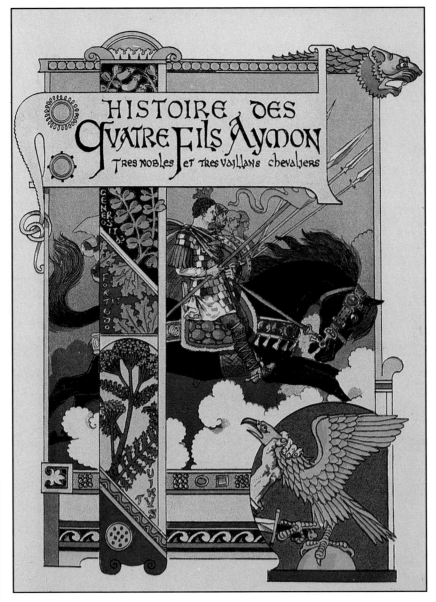

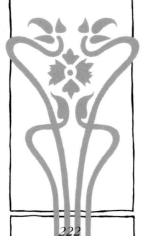

The Art Nouveau style found its most complete expression in the graphic arts. The emphasis on line, the whiplash line of a plant stem, a swallow's wing or woman's hair was clearest in a medium in which line was the principal, or only, element. In every other medium the Art Nouveau artist was most successful when he was able to concentrate upon linear elements, whether it was in the design of a wrought iron balcony or stained glass. Book illustration, poster design and typography were all media in which the demands of mechanical reproduction limited the possibilities for nuances of tone, colour, atmosphere and light, which are the tools of the painter. Instead, the graphic artist concentrated upon strength of design and linear inventiveness. The strongest design was very often that which acknowledged the flatness of the medium, and therefore concentrated on patterning the surface. Ironically, this was also the style of avant-garde French painting of the 1880s and 1890s, particularly of Gauguin and his followers and the transition from fine to decorative art was easier to make at this time than at any other in the nineteenth century. It was in some ways paradoxical that the increasingly abstract and decorative tendencies of painters had an influence on the discovery of the essentially decorative element in the graphic arts.

It was natural that Symbolism, as a movement involving both painters and writers naturally encouraged a meeting with Art Nouveau of the two via illustration. Literary themes and allusions were common

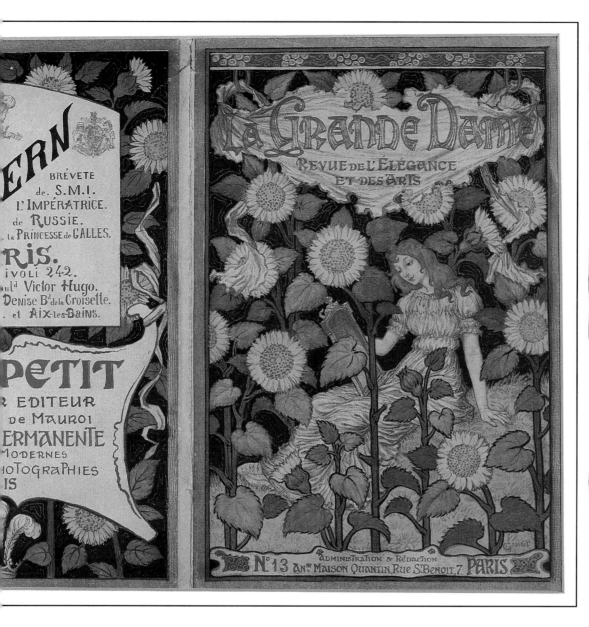

LEFT: La Grande Dame *cover by Eugène Grasset, showing a developed Art Nouveu style, complete with the characteristic young girl. Grasset's typeface is increasingly freer but still retains echoes of his Gothic inspiration.*

in painting and it was a small step to actual illustration, as practiced by Manet, Redon, Denis and others. This was part of a general drift away from realism in the arts to fantasy and stylization, the impulses behind Art Nouveau decoration. Combining visual images with text also resulted in a work that was more than a sum of its parts. It approached the mysterious, all-embracing work to which writers of the time aspired. The many references by writers, to painting, music and to the neglected senses of taste and smell, were used to enhance the breadth of their symbolist moods. Literary references could have a similar use in the arts and crafts. Gallé's *verre parlant* is perhaps the best example, using quotations to add a further dimension to his work.

This was the theoretical background but, for the illustrator, approaching a text with the aim of creating a unified work of art presented certain practical difficulties. The ideal was an integration between text and image rather than the use of a few isolated plates throughout the volume. This integration of various elements into an overall design was very much the forte of Art Nouveau. Made possible by the versatility of the designers involved, it has been clearly seen in interior design, where a uniform style involved even the smallest objects in a stylistic harmony with the whole. The fact that many of the leading Art Nouveau figures were literary figures too, frequently authors in their own right, naturally strengthened the visual and literary relationship.

Book production was generally acknowledged to be of poor quality in the 19th-century. 18th-century typography styles and bindings were still being used in a rather debased form. In France, bibliophile societies were formed at an increasing rate as the century progressed in order to encourage higher standards of paper production, printing and binding. Limited deluxe editions were commissioned from craftsmen, parallel to the production of ordinary 'edition bindings' in larger quantities for the general public. The effect of this enlightened patronage was apparent only in terms of the quality of materials and binding. A corresponding improvement in artistic quality had to come from the designers themselves.

In 1891 William Morris turned his attention from interior design to the problem of artistic quality in book design. The first publication of his Kelmscott Press appeared in that year and the revival of the printed book began in earnest. Morris designed new typefaces, and used text and illustration as elements in an integrated page design. Morris's work was of great importance though the Arts and Crafts style did not develop an Art Nouveau curvilinear style. Arthur Mackmurdo's revolutionary title page to *Wren's City Churches* of 1883 had created a remarkable union of lettering and decoration in an Art Nouveau manner, but it was Eugène Grasset's production of *L'Histoire des Quatre Fils Aymon* in the same year which was the first totally integrated publication. Grasset had chosen a medieval legend and had spent over two years developing the decoration and illustration so that they became integrated, or even fused, with the text in a great variety of different ways. The actual style of graphics was not yet Art Nouveau but it was certainly derived from the sources that were to give it birth; flat areas and an emphasis on outline came from Japan and intricate patterned borders from Celtic illumination and carving. Grasset himself continued to be one of the most influential Art Nouveau illustrators and poster designers.

An important part of Grasset's subsequent work was the treatment of lettering itself as part of the whole design. This was far easier to do when the written element was limited, as in a poster, magazine cover or advertisement, and Grasset's creation of new forms was echoed by other artists in these fields. On a larger scale, Guimard had created his own lettering style for his Métro work to blend into his total composition. As in Art Nouveau as a whole, Art Nouveau lettering avoided the straight line as far as it was possible. Lines flowed into gently curving shapes and where they met they were looped together with intertwined tendrils. The intention was to remove the letters as far

HOW SIR TRISTRAM
DRANK OF THE ■■■
LOVE DRINK ■■■

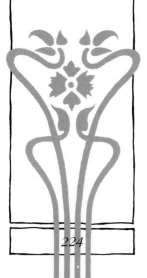

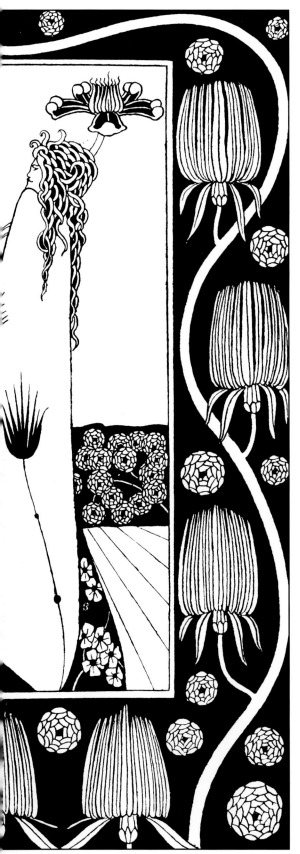

as possible from the idea of print and mechanical reproduction. Oriental calligraphy was the model: the Japanese and Chinese scribe had the freedom to adapt shapes and express himself by the nuances of his brushwork without losing meaning. By including poetry or criticism in a woodcut, and making it attractive by virtue of the beauty of the calligraphy and its disposal in relation to the overall design, Japanese art had also shown the West how image and script could be successfully combined. While most Art Nouveau designers created individual letter types to suit the commission, in 1898, Grasset progressed to create a complete typeface, the first in Art Nouveau, enabling the style to spread more easily into commercial art. In 1900, Grasset's example was followed by Eckmann, who designed the heavier, more moulded typeface associated with the Austro-German Jugendstil.

In England, the Arts and Crafts allegiance of most designers inhibited anything emphatically curvilinear in the graphic arts. Walter Crane's illustrations often exploit sweeping curves and rather intricate decoration, but even he later repudiated this tendency in his art. Despite the general climate, the greatest figure in Art Nouveau illustration developed in England during this time. This was the brilliant young illustrator Aubrey Beardsley, who began his career in 1893 illustrating *Morte d'Arthur* for Morris's Kelmscott Press. Morris was outraged by the result, rightly seeing it as a style antipathetic to that which he was trying to encourage, and this provoked an acrimonious dispute. Beardsley was developing his own highly personal version of the Art Nouveau style. He favoured asymmetry in the layout of the page, and natural detailing was stylized into essentially artifical and over-refined forms. Movement was conveyed through great unbroken, sinuous curves, and, most importantly, any sense of space was sacrificed in favour of a dramatic interplay between large simplified areas of black and white. Beardsley's sources were those of most Art Nouveau artists — the orient, an element of the medieval, an increasing fascination with the 18th century and a very distinctive re-intepretation of some early Renaissance decoration. Yet Beardsley's work is startlingly original, deriving most of its impact from his peculiar literary sense and the heightened sensibility of an invalid's delicate constitution. Beardsley was fascinated by the decadence of the time; his most characteristic illustrations are those for Oscar Wilde's *Salome*, in which he creates a world of cruelly perverse sensuality, of great visual refinement, exoticism and occasional sardonic wit. It has the studied amorality of the *fin-de-siècle* dandy epitomized by Beardsley and Wilde. Beardsley's sinister eroticism

RIGHT: *Another* Morte d'Arthur *illustration by Aubrey Beardsley. Beardsley's erotic style shocked the British public and was long out of favour.*

and cruel distortions were very distant from the freshness of much Art Nouveau flora and fauna, yet they were given form by the same sinuously active line, and had the same asymmetrical elegance.

The character of Beardsley's world was very much his own, and it fostered many imitators across Europe and America. The use of simple black and white, and areas of heavy decoration set against areas of space, was a technique that was easy to copy and provided a strong impact with great economy. Many of Beardsley's imitators were extremely derivative, but his style could be used intelligently as part of a broader synthesis; in the graphic work of the Glasgow Four, it was combined with the distortions of Toorop and their own stylized Celtic to create a very distinctive variation. Like every all illustrator's work, Beardsley's designs penetrated widely because in a book or magazine format they were very easily transportable and were available in large numbers. This was particularly true of Beardsley's work for the *Yellow Book*, the journal of the English decadents, and the *Savoy Magazine*. Beardsley died of consumption at the age of 26.

While typography and illustration were being revolutionized by Art Nouveau artists, bookbindings themselves were also being produced. Deluxe of editions of books were often produced in flimsy bindings to allow a wealthy owner to commission his own, and this demand was being satisfied by a growing number of leather craftsmen. Of these, René Wiener of Nancy was one of the most highly skilled. Flaubert's *Salammbo*, an exotic historical fantasy, provided the theme for his most spectacular binding, which was designed by Victor Prouvé and had enamel corners by Camille Martin. The cover is an elaboration of Art Nouveau themes — swirling veils, writhing snakes, a naked Salammbo with long, unbound hair, fish, flames, insects, all reduced to flat areas of glowing rich colour.

The development of posters in the nineteenth century created a whole new area for the graphic artist. By the end of the century poster art had become a vogue with its own collectors and galleries, its commercial aspects underplayed and its artistic value emphasized. This situation had been largely brought about by the pioneering work of Jules Chéret in the 1870s and 1880s. Chéret rejected the traditional format of the poster as a concentration of written information relieved by occasional illustrations, and instead concentrated upon one large, brightly coloured eye-catching image supported by the barest information concerning the actual event advertised. Chéret concentrated on the maximum possible impact since he knew his poster would be competing for attention with all the distractions of the surrounding street. He was forced to simplify — colours became strong, shapes simple and flat — and dynamic and exciting movement was conveyed purely through an active linear design. Chéret's images of lively gay dancing girls were admired by painters and designers alike and anticipated the simplifying trend of the Art Nouveau. Chéret's line was still a little hesitant and fractured, as in an Impressionist painting, and it was Eugène Grasset who created the Art Nouveau poster proper by using stronger outlines and more fluid contours. The flatness and outlining of Grasset's forms emphasized an affinity with stained glass design, which he also produced. Grasset's work concentrated upon the central image of all Art Nouveau graphic design — the wistful, willowy young girl whose long hair and loose clothing billowed out into fanciful, fluttering forms.

Grasset's strong sense of structure, his occasionally intricate patterning and his colour, paler and subtler than Chéret's, appealed more to an aesthetically-inclined audience than the more vivid and energetic, extrovert images of the latter, and formed the basis of the development of the Art Nouveau poster. After Grasset its best know exponent was Alphonse Mucha, a Czech-born painter of some obscurity before his first poster for Sarah Bernhardt, then appearing in 'Gris-

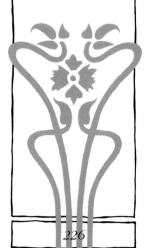

GRAPHICS

●

LEFT: *Dubonnet Aperitif advertisement from the Chéret studio. Chéret concentrates on one lively image with the minimum of lettering.*

RIGHT: La Samaritaine -
*Alphonse Mucha.
Advertising a vehicle
for Sarah Bernhardt,
Mucha successfully
adapts Hebrew-
inspired lettering into
the Art Nouveau style.
The red lettering
behind the head is in
real Hebrew.*

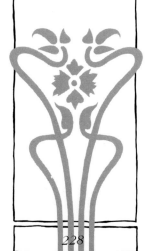

monda', made his name overnight. Bernhardt continued to patronise Mucha for her posters as well as for
the stage jewellery he began to design for Georges
Fouquet. Mucha based his whole career as a poster
artist upon his successful formula of reducing the poster to an elegant, narrow strip, featuring a single,
usually full-length, female, simplifying the structure
to a few simple forms and using complicated and
intricate patterns to ornament the surface. The pale
colouring and wealth of intricate detail demand close
attention in Mucha's work and make it the opposite of
Chéret's direct imagery. Mucha was particularly
skilled at synthesizing his enormous range of sources
for decorative motifs into some kind of exotic homogeneity that still managed to be very much of its time.
The only influence Mucha ever publicly acknowledged, with the confidence of its originality, was that of
the folk art of his native Czechoslovakia. This is indeed
much harder to detect than many more recognizable
sources: Japanese woodcuts, Arab and Moorish
decoration, Byzantine mosaics, Romanesque and Celtic interlacing, quite apart from the influence of such
contemporaries as Grasset. In his weaker moments,
Mucha seems to use these in what is almost a pastiche
of Art Nouveau, but elsewhere they are very skilfully
combined and bound together by flowing hair with an
active life of its own, or by carefully observed flowers
and foliage. Mucha's output was enormous throughout the 1890s. Apart from the more prestigious posters
for plays and exhibitions he was widely employed for
advertisements, and also produced independent graphic work, posters without a theme or event other than
Mucha's own creation. They relied increasingly on
scantily-clothed females until these coyly provocative
maidens effectively became pin-ups, under the guise
of being 'Spring', 'Music' or 'Night'. These images have
a fluid grace and light charm that is very much of its
epoch.

A more refined sensuality is offered by the elegantly, and fully-dressed ladies of Georges de Feure's
graphic works. Georges de Feure's interior designs
represent a very soigné form of Art Nouveau, moving
ever closer to classical 18th-century simplicity and
always adorned richly but with restraint. However,
before he began designing for Bing and before an
involvement with symbolist painting, de Feure (whose
real name, from his Dutch father, was van Sluyters)
had trained under Chéret. His graphic work has a
vitality that immediately recalls Chéret, rather than
his own work in the decorative arts. De Feure relied,
too, on the emphatic linearity of Grasset, but produced
much more animated work. His swooping line and
proclivity for bizarre dwarfish grotesques and exag-

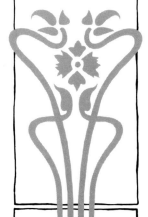

gerated costume details, best seen in his illustrations for Marcel Schwob's *La Porte des Rêves*, also reveal a strong debt to Beardsley. Like Beardsley, de Feure was more concerned with book and magazine illustration and covers than commercial advertising. His posters are concerned with galleries and exhibitions associated with his own style. The de Feure female of these works is generally a fur-coated, hatted, literary and artistic lady, refined, poised and closely related to her English cousin in the work of Beardsley.

In Holland, Jan Toorop had been involved in much the same quasi-mystical symbolist painting as de Feure. His images had blended fashionable eroticism and the occult with distorted, elongated forms derived from the shadow puppets of Java. It is one of the characteristic surprises of the Art Nouveau that such an artist could make the transition to advertising peanut oil as successfully as he did with his Delftsche Slaolie poster of 1895. Toorop's painting was certainly a geat deal more decorative than his rather portentious themes might suggest, and closer to the demands of commercial graphics. Yet examined from the other end of the spectrum, the poster is immediately identifiable stylistically with the most avant-garde type of painting in a way remarkable for a commercial poster of any age. It serves as atribute to the success of Art Nouveau in achieving some degree of unity across the arts and vastly increasing the artistic significance of what were hitherto banal media. Toorop uses the flow-ing hair of the two female figures to fill every available area of space in the design so the whole becomes a mass of hypnotically undulating rhythms.

Henry Van de Velde's Tropon poster, his only experiment in the medium, is comparable with Toorop's Delftsche Slaolie poster in its lack of stylistic compromise. Although an advertisement for a concentrated foodstuff, it is primarily an autonomous composition around the word 'Tropon' which makes no concessions to commercial concerns yet is unarguably striking and memorable. It almost has the right to stand as a work of abstract art in its own right and was certainly afforded a great deal of importance, then as now. Van de Velde holds to his rejection of the anecdotal natural detail of Mucha or Gallé. Instead, he concentrates upon shapes that suggest growth or liquid movement but cannot be tied down to any one source. Van de Velde's deeply held artistic ideals, of which this is one, and his socialist sympathies, would have made him a poor poster artist in commercial terms. He lacked Mucha's ability to adapt and develop a directly appealing subject matter for a variety for purposes, and so Tropon remains a brilliant but isolated example of his poster work. Instead, van de Velde's great graphic talent was concentrated upon a linear Art Nouveau style in other artforms. He had first started working in a purely graphic vein during a convalescence after his mental breakdown in 1889,that forced him to abandon his painting career. Graphic art was

the path which led him to the Arts and Crafts movement and the ideals of Morris, reshaping his life to serve the social mission of an improved aesthetic standard in every branch of design.

The wide circulation of printed material ensured that graphic art was more easily seen in America than many other forms of Art Nouveau. Grasset also produced covers and illustrations for *Harper's Bazaar* and the *Century Magazine* in the early 1890s with great impact, particularly on Lhouis Rhead, an English immigrant who produced his first poster in 1890 and subsequently left to further his career in Paris. Rhead worked in the Grasset style and produced a cover for one of the prestigious Estampe Moderne portfolios of contemporary French prints. On his return to America, his Grasset style proved successful and he pursued a career in posters and magazine illustration. Will Bradley worked in Chicago and was self-taught, without the benefits of European travel. Like most American designers he based his style on the Arts and Crafts movement, but as an illustrator he was drawn toward the early Beardsley illustrations of *Morte d'Arthur.* Bradley employed the fluid line of Art Nouveau, separating the white and black of Beardsley, but retained a freshness and innocence almost entirely absent from Beardsley's later development. Bradley became sufficiently successful to publish his own occasional magazine, resoundingly entitled *Bradley: His Book.*

OPPOSITE: La Plume *calendar by Mucha. Mucha's treatment of hair as semi-abstract fronds is typical. Also notable are the jewellery, recalling his work for Fouquet, and the Egyptian motifs of the horoscope.*

ABOVE FAR LEFT: *Bookplate by Koloman Moser. The combination of lively natural detail with an essentially orderly elegance is typical of the Viennese Secession.*

ABOVE LEFT: Reine de Joie *by Henri de Toulouse-Lautrec. Inspired by Chéret, the artist simplified the image still further by using flat, strong areas of colour. Lettering continues the active line.*

BELOW LEFT: Delftsche Slaolie *poster by Jan Toorop. Even the group of peanuts in the top left-hand corner of the poster have been endowed with an almost sinister Art Nouveau vitality, wriggling like amoeba.*

A GUIDE TO

·ART· DECO

STYLE

ARIE VAN DE LEMME

Art Deco is a style of design and
decoration that reached its peak
between the two world wars. Its
name derives from the Exposition des
Arts Décoratifs et Industriels, held in Paris in
1925, although not everything that was on show
at the Exposition would now be described as Art
Deco. The term Art Deco is used to describe, in
somewhat simplified terms, the diverse developments that took place in the world of design
between the wars. It is, however, an apt title for
the style that followed on immediately from Art
Nouveau at the end of the 19th century. The
latter had mostly relied on floral motifs to pattern
and ornament its buildings and other artefacts,
whereas Art Deco was thoroughly modern in
turning away from the winding, sinuous qualities
of Art Nouveau, looking instead to those of
abstract design and colour for colour's sake; and
when turning to nature for inspiration, it preferred to portray animals, or the beauties of the
female form.

While Art Deco upheld the importance of
craftsmanship in the teeth of the new mass production, it often benefited greatly from this
development. Although Art Deco objects were
originally made with expensive and rare materials,
many ideas were copied and manufactured in
cheaper alternatives.

Art Deco was a style that spread through every
aspect of daily life between the wars; every form
of art and craft used the new sensibility, whether
it was the cinema, or the design for a radio set or
motorcar.

Where Art Nouveau had been heavy, complex
and crowded, Art Deco was clean and pure. The
lines in Art Deco did not swirl around like the
centre of a whirlpool; if they curved, they were
gradual and sweeping, following a fine arc; if they
were straight, they were straight as a ruler. Art
Deco could be light-hearted on one level and
deadly serious and practical on another. As the
style in a time of unprecedented change, it was
fluid enough to reflect that change.

LEFT 'Innocence' by
Demetre Chiparus, made
from ivory and bronze
with a marble base and
signed by the artist. A
delightfully coy little
sculpture, and beautifully
worked.

ART DECO
■

RIGHT Leaded glass skylight, designed by Frank Lloyd Wright for the B. H. Bradley House, Illinois, 1900. The geometric design of the window is convincing proof of Wright's advanced taste, securing him as one of the sources for the Art Deco style.

CENTRE This luxury Bakelite box made by the Paris company Edition E. Furnels, is an example of a more expensive range of plastic objects. The motif stamped into the lid is of a bacchanale, including nude women, a deer and oak trees.

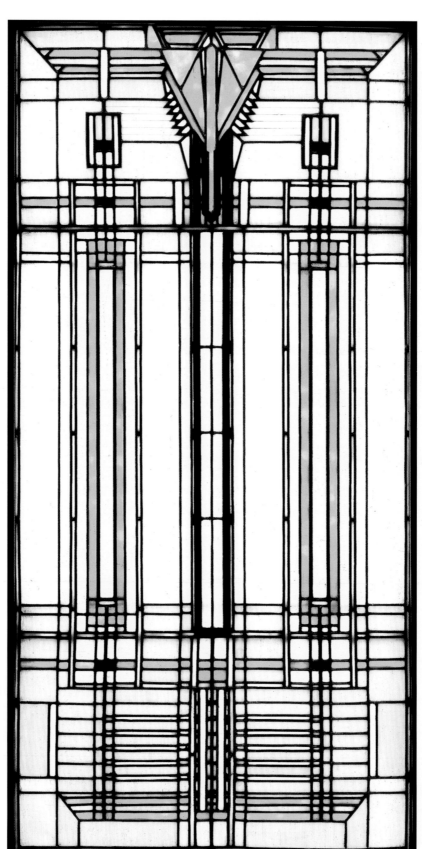

LEFT Enamelled 'minaudière', or compact, with portrait of the opera singer Enrico Caruso, by Lacloche Frères, Paris. This kind of artefact would be used by ladies as a fashion accessory for evening wear. The compact opens out to reveal a clip for bill money, a separate powder and lipstick compartment, along with a mirror, an ivory note pad and propelling pencil.

BELOW This elegant and luxurious bathroom was designed by Rateau for Jeanne Lanvin between 1920–22 and incorporated the use of marble, stucco, wrought iron and patinated bronze.

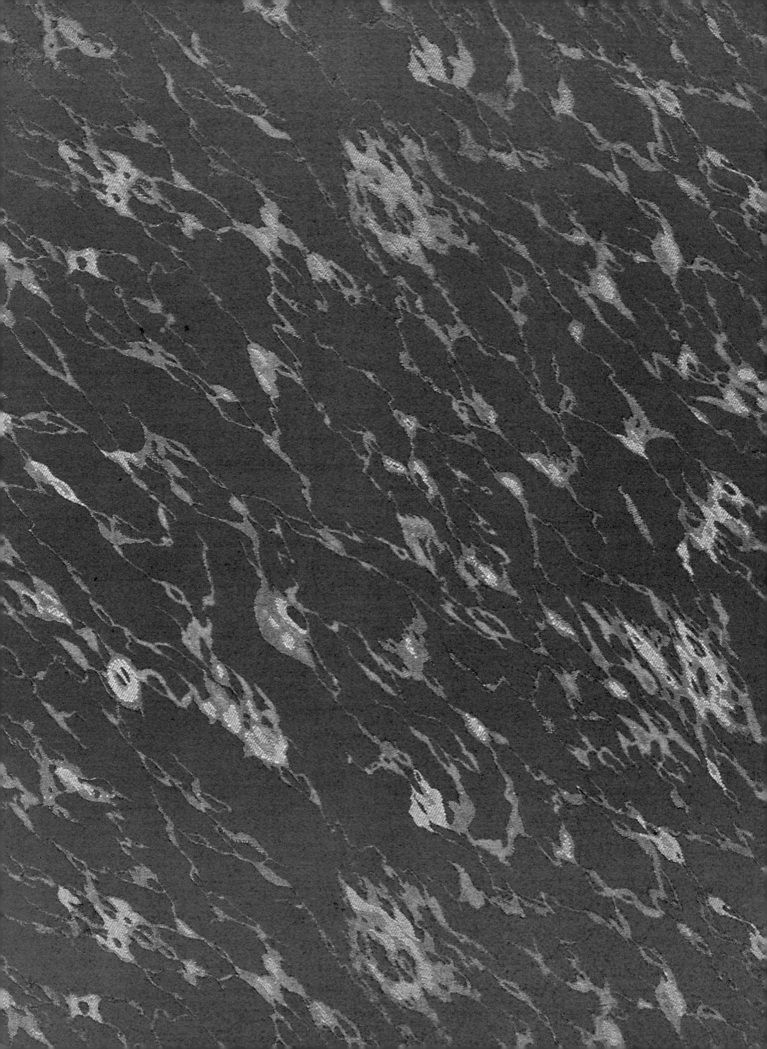

CHAPTER ONE

THE AGE OF
ART DECO

Unemployed men eating their bread and
soup at one of the many New York soup kitchens
set up during the Depression to prevent mass starvation.

RIGHT Unemployed men
eating their bread and
soup at one of the many
New York soup kitchens
set up during the
Depression to prevent
mass starvation.

There are many people still alive today for whom the inter-war period is a vague memory of childhood, or a difficult adolescence preparing for a military service that might, or might not, terminate their life. Others will remember the early Hollywood films, dancing, and the courtship of their prospective husbands and wives. All were part of the same world. Sandwiched between the two world wars, the period from 1918 to 1939 had a very distinct, if contradictory, character. It was the age of economic depression throughout the western world yet also the era of feverish, youthful vitality which attempted to ignore what in retrospect seems obvious, the coming war.

In 1918 the Allied forces joined together to form the League of Nations. Following the carnage of the First World War they hoped to ensure that nothing so awful would ever happen again. It all turned out very differently. The 1920s and '30s were, in fact, just a pause. There are as many titles for, and descriptions of, that period as there are historians. It was not only the Age of Jazz, the Age of Swing, the Charleston, the Age of the Flapper, of Hollywood, of Christopher Isherwood's *Goodbye to Berlin*, and of course the Age of Art Deco, but also the Age of the Great Depression, the Wall Street Crash, the Age when money went mad, the Age of Fascism.

It is perhaps a typical quirk of human nature that even in the periods of deepest gloom and depression, the spirit calls on its resources to create and sustain something of beauty. In a small and very practical way the innumerable Art Deco teapots, cups, saucers, plates and cigarette lighters, with their clear colours and simple designs, affordable by almost everyone, provided an innocent boost to flagging spirits. Something else new had also happened with the turn of the century, namely, mass production.

The industrialization of the late 19th century, which in passing had been responsible for destroying many of the age-old arts and crafts that passed from father to son, had also spawned a brand-new marketing system that was, on the whole, efficient, which could produce in quantity for an attractive price. In the United States, the Sears Roebuck mail order catalogue was a hugely successful example of how consumer goods were now easily available to the most distant prairie-dweller or backwoodsman. What this meant in actual terms was that even for the

average person, it was now possible to be up-to-date and "modern". An object seen at the 1925 Exposition des Arts Décoratifs et Industriels could be copied, probably with a few alterations, and ready for mass production within the year. To be in style was no longer the domain of just the wealthy European. The flavour of France could be savoured in Eastbourne, England, Munich, Bavaria or Memphis, Tennessee. The Age of Speed had telescoped diverse experiences one into another. Unusual objects from the far-flung corners of the world could be enjoyed at home. Although all of this could have promoted the spread of a greater and deeper understanding between the nations and races, the reality was different. If it was the Age of the Motor Car and the elegant transatlantic liner; it was also the Age of Empire.

The British Empire 'on which the sun never set', the Belgian, French, and more dangerously the Italian and German empires, had controlling positions that ensured the supply of cheap labour

LEFT The immediate effects of the Wall Street Crash were felt throughout the stockmarkets and business communities of the world. By the early 1930s the effects were felt by almost every community, even the most far flung. Those communities that relied on a single industry or agriculture often took a great deal longer to recover. This is a pathetically sad image of the poverty of a single family in Tennessee, United States.

and materials. If nations were powerful, so were their leaders. The 1920s and '30s were the last decades during which private palaces, country houses and yachts could be staffed and used as if their owners had an absolute and divine right to the comfort and pleasure that went with those assets. In the early 1920s, with the First World War far behind them, it must have seemed to the wealthy that nothing would ever change. It was a time to amass riches and enjoy them.

After Art Nouveau, with its intricate, heavily-worked floral patterns and intertwining vines, and Empire and Consulate furniture, the coming of Art Deco and the pure, no-nonsense simplicity of everyday objects must have filled their users with a sense of relief and clean, uncluttered well-being. If Art Deco design was bold, bright and innocent, the reality of the age was far more sinister, far less comfortable and secure.

W H Auden, who had emigrated to America in the early 30s to escape from the Nazi threat, wrote a poem called *September 1, 1939*, a title as unromantic as its subject matter. From that vantage point he wrote hauntingly and hope-lessly:

> I sit in one of the dives
> On Fifty-Second Street
> Uncertain and afraid
> As the clever hopes expire
> Of a low dishonest decade:
> Waves of anger and fear
> Circulate over the bright
> And darkened lands of the earth,
> Obsessing our private lives;
> The unmentionable odour of death
> Offends the September night.

The indication that all was not well with the world, after the high expectations of the League of Nations' founders, occurred as early as 1926. Inflation raged in Germany until finally the currency became utterly worthless. Wealthy shipowners and businessmen went broke over-night. Stories abound; the elderly couple who

$100. WILL BUY THIS CAR MUST HAVE CASH LOST ALL ON THE STOCK MARKET

FAR LEFT On the worst day of trading, 24 October, 1929, mounted police are called in to keep law and order outside the New York Stock Exchange building on Wall Street.

LEFT One of the many losers on the stock market seeks to sell his car at a knockdown price.

CENTRE Following the Wall Street Crash, welfare services were stretched to their limits in order to prevent destitution and starvation. These men are waiting for the opening day of a new lodging house.

BELOW Crowds of anxious businessmen wait for news outside the sub-treasury building across from the New York Stock Exchange on the day of the worst collapse in stock market history, that signalled the beginning of the Great Depression.

cashed their life savings and found they could buy only a few strawberries, and the man who took a wheelbarrow full of money to buy a loaf of bread and, leaving it unattended for a few seconds, came back to find a pile of money and no wheelbarrow, are but two examples. The immediate effect of this was limited almost entirely to Germany, but it would take only another ten years for the repercussions to affect the rest of Europe and eventually the whole world.

The Wall Street Crash in October 1929 was of far greater importance. The stock market had been driven up to unprecedented levels, first by professional investors and then by anyone who could release enough cash to speculate on the buoyant market. The fickleness of the stock market is notorious, a sudden loss of confidence can radically alter the state of the market. That was exactly what happened. A sudden run on shares encouraged a further spiralling down, until paper fortunes were not worth the ink they were written in. Companies and banks were dragged down into the morass of bankruptcy, and the shock waves went right through the world economy. Fitful recoveries lasted only a few months as unemployment stayed at record levels in most of the western world. It took well into the mid '30s for the economy to recover, but by that time other, more serious problems, those of Fascism and Nazism, became more pressing.

To describe the 1920s and '30s as a sorry episode in history is perhaps making light of the enormity of the misery and desperation that most experienced. What is surprising is that Art Deco managed to survive and become the style of the age, when its designers and practitioners had such little support. It was partly due to the farsightedness of the French government's patronage.

RIGHT Revealing yet teasing photo of Josephine Baker in 1926 at the Folies Bergères, wearing the barest amount of Art Deco jewellery.

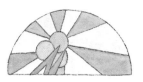

LEFT During the Depression, young couples would literally dance until they dropped in dance marathons that offered prize money to the winning couple. As this touching photo shows, it was a cruel burlesque of all that we associate with dancing: romance, energy and excitement. No picture could contrast more strongly with the hundreds of Hollywood publicity shots of the well-groomed hero looking deep into the heroine's swooning, lovesick eyes.

BELOW With all their worldly belongings, an Oklahoma family trudge westward to California along the Pittsburgh County Highway, in a tragic 1930s parody of the 19th century Wild West pioneers, with seemingly less hope.

■

RIGHT Couple dancing the
Charleston, just one of the
new dance crazes of the
1930s.

LEFT The Charleston dance and Jazz music were two of America's most important contributions to the spirit of the Art Deco age. This humorous photo has more serious undercurrents. Oblivious to the outside world, it was as if the Charleston dancers were dancing on top of a volcano, blissfully unaware.

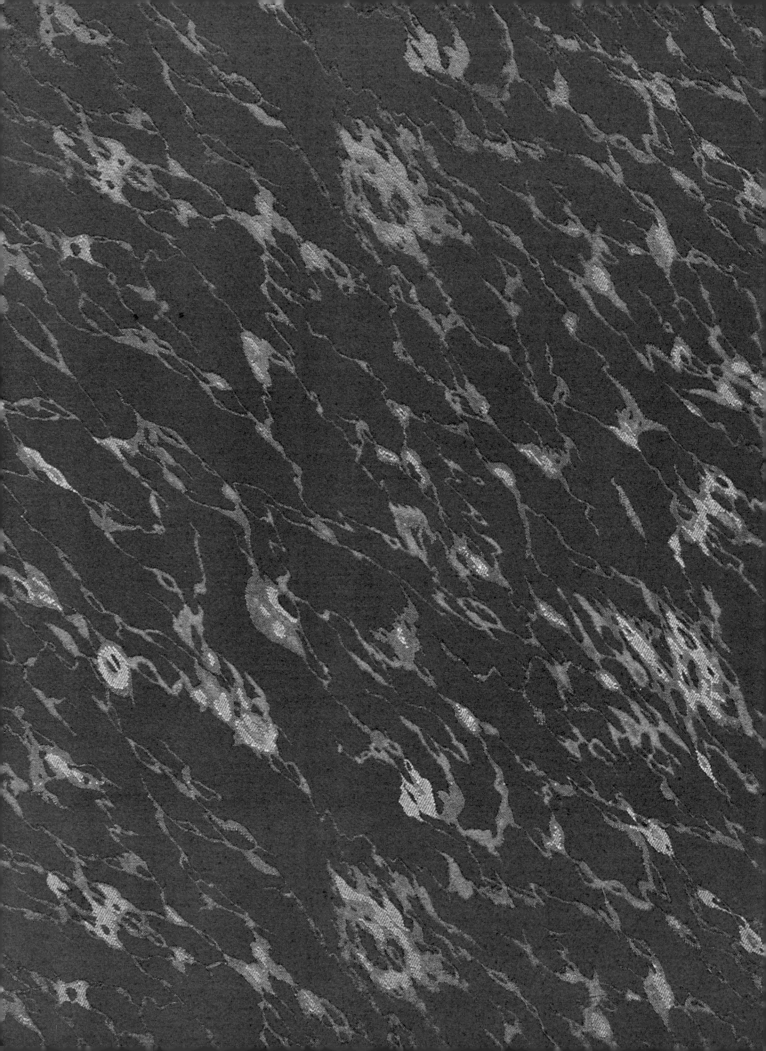

ART DECO STYLE

The tennis ball ashtray is an
ingenious creation for the Dunlop rubber Company.

RIGHT Examples of British Art Deco porcelain design from the 1930s by Henry Nixon and W. S. Coleman for the Royal Doulton works.

BELOW RIGHT Two fine examples of promotional advertising objects made of new synthetic materials in a simple Art Deco style. The Bakelite hot drink mug promotes the Bournvita brand for Cadbury's of England, and comes across with 'jolly night cap' lid. The tennis ball ashtray is an ingenious creation for the Dunlop rubber Company. The spherical body is made from urea formaldehyde, while the actual cigarette holders are made from a sister material, phenol formaldehyde.

 As with all works of art, it is difficult to pinpoint exactly where the ideas, or inspiration for a style come from.

But why was Art Deco so special, and different? There are many reasons. Art Deco was the first truly 20th-century style, moreover, it was international. Arriving when it did, and such timing is seldom by accident, it was a style that could be adapted to every single man-made object, regardless of application or budget. It also arrived at a time when new forms of communication ensured its rapid spread. Finally, and most important, it was the last total style. Like Baroque, Classical or Regency, Art Deco could ornament a house, a yacht, or a knife. Nothing has coloured and illuminated our life so extensively since.

That Art Deco was *the* style in the period between the wars is without question, but why this particular style? Fashions tend to be cyclical; why not neo-Baroque, for instance? Why did people go for the new when they could have revamped the old? That is where the secret lies. Art Deco did exactly that — it re-presented the old but spiced it up with new ingredients. Part of today's interest in Art Deco is pure nostalgia — the Charleston and the early movies — but at the time, the perspective was entirely different.

The spirit of Art Deco was the spirit of the modern. Even though it adapted older styles for its own use, it was still the style of the new. An Art Deco piece can be enjoyed for its form, the craftsmanship involved in the making and, because any object has its place in history, also because it is an indicator of times past. In the 1980s, only our grandmothers and grandfathers can still recall the surprise and excitement of owning their first motor car (automobile), their first trip in an aeroplane, their first radio, telephone and, later, television. Spoilt and jaded by the current overabundance of new technology, it is easy to forget that there is always a first time. Every advance to them must have had the impact of the first man on the moon. Art Deco was the style of the age that wouldn't stay

LEFT Poster advertising the Grand Bal de Nuit, designed by the Russian artist Natalia Gontcharova, who also designed stage sets for Diaghilev's Ballets Russes.

still and looked to that age for its content, its meaning, and often its subject matter.

However, Art Deco may have been the modern style, but it emerged from as many different directions as it had applications. Art Deco was given its greatest cohesion in the Paris Exposition of 1925, but it was also the Paris of Pablo Picasso, Georges Braque, Fernand Léger, and Robert and Sonia Delaunay. Such Art Deco pieces as a decorated cigarette lighter by Gérard Sandoz, a silver tea service by Jean Puiforcat, and a plate by the Royal Doulton works, could not

have come from any time earlier than 1910. Art Deco is essentially a style applied to applied art, though most of its sources are in the fine arts, architecture, sculpture and painting.

Paris was the stage on which almost all the battles of modern art were fought. The rapidity with which style has since followed on style has made it almost impossible to discern any lasting direction today. From Impressionism through post-Impressionism, Symbolism, Cubism, Futurism, Orphism, Constructivism, Purism, Surrealism, Vorticism, one "ism" has replaced the

TWO TYPES OF CUNARD

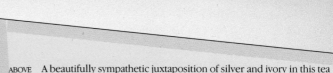

ABOVE A beautifully sympathetic juxtaposition of silver and ivory in this tea service by the master craftsman Jean Puiforcat. The spouts and handles are reminiscent of the ocean liners of that age.

RIGHT Two of the Cunard's most famous liners in a poster from the 1950's.

LEFT Portrait of the illustrious Nancy Cunard by the society photographer Cecil Beaton. Lively, well-connected, and beautiful, this photo shows why Nancy had so many supporters and admirers.

In 1840 Samuel Cunard, based in Halifax, Nova Scotia, established the Cunard Line, a trans-Atlantic passenger service. By the first decade of the 20th century the Cunard liners became so sophisticated they could properly be called "floating palaces". Massive ballrooms, casinos, swimming pools, and restaurants that served the best cuisine were only some of the facilities that passengers could expect. In 1907 the *Mauretania* was launched, and along with her sister ship the *Aquitania*, became standard bearer of the Cunard Line. They were important,

not just because they provided the quickest transport between America and Europe at the time, but also because their design played a decisive role in the development of modern architecture, and the Art Deco style.

At the 1925 Exposition des Arts Décoratifs et Industriels there had been one pavilion which seemed completely out of keeping with all the rest. The now famous architect Le Corbusier, arguably the greatest of this century, suggested a pavilion which would be used as a forum in which to discuss his latest ideas. The organisers attempted to dissuade him from entering, but finally had

to allow him a space, stuck in a corner behind the Grand Palais. The result was the Pavillon de L'Esprit Nouveau. It was a curiosity, a statement which argued forcefully against the decorative arts that the whole Exposition hoped to promote. Rectangular, and cube-like, with large, plain windows, it was the very latest in modernist architecture. It was as Le Corbusier himself had written in his book *Towards a New Architecture* two years previously, "a machine for living in." Le Corbusier had split *Towards a New Architecture* into sections, of which the major part concentrated on the possibility

of looking towards aeroplanes, motor cars, and liners as possible sources of inspiration for the new architecture. The *Aquitania* displayed numerous possible applications for domestic architecture. Le Corbusier's message was that the artist should control the machine and apply it to all aspects of modern life. Liners were supremely functional; the *Mauretania* held the Blue Riband, the transatlantic prize for the fastest crossing, for 22 years, averaging over 27 knots at its fastest. They were also elegant in their simplicity; long colonnaded walkways, metal staircases, and an approach to new materials that had not been thought of pre-

NEW YORK DIRECT
O QUEBEC & MONTREAL

viously. This spirit of the new that Le Corbusier spoke of later on became of great importance to a whole stream of Art Deco. In the silver-gilt teapot with rock crystal handle by Jean Puiforcat the elegance of the ocean liner can be clearly seen.

When Samuel Cunard set up the Line in 1840 he could not have predicted the uses that some of his liners would be put to. He would probably have shuddered also had he foreseen the life of Nancy Cunard, one of his granddaughters and the epitome of the foreigner in the Art Deco Paris of the 1920s. Her link with Art Deco could not have been more direct. She was

the daughter of an English aristocrat and a wealthy American mother, Lady Emerald Cunard, "Maud" to her friends, who was the leading hostess of the day, who rented their London home, 20 Cavendish Square, from the then Prime Minister, Herbert Asquith. Familiar with the wealthy and powerful, Lady Emerald's tastes also ran to the advanced in art. Her walls were covered in green lamé and other exotica, in direct response to Leon Bakst's designs for the Ballets Russes. Her companion for many years was the conductor Sir Thomas Beecham who, when Diaghilev came to London, offered him his ser-

vices. From this early education in pre-Art Deco style Nancy Cunard escaped the influence of her powerful and overbearing mother and went to Paris in 1920. From one élite she stepped into another, the intelligensia of the avant garde. Her hectic beauty and manners symbolized the age; reckless, bright, flying in the face of convention. Cecil Beaton's photograph of her reveals much about her and her time. Nancy loved the primitive and the new Art Deco in equal quantity, and revealed in her dress the close relationship between the two.

Weighted down with heavy primitive bracelets, Nancy,

like many others, was fascinated by all things African. In her case it also extended to black Jazz musicians, which finally, when Nancy published her defence, *Black Man and White Ladyship*, led to a split with her mother, and the traditions she represented. She was typical of avant-garde taste in other ways; she frequented the bookshop Shakespeare and Co., where she bought a first edition of Joyce's *Ulysses*, and set up her own press "The Hours Press" in the late 1920s to promote modern writing.

In the *Mauretania* and Nancy Cunard, Samuel Cunard produced two of Art Deco's most vital emblems.

RIGHT Advertising poster from 1930 for the German passenger airline Deutsche Lufthansa by Otto Arpke. The stark outlines of the woman's costume and appearance are characteristic style indicators, creating an air of chic that accompanied the kudos of air travel.

next, with disarming regularity. What many of these "isms" had in common, which would be of great importance to Art Deco, was that they shared a tendency towards abstraction, a move away from obvious subject matter towards a concern for the basic elements of picture-making or sculpting, so that form, colour, line and volume became important in themselves. The artist's feelings and sensibility could be read, it was hoped, through the manipulation of those infinitely flexible variables. Architecture had the additional need to be functional, to keep out the rain, keep in the warmth, and provide a living space. Ornament is not absolutely necessary on a building, nor on everyday objects. Teapots are for pouring tea and keeping it warm, a plate is for eating off.

As for the decorative arts in the Art Deco style, they ranged from the purely functional, through simple and clear decoration, to pure ornament. That is why it is impossible to talk of one Art Deco: there were as many directions, hybrids and strains as there were practitioners. The easiest way to understand and unravel the puzzle is to

see where Art Deco came from and what sources it may have used.

When Picasso and Braque set off together in 1907–8 on the journey through their radical discoveries that would lead to Cubism, "roped like mountaineers", they turned art, as it had then been understood, on its head. The shock waves pulsed across Europe into Russia, and across to North America in less than five years. The Italian artists Severini, Boccioni, and Marinetti quickly united under their Futurist banner; in Holland the architects, designers and painters Gerrit Rietveld, Bart van der Leck and Piet Mondrian formed de Stijl, and Constructivism was conceived in the U.S.S.R. In England there was Vorticism, in Germany the Bauhaus was formed a few years later, and back in Paris Orphism appeared. Out of Picasso, Abstraction had been born. The process of art had become a search, an experiment. Modernism came into being, the avant-garde invented. It had become viable, and ultimately necessary to test out all the infinite options, to play intellectual games, and extend and expand the boundaries of art. To be ahead of one's time, or at least up there with it, pushing forward, was to be a modernist. Like-minded designers could apply these principles to the decorative arts and arrive at something wholly novel. In a lesser way they could apply the colour schemes of a Mondrian painting, a Goncharova, El Lissitzky, a Wyndham Lewis, or, simpler still, Malevich's painting *White square on a white background*, and arrive at simplicity itself. In the transition from fine art to applied art, the most simple motif had passed from being shocking, avant-garde and bewildering, to being accepted and merely decorative.

Art Nouveau was of central importance to the

LEFT Bakelite radio set of the 1930s inscribed receiver type 439 is an example of Art Deco applied to the latest technology. How many of these must have been thrown out with the rubbish when technology improved, and styles altered.

BELOW LEFT The M-speaker is typically Art Deco in design. The letter M is distinctly of the period, as are the sound box grilles and the pseudo-classical scrolls at the base. Made in Bakelite by Wavox in Britain, it must have been one of the least expensive speakers on the market.

RIGHT Cologne bottle, inscribed 'HIS' for the Northwoods company, Chicago, Illinois. The stylized cubist head is in cream-coloured Bakelite; the maroon bottle is made of glass.
This hexagonal box with a motif of two birds is an exceptionally fine example of marbleised Bakelite employing various colours.

OPPOSITE ABOVE Simple yet eccentric side-table of 1923 by Pierre Legrain clearly showing African inspiration and displaying Legrain's love of the primitive.

OPPOSITE BELOW 1979–81 reconstruction by Martyn Chalk of a relief produced in 1914 by the Russian avant-garde artist Vladimir Tatlin. Using materials as diverse as sand, plaster, wood, glass, iron and bitumen, Tatlin spearheaded the Russian avant-garde movement that would later produce fine examples of porcelain.

rise of Art Deco, if only as a style to react against. Equally, the work of Hoffman, Olbrich, Peche, and Moser, who founded the Wiener Werkstätte at the beginning of the century, were early practitioners of a style which, when refined, looked like very early Art Deco. Another influence, which probably became the most important of all, was a response to primitive art. Painters such as van Gogh and Whistler had earlier looked at Japanese prints for inspiration. Later Derain and Picasso looked at African art, and later still Matisse looked at the decorative potential of Morocco. What had happened throughout the late 19th century was a reappraisal of primitive art. Museums throughout Europe had rearranged their collections of primitive art, dusted them down, opened up the old showcases jumbled and heaped up with old artefacts, and redisplayed them as works of art. Anything that was not European was recognized at last as having some artistic worth. Indeed,

Europe looked away from the products of a diseased society that had chosen to massacre its youth across the battlefields of the Somme, to an art that was primitive, untouched and natural. This was particularly relevant to Art Deco, because by the time the style began to develop, a tendency towards the primitive was not just an option, it was obligatory.

Nobody looking back at Paris in the first quarter of this century could ignore the impact of the Ballets Russes on the arts. Driven by its passionate Svengali and impresario Serge Diaghilev, its stage designs and costumes mixed the oriental with the westernized, the avant garde with the primitive. Leon Bakst, its most famous designer, produced costumes whose lavishness and orientalism came as a complete shock to the Parisian public. Diaghilev's production of *Scheherezade* was a riot of deep, rich colour which inspired the heavier decorative side of Art Deco and interior design. Even more

ART DECO WIT

Designers have a habit of taking themselves too seriously. Most styles can be elegant, impressive and imposing, but no fun at all. The Parthenon, the Eiffel Tower and Versailles amaze rather than amuse. One of Art Deco's most endearing qualities, therefore, is its playfulness, its sense of the ridiculous, its knack of taking something out of a context which we all recognize and putting it into another. Often it is downright silly. Art Deco has been responsible for the most tasteless of kitsch. If the dog with the nodding head wasn't invented then, it should have been.

That teapot by Puiforcat looks like an ocean liner but for the perversion of scale involved, so that massive areas become small domestic details — imagine crossing the Atlantic in it. The tables and chairs by Pierre Legrain with their strong African flavour could be just as easily worn as bracelets or strung on a necklace as sat on.

Art Deco produced teapots disguised as cars, bears and elephants, and table lamps of a landing female parachutist. Some of the most common objects of all, and still among the easiest examples of Art Deco to collect, are the hundreds and thousands of plaster heads. Based on the tradition of portrait busts, these are pure comedy. The simpering dancer, or the haughty, fashion-conscious woman, the golfer, and the pipe smoker, are all distilled into caricatures — cartoons of themselves.

ambitious in the Art Deco style were the thousands of gouache drawings for set designs of Erté. The sinuous, sweeping curves of dresses and curtains fell across a rigidly simple, but still evocative backdrop. Elegantly arched windows looked in on interiors bedecked with leopard skin rugs and abstract rectilinear furniture, enlivened by dancers in oriental costume. That was part of Diaghilev's legacy to Art Deco. If that was not enough, he also incorporated the latest in contemporary dance, design and music. In 1917 the ballet *Parade* employed the talents of Picasso as stage designer, Erik Satie as composer, and Jean Cocteau as the scenario writer. In later years Diaghilev would also involve Russians like Naum Gabo, Antoine Pevsner, and Larionov, whose constructivist sets would display an outrageous purity of form that continued to fuel the starker and more minimal extremes of Art Deco.

If oriental art had been made fashionable by the Ballets Russes, Mexican, Egyptian, North American Indian and South American art was of equal importance. The Egyptian influence, and also that of Africa, are obvious in the chairs of Pierre Legrain. Heavy, solid pieces of furniture they are crude and built to last, much like the early radio sets and triangular clocks for the mantelpiece that instantly recall Egyptian pyramids or Aztec temples. What Art Deco learnt, and taught the public, was bold design. If colours were to be bright, they should knock you over, if lines were to be clear, they should be as stark and severe as the steps up a temple. The obvious could be chic.

The final, and one of the most obvious, influences on Art Deco was there to see at every street corner, in every house, factory and shop, on the sea and in the air. The 20th century was the machine age. Art Deco was modern because it used aspects of machine design as inspiration, the wings of an aeroplane, the bow of a yacht, the porthole of the cabin window of the new ocean liners, the cogs and wheels of a sewing machine or a motor car engine. It was even more modern because it accelerated the adoption of new materials such as plastic, bakelite and chrome.

The mixing of all these influences made Art Deco the style it is. In the hands of genius, the objects transcended their sources. In the hands of competent designers, or plagiarists, they might become drab or garish, but they were, nevertheless, truly Art Deco.

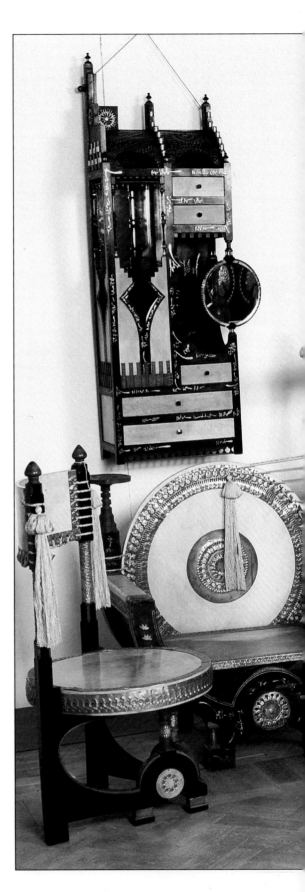

LEFT Drawing room suite
by Carlo Bugatti. As
eccentric in its middle
eastern and oriental
flavour as any piece by
Armand J. Rateau, Bugatti
furniture runs totally
counter to the modernist
strain in Art Deco
furniture.

CHAPTER 2

■

LEFT Two mechanical toy
cars in Bakelite, fully
operational and hardy
enough for the most
demanding child.

A R T   D E C O

■

RIGHT Interior design for
dining room by André
Groult, c. 1920. The
furniture has a traditional
look but the drapery and
wall decorations favour
the austere look of the
twenties.

THE REDISCOVERY OF THE LOST ART DECO · GERMANY AND RUSSIA

Art Deco has become so closely associated with France and to a lesser degree, Britain and America, that people tend to forget, or ignore, the fact that the decorative arts were alive and well in Weimar Germany and post-revolutionary Russia. Perhaps uninformed opinion of what Russia must have been like immediately after the revolution fostered the assumption that the "luxury" nature of the decorative arts made it impossible for Art Deco to exist there at all. Such an assumption was quite wrong, denying Art Deco one of its most important attributes, that of flexibility. The principles of Art Deco could be applied as successfully to mass-produced clothing or cheap pottery as to the most expensive and opulent piece of Cartier jewellery or piece of inlaid furniture by Ruhlmann. It was a style fit for kings, while at the very same time it was being absorbed and used by the people.

Weimar Germany may have suffered economically under the harsh conditions laid down under the Treaty of Versailles, which resulted in the financial collapse of 1926, and in the Great Depression a few years later, but there was always a demand for the most basic commodities such as a plate, a cushion, a teatowel, or a milk jug. In fact by 1930, the German porcelain and ceramic industry, far from being run down, was the largest in Europe. Companies like Villeroy and Boch, based in Dresden, flourished by meeting the realities of the situation head on. Good, cheap design did not have to be a luxury. Until 1933, at least, it would be true to say that if the supremacy of France as the centre of the art world was under any threat, it was from Germany. From that year on, following Hitler's rise to power, the leading lights of German culture emigrated to America, mostly via London. Figures like Walter Gropius,

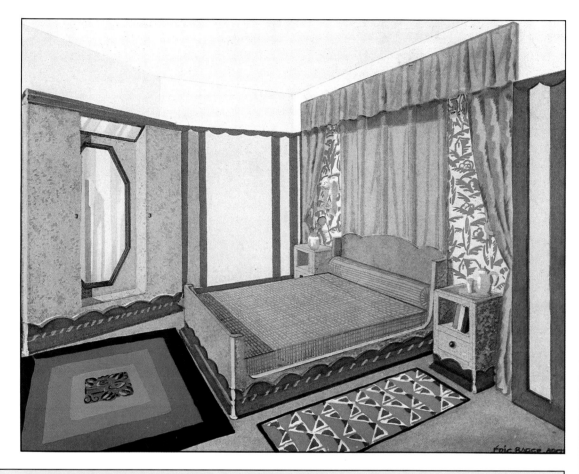

LEFT Interior design for a bedroom by Eric Bagge, c. 1930. Note the starkness of the walls, the absence of pictures, and strong, plain outlines of furniture and fabrics.

Mies van der Rohe, Marcel Breuer, Kurt Schwitters, and George Grosz, were as vital to contemporary German culture as Le Corbusier was to the French. The Bauhaus was the laboratory of the avant-garde. The design of a chair could be broken down into its most basic components, a plywood plank for a seat with bent chrome legs for support. What could be cheaper yet more novel?

The situation in Russia was even more interesting and experimental. Following the revolution, there were two immediate problems to be resolved: initially, how to revive and restore industries that had been disrupted during the revolution, and secondly the role of the artist in the new society. The artist could no longer just serve and respond to the whims of an élite, he had to climb down from his ivory tower and work in harmony – or conflict – with the people. The constant examination of these questions in such conditions promoted exciting new developments and resulted in many fresh approaches.

For many spectators, the Soviet pavilion at the 1925 Exposition must have seemed shockingly innovative.

Designers like Nikolai Suetin and Ilya Chesnik applied their Suprematist designs to dinner services. Highly abstract and directly derived from contemporary painting, these had a clarity and straightforwardness that was marketable – and close to Art Deco. Even when obvious symbols of the revolution were employed, like the hammer and sickle, the worker or the farm hand, they could be incorporated into the most advanced textile or ceramic designs. Even artists of the stature of Rodchenko or Tatlin, whose reputations as avant-garde leaders were without question, turned their hand to dress design. If artists were to be artists at all, their art had to be applied. In Europe the situation was different, and that was one reason why the decorative arts were always thought of as secondary in importance to fine art.

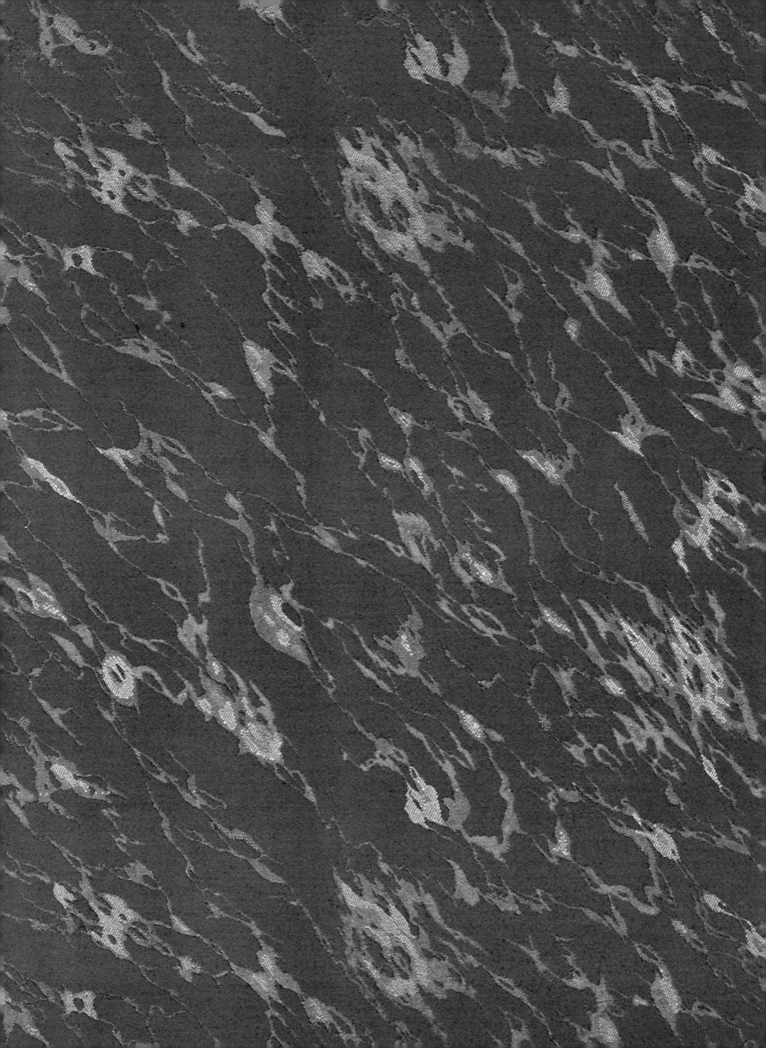

THE GREAT
COMMISSIONS

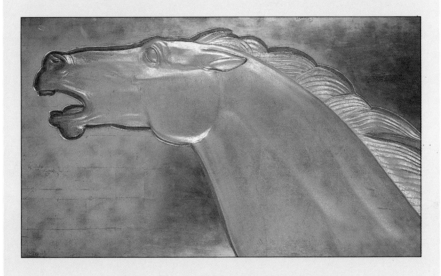

ABOVE Gold-lacquered panel depicting the head of a
stallion with streaming mane by Jean Dunand. The design
and application link it closely to the designs for the
Normandie.

RIGHT Ten of the surviving mural panels designed by Jean Dupas and executed by Champigneulle in 1932–4 for the liner Normandie. These were part of a series on the theme of the history of navigation.

BELOW RIGHT The grand salon of the Ile de France. The decoration of the main public rooms aboard the liner were by Jeanniot, Bouchard and Saupique. A foretaste of the grandeur to come with the Normandie.

OPPOSITE RIGHT An exotic painted panel in the Normandie Salon.

OPPOSITE BELOW RIGHT West elevation of the New Victoria cinema (movie theater), London, England. A grand imposing Art Deco façade

Art Deco was very much a case of reinterpreting old ideas in a new way. Since the middle of the 19th century, there had been great concern about the alienating effect of the industrial revolution. Although welcomed by many, it posed the very immediate problem of how to retain the medieval sense of pride in craftsmanship. Many forward-thinking people were genuinely worried that industrialization would culminate in a situation in which workers would be totally divorced from the creative process, and would ultimately become the tools of the machinery that had been meant to serve them. The concern was genuine. The reality became worse. In a city such as Manchester where the average life expectancy of factory workers had been reduced to thirteen years by the early 1860s, there was a real need to curb the more extreme aspects of the industrial process. It was not very surprising that Britain, the country that had industrialized first, was also the first country to attempt to re-establish an equilibrium between the individual and his workplace.

Following the teachings of Thomas Carlyle, Pugin and Ruskin, William Morris attempted to find some answers. Morris was the founder of the Arts and Crafts Movement; and his follower C R Ashbee attempted to reintroduce a sense of humanity to the workplace. In the face of accelerating industrialization it was a brave attempt to make time stand still.

The most important legacy of the Arts and Crafts movement for Art Deco was the concept of collaboration between craftsmen. The heroic example of the Renaissance Man who could turn his hand to anything had been replaced by specialization in particular trades and crafts. At the turn of the century, there were two men who singlehandedly proved themselves exceptions to the rule. The American, Frank Lloyd Wright, and Josef Hoffman, an Austrian, were geniuses, giants in the history of architecture and design. Both proved to be invaluable examples of and fore-runners of the Art Deco style. Frank Lloyd Wright's massive project for the Midway Gardens in Chicago, contemporary with the zenith of the Art Deco style, and his 1912 designs for the Avery Coonley Playhouse in Chicago, Illinois, are well ahead of their time. Hoffmann's Palais Stoclet in Belgium shows a similar attention to detail while still maintaining a sense of the whole. Their work was extraordinary, visionary

RIGHT Interior of the Odeon, Muswell Hill, London, England, a splendid example of an Art Deco cinema (movie theater) interior. Particularly interesting is the octagonal clock with 'The Odeon' on its face, of which there are very few examples still in existence.

FAR RIGHT View of the Odeon cinema (movie theater), Woolwich, near London, England, looking down across the River Thames to the London docks. The brickwork entrance is set at a right angle to the auditorium.

but, particularly for the Art Deco movement, almost impossible to emulate.

The introduction of new materials brought new problems, and the search for a new style demanded a new approach to the large commission or project. What was needed was co-operation between all the mastercraftsmen. The example of Modernism which stressed a need to reappraise all given ideas promoted an atmosphere in which interchange between different disciplines was encouraged and promoted. Why bother to learn to weld, inlay wood, work with lacquer, bend chrome, blow glass, mould plastics, cast bakelite, when all you needed to do was seek out the relevant craftsman? Art Deco was revolutionary in that it promoted the concept of the designer. The designer could be at worst a dilettante or mediocre amateur, at best a brilliant innovator and promoter of the possibilities created by other people's expertise.

Although Art Deco is best known to us through its smaller objects, such as posters, textiles and ceramics, it is the large commissions which display the full possibilities of the style. The Exposition des Arts Décoratifs et Industriels, the magnificent French ocean liner, the *Normandie*,

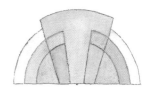

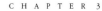

LEFT Exterior view of the corner tower of the Rex cinema (movie theater).

BELOW LEFT The Harrogate Odeon cinema (movie theater), England. This view highlights the contrast between the faïence tiling and the plain and patterned brickwork. It still has the original corner tower with the neon cinema sign as advertisement.

the glass entrance to the Strand Palace Hotel, now in the Victoria and Albert Museum, London, the preserved splendours of the ballroom in London's Park Lane Hotel, and New York's Radio City Music Hall, or the stylized elegance of the Hoover factory in England, marooned on the A40 London to Oxford road or, more spectacularly, the dizzying, skyscraping summit of the Chrysler building are just some examples of Art Deco at its most ambitious and successful.

The massive scale of the Exposition des Arts Décoratifs et Industriels has already been discussed, but what needs further explanation is the detail of some of the best pavilions. Perhaps the most remarkable of all was the pavilion for the Au Bon Marché store designed by the house of Pomone, specifically by Louis Boileau. The squat aspect, like that of most of the pavilions, was dictated probably as much by necessity and other practical considerations as it was by any aesthetic. Huge doors, like those of some gigantic tomb, adorned the frontage. From the outside it looked severe, each layer of the building echoing the entrance steps divided by low hedging, forcing the eye upward to the flat roof. All the flat surfaces of the walls were decorated with

RIGHT The massive scale of the Normandie is seen in this photo of the building of the ship at Saint Nazaire, France.

BELOW RIGHT The Grand Staircase on the Normandie leads the passengers up to Baudry's sculpture *La Normandie*.

abstract patterns and, in keeping with many of the other pavilions, leaded windows were employed wherever possible to lighten the effect. At night, these windows were spectacularly transformed. As light poured through the coloured glass, the Pavilion Au Bon Marché became fragile and glowing. Another particularly striking pavilion was that of the Diamond Dealers, designed by Lambert, Sacke and Bailly. Using very little floor space, its elegance relied on the high oval roof with its shallow rectangular planes. Like a massive Fabergé egg, or vast precious stone, this alerted the viewer to its purpose, the promotion of the diamond industry. The simplicity and clear lines of many of the pavilions were countered by the opulence of the Ruhlmann Group's pavilion, Hôtel d'un Collectionneur. Emile-Jacques Ruhlmann, the prince of modern furniture, imbued this with a panache and sophistication that even he would react

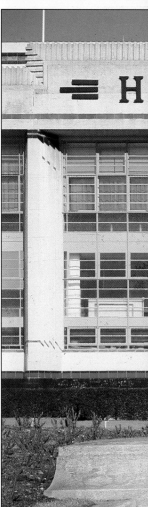

against in favour of the modern Deco style. The diversity of the exhibition was reflected in its scale, which was enormous. It was a showcase for the world, but was dismantled as quickly as it was constructed. If the French needed a more permanent display for their craftsmen they very soon found a solution.

In 1932, the ship *Normandie* slid into the water at the St Nazaire dock. Run by La Compagnie Générale Transatlantique, the *Normandie* project enjoyed the sponsorship of a government who had wisely recognized that a floating showcase of the decorative arts, in which the passengers would be a captive audience for at least four or five days, would enhance French prestige abroad. The success of the *Normandie* had as much to do with the latest engineering as it did with the luxury aboard. It set off on its maiden voyage from Le Havre on 29 May, 1935, arriving at New York on 3 June, having averaged

LEFT Interior view of a Paris cinema (movie theater), the Rex. A perfectly-preserved and wildly baroque example of Art Deco. Designed as an inside-out cinema, the impression the spectator gets is of sitting out amongst the stars. During the intervals the ceiling is lighted with cloud effects. The red-lighted proscenium arch is reminiscent of Radio City Hall, New York.

BELOW LEFT The shrine of British Art Deco, the colourful exterior of the Hoover Factory by Wallis Gilbert recently rescued at the last minute from threatened demolition.

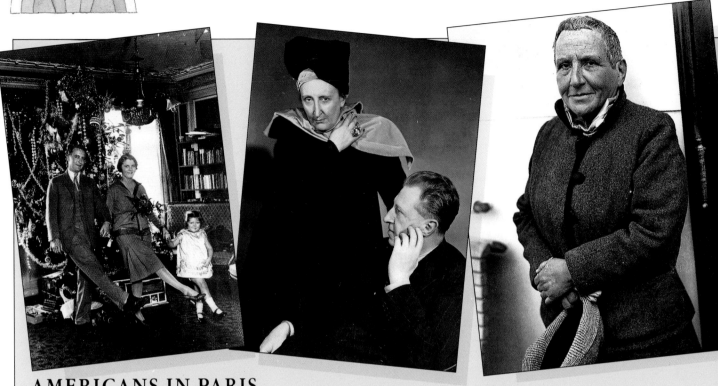

AMERICANS IN PARIS

"If you are lucky enough to have lived in Paris as a young man, then wherever you go for the rest of your life it stays with you, for Paris is a moveable feast."

Ernest Hemingway

For architects, designers and craftsmen in Paris 1925 meant the demands of meeting deadlines for the Exposition de La Société des Arts Décoratifs et Industriels. For the Americans in Paris, the capital of Bohemia, that year was more aptly described by Scott Fitzgerald, of *The Great Gatsby* fame, as "the summer of a thousand parties".

The hordes of young American men and women who had come eight years previously to save a sinking Europe, and had confronted the bloody horrors of the war to end all wars, also discovered the unique romance of Paris. Paris, the lovers' city,

was also the cultural centre of the world. It was where intellectual Americans had to come and test themselves against the competition and come into contact with the avant garde. Although the move to Paris was often disguised behind the heavy veils of cultural exchange, the reality was more prosaic. For those with an independent income from generous relatives or inherited wealth, the strength of the dollar, cheap accommodation, good food and, following the introduction of Prohibition in January 1920, legal access to cheap alcohol, made Paris a happy and exciting experience. If they came for literature and art they got a lot more besides.

Scott Fitzgerald and his wife Zelda moved to Paris in 1925, where he was to write *Tender is the Night*. Arriving there, he found a milieu of

fellow writers and artists among which, during the 1920s were the Americans Djuna Barnes, Robert McAlmon, William Carlos Williams, Henry Miller (*Tropic of Cancer*), the photographers Berenice Abbott and Man Ray, Ernest Hemingway, who was busy writing *The Sun Also Rises* and *Fiesta*, and Sherwood Anderson, as well as the wealthy publishers Harry and Caresse Crosby (Black Sun Press), the modern dancer Isadora Duncan, and the poets T S Eliot and Ezra Pound. Travelling between Paris and Antibes in the South of France throughout the summer of 1925, the Fitzgeralds united the heady world of Hollywood and its Rudolf Valentinos, the French aristocracy, and the Bohemian writers. The Americans had come to lie on the beaches, worship the

sun, and sit at the feet of the muse of European art.

Writers such as Hemingway, Fitzgerald and Malcom Cowley, had come to a Paris that other Americans had already annexed before them. More than 20 years earlier, the Sybil of Montparnasse, Gertrude Stein, and her companion Alice B Toklas had been central to all that was advanced in art. Gertrude Stein, famous for the enigmatic phrase "A rose is a rose is a rose", had also claimed that if America was her country, Paris was her home. This Laurel and Hardy of the art world had patronized and collected the work of, among others, Pablo Picasso, Georges Braque, Henri Matisse and the Delaunays, from as early as 1906. Not overburdened with humility, and quite, quite assured of her genius as a writer, Gertrude Stein effected a bridg-

ABOVE LEFT Ernest Hemingway, the macho Nobel prizewinning action man of American letters, pictured here with his second wife (he had four), Pauline Pfeiffer. One of the founding fathers of modern literature, Hemingway was the acknowledged leader of the emigré bohemians who congregated in Paris in the 1920s. His posthumously-published *A Moveable Feast*, claims 'If you are lucky enough to have lived in Paris . . . then wherever you go for the rest of your life, it stays with you, for Paris is a moveable feast'.

BELOW LEFT Sylvia Beach, owner of the Shakespeare and Company bookshop, and publisher of James Joyce's *Ulysses*, pictured with Joyce in her shop.

FAR LEFT F. Scott Fitzgerald, his writings and his tragic marriage, are symbols of the glamorous and fated Jazz Age. This photo of Scott Fitzgerald's family was sent as a belated Christmas card to friends. Taken in their hotel room in Paris at Christmas 1925, at the end of the 'summer of a thousand parties', the glamorous trio are pictured at the height of their happiness and contentment.

CENTRE Brother and sister, Osbert and Edith Sitwell, represented the aristocratic and fashionable extreme of the Modernist movement in writing. Stylishly eccentric, they were closely allied to other writers of notoriety, such as Ezra Pound and James Joyce, and gave readings of their work at Sylvia Beach's bookshop, Shakespeare and Co., on Paris's Left Bank.

LEFT Gertrude Stein the writer, Svengali of modern literature and the arts. Through cajoling, bullying, encouraging, and by her own example, Gertrude Stein, from her salon at Rue de Fleurus in Paris, sponsored and assisted the talents of the soon-to-be-famous Picasso, Matisse and the ingrate Hemingway.

ing between the worlds of French culture and the English-speaking peoples.

If Gertrude Stein was the severe autocrat of the visual arts and writer supreme, Americans in Paris would find a warmer welcome at Shakespeare and Co., the bookdealers and publishers, on the rue Odéon. The informality of the bookshop, which also acted as a post office for emigré Americans and a lending library, disguised a solid pioneering support for the most advanced in literature. Its gentle and sensitive founder, the ever-patient Sylvia Beach, ran a haphazard business on a shoestring and a large quantity of goodwill. Her publishing of James Joyce's *Ulysses* won her notoriety and customers. Written about in American newspapers, Sylvia Beach was one of the best possible ambassadors that

France could have called on. American reporters quipped, "Grab your towel and let's go down to Sylvia Beach." If painters and writers came because of her, so too did the designers, and what they saw was Art Deco.

Of course many who came had little or no interest in the more *recherché* areas of modern art. They ate, drank, and enjoyed themselves as all tourists do. What they did was to boost demand for consumer items; Deco jewellery for their relations back home and other examples of French chic as gifts. In rare cases whole interiors from cutlery to curtains made their way across the ocean to America. In 1927, the wealthy American, Templeton Crocker, well in advance of the taste of his peers, commissioned Jean Michel Frank to design his San Francisco apartment in the French Art

Deco style.

The tide flowed both ways. While Americans discovered and became attached to a rich European cultural heritage, Parisians discovered Walt Whitman, watched the gauche and wistful cinematic comedy of Charlie Chaplin, admired the vitality and eroticism of Josephine Baker's dancing and listened to the deep, resonant singing of Paul Robeson.

Importantly for the development of Art Deco, the showcase of the Exposition des Arts Décoratifs et Industriels displayed to Americans the possibility of making high-quality furniture, jewellery and porcelain, in good, innovative design. The Metropolitan Museum of New York would only take a few years to realize the sense of putting money aside to invest in the best examples of Art Deco objects. The beginnings of

the migration of Art Deco to America were assured. A year later Mina Loy, backed by Peggy Guggenheim's millions, opened an art gallery in Paris selling, among other things, American design.

Few autobiographies, collections of letters, diaries of American men and women of letters of that period fail to mention Jimmy the barman at Dingo's, Kiki of Montparnasse, argumentative, drunken evenings around the tables and at the bars of the Dôme, the Rotonde, the Clôserie des Lilas, or La Coupole, the Brasserie Lipp and the Café Flore, and the inevitable reconciliations the next day. Many tourists today find their way straight to the Left bank to sit outside the Deux Magots, where Hemingway sat, order a kir, and breathe in the nostalgia, conjuring in their mind's eye the myth of Paris in the '20s.

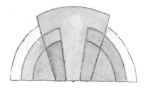

more than 30 knots per hour. If its efficiency was the main attraction for transatlantic travellers, the *Normandie*'s decor was the icing on the cake.

The *Normandie* was the latest of the great French liners, double the tonnage of its predecessor, the *Ile de France*. An important innovation in ship design, it increased the luxurious accommodation for passengers by dividing the funnel uptakes to the three characteristic red chimneys, thus providing a long sweep of massive reception rooms, one after the other, down its length. The main dining-room alone measured more than 300 ft, and could seat 700 people for dinner. The scale of the boat and the massive investment in it allowed for an unrivalled decorative commission.

The list of craftsmen who worked on various aspects of the *Normandie* reads like a catalogue of the cream of Art Deco. Few of the leading French designers of the time passed up the chance to display their talents, but for all of them the eventual glory and fame they derived from working on the commission was tragically short-lived. In 1941, the ship was commandeered by the United States government to be used as a troop carrier. While stripping the ship of its decorations in order to modify it for its new role a workman accidentally set fire to the ship that boasted it was 100 per cent fire proof. Most of the greatest works of Art Deco ended up at the bottom of New York harbour.

In creating the *Normandie* its sponsors deliberately chose to be as modern as possible. Not only was it a chance to promote the French decorative arts, but it was also used as a vehicle to display the extent and glory of the French Empire. Shamed by the defeat of the First World War, a whole movement in literature and arts arose that chose to look beyond the confines of mainland France toward the French colonies. Many of the designs were of an exotic nature, both oriental and African in flavour. The most famous single commission for the ship were the four panels designed for the main lounge by Jean Dupas on the theme of the History of Navigation. Each panel measured 50 by 22 feet, and the whole ensemble stretched round the two walls. Of the four panels only one survived, and can be seen at the Metropolitan Museum in New York. Working in reverse, the glass panels were both painted and etched on the back by the craftsman Charles Champigneulle, using a method known as *verre églomise*. It was typical of the Art Deco

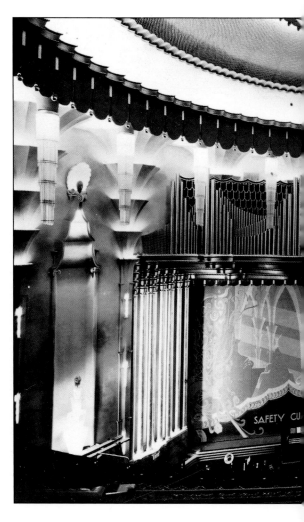

attitude prevalent at the time that craftsmen revived and invented working methods as well as experimenting with new materials. Traditional industries like the Sèvres porcelain works designed the service for the *salon de thé*, and the Aubusson tapestry studios were given a boost by commissions for the stateroom "Trouville" by the designer and cabinetmaker Jules Leleu. Other staterooms named after French départements or cities gave ample opportunity for new designers to create unique work. Pierre-Paul Montagnac, the President of the Société des Artistes Décoratifs, executed the "Caen" suite. The decorating firm of Dominique, which had previously won the prestigious commission to decorate the Paris private residence of that most quintessentially Art Deco of designers, Jean Puiforcat, created the four rooms of the stateroom the "Rouen".

Some of the designers, like René Prou, specialized almost exclusively in commissions on

LEFT Hollywood Greats: Buster Keaton and other show business personalities aboard the Ile de France.

the scale of the *Normandie*. Prou also executed work for the first-class carriages on the French railways.

Although it has been suggested that the furniture in some rooms was designed by Emile-Jacques Ruhlmann, his premature death in 1933 robbed the *Normandie* of one of its most inspired designers. The metal furniture attributed to Ruhlmann in two large staterooms, harmonizing with the metal-clad walls, must have been designed very early on in the *Normandie*'s decorative scheme. Blanche J. Klotz worked on very similar lines to Ruhlmann, also using metal, but Ruhlmann's innovative capacity would surely have been stretched by such a demanding and lavish commission.

Another great loss, as a result of the stripping of the *Normandie* in preparation for its wartime role, was the disappearance of much of the metalwork. At least three of France's greatest specialists worked on the commission: Adelbert Szabo, Edgar Brandt and Raymond Henri Subes. Presumably, because metal is one of the easiest materials to melt down and recast for use in the armaments industry, most of the more basic design elements such as the sweeping handrails and doors which added the practical and finishing touches to the ship's design were lost forever. Adelbert Szabo had created doors for the first class dining room, and Edgar Brandt was also commissioned to design doors and gates. Raymond Henri Subes, who worked both in wrought iron and later in steel lacquered in Duco varnish, was, in collaboration with the architects Patout and Pacon, one of the few people to display his designs for elements of the *Normandie* at the Salons des Artistes Décorateurs in 1933 and 1935, also in Paris. Along with all the press photographs, and the famous poster by Cassandre, these must have given those who had neither the money nor the desire to travel on the *Normandie* an idea of the style and chic aboard the boat. The influence of the *Normandie* commission spread through all branches of the decorative arts. It is tragic that so little has survived to the present day.

If premature decline was to be expected of the large liners, very few of which are still in service, superseded by the speedier aeroplane, this was less the case with large building commissions for hotels, cinemas and factories, but even these projects were always in danger from the elements, changing taste and rebuilding schemes.

Conservation departments all over the world

RIGHT The staircase of the Strand Palace Hotel, Westminster, London, 1930. A fine example of an Art Deco interior in a public building employing a sophisticated use of abstract design.

BELOW RIGHT The manicure saloon of the Strand Palace Hotel, London, England.

have taught the public that there are always examples of taste that are in continuous danger from the necessity to maximize the use of land in urban centres, and modernization. Yet the generation that grew up with Art Deco also grew out of it into other styles. For them it was a retrogressive step to hold onto something that was passé. It is only with the advantage of hindsight – and the foresight of some great collectors – that Art Deco has been saved, in its grander, more elaborate manifestations. Not long ago the quiet, serene design of the Hoover factory seemed laughably out-of-date. With its survival now almost completely assured, the public have an opportunity to see Art Deco in its application to industry. Technological advance would undoubtedly have necessitated improvements inside the factory were it to remain competitive, but the neo-Egyptian exterior is still a pleasure to the eye.

No one can deny that New York's skyline would be hugely impoverished by the loss of the Chrysler building. Its steep, rapier-like point adds a unique quality to what is after all just a high-rise block, of which hundreds and thousands are to be seen in capital cities all over the world. The gradual and gentle half circles that edge the eye smoothly up to that final rapid sweep are typically Deco. The inset darts on those half circles are a motif that recur again and again, on anything from cigarette lighters to large pieces of furniture. These "sun rays" tell a great deal about Art Deco's optimistic and joyous quality – even at its most cumbersome it also has details expressing lightness. If the Chrysler building is the cathedral of Art Deco then its holy shrine is without a doubt Radio City Music Hall in the same city. It is along the length of America's Eastern seaboard, from New York right down to Miami, that fine examples of Art Deco buildings

LEFT The interior of the famous Claridges Hotel, London, England.

still survive in the most unlikely of places.

For serious students of Art Deco and lovers of the style, the small suburban cinemas surrounding the heart of London, England still give an accurate indication of Art Deco's application to public buildings. The cinema has always been the setting for an evening out, an occasion for escaping into another world, and the interior of, for example, the Odeon Cinema, Camberwell (a London suburb), with its elegant curves,

spacious carpeted halls, and potted palms, treads that difficult dividing line between discreet and calming elegance, and a sense of occasion.

Without the examples of the Park Lane Hotel ballroom, the Muswell Hill Odeon, the Coca-Cola bottling plant in Los Angeles, or the Grand Hotel, Dax, in France, Art Deco would seem to the onlooker from the end of the 20th century merely a style of the domestic interior and of small objects.

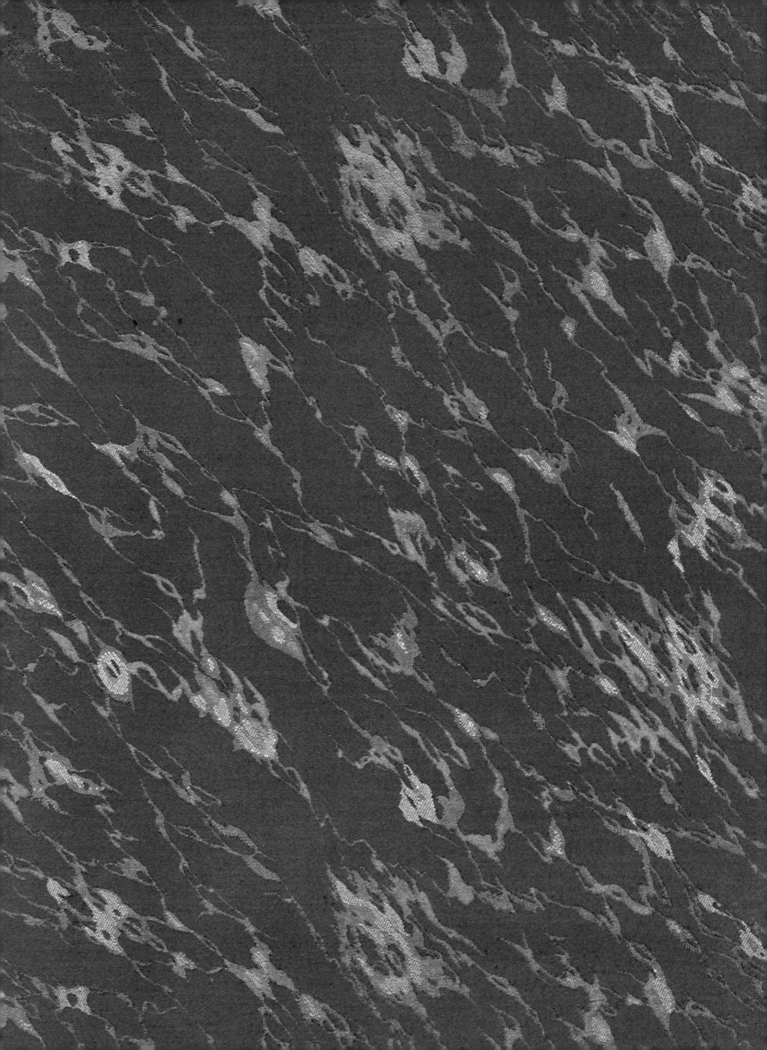

CHAPTER FOUR

FURNITURE

ABOVE Five-piece giltwood and Beauvais tapestry drawing
room suite by Maurice Dufrene. This type of application
of tapestry to furniture, by no means unique, provided a
boost to an ailing industry. Note in particular the
giltwood layering down the stubby feet.

If anyone nowadays were to start collecting Art Deco the most difficult thing of all to obtain would be Art Deco furniture. Most pieces of any sophistication are in the Musée des Arts Décoratifs in Paris, or New York's Metropolitan Museum. A few other museums around the world have examples, and a few private collectors like Alain Lesieutre, Felix Marcilhac, and Mr and Mrs Peter M Brant have substantial collections. Scarcity is one of the obvious difficulties facing a new collector, but price is even more prohibitive. For a piece of furniture by Jean Dunand, Emile-Jacques Ruhlmann, or Pierre Legrain the price would now be in the hundreds of thousands. Art Deco furniture is certainly one of the most interesting and inspired applications of the style. The high prices nowadays are certainly due to its rarity, but they also reflect another factor, that of the value of quality craftsmanship. Even when Emile-Jacques Ruhlmann sold his furniture in the 1920s, such pieces were only affordable by the wealthiest of wealthy clients, such as maharajahs and princes. If his work commanded such prices, it was not because of commercial greed but because of the months and months of skilled labour and the use of the most expensive materials as expressions of his genius. If such a piece of furniture were to be copied today it would be next to impossible to find a cabinetmaker capable of producing it. What men like Ruskin and William Morris had feared, the loss of the crafts due to industrialization, had become a reality. The 1920s and '30s witnessed, among so many things, the dying of the old crafts. Skills like French polishing and marquetry had been passed down from father to son, and the apprentice system protected and maintained expertise. Even today, craftsmen jealously guard their secrets, and find it difficult to pass on the experience that comes from years of perfect co-ordination between hand and eye.

Art Deco furniture, therefore, more than any other expression of that style deserves preservation. It is the final chapter in the craft of cabinetmaking.

Within Art Deco furniture design, there were two distinct trends. On the one hand, there were the early experiments in what we have now come to recognize as modern furniture, using metals and plastics in forms which could lead to eventual mass production, and on the other the high-quality craftsmanship of which Ruhlmann was the greatest exponent. Purists would say that Art Deco furniture is truly only that of the highest quality of production.

At the turn of the century, most quality furniture that was built to last was in the Louis XVI or Empire styles. Solid it might have been, but in no way was it modern. The achievement of

■

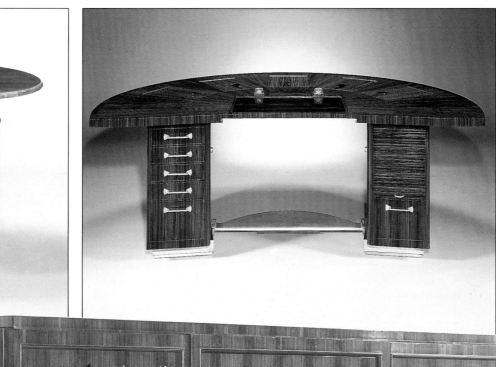

LEFT Fan-shaped Macassar ebony and gilt bronze desk of 1929 by Emile Jacques Ruhlmann. Note how the grain on the left-hand side continues without interruption up across the drawers, and the exquisite coupling of the luxury materials. Masterpieces like this desk justly place Ruhlmann amongst the best of all cabinetmaker-designers.

BELOW LEFT Delicate and decorative wardrobe by Jules Leleu, with mother-of-pearl and ebony inlay.

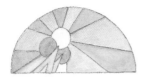

RIGHT Inlaid secretaire by
Süe et Mare that
capitalises fully on the
grain and character of the
wood, in contrast to the
delicate ivory detailing
round the keyholes and
the theatrical yet precise
geometry of the lid.

Ruhlmann, Süe et Mare, Jean Dunand and others, was to re-evaluate the furniture styles, take the best and subtly alter and revamp them. Many of the people responsible for furniture design, including those just mentioned, were not themselves great craftsmen, but they were capable of running large workshops, and using the talents of their own and other studios' craftsmen to the best effect. They were virtuoso performers, and they showed off their abilities to the utmost. The materials they used were equal to their skills. France's vast empire provided them with the most exotic of materials: macassar ebony, mother-of-pearl, abalone, ivory, tortoiseshell, amboyna wood, burr walnut, palmwood, silver and gold and the inspiration of oriental techniques such as chinoiserie and lacquerwork.

Expensive and élitist as the luxury trade undoubtedly was, its resurgence depended on other factors. Apart from a few specialist shops, the outlet for contemporary furniture was limited. When the new department stores realized that design could be of great use to them, the situation altered. Au Printemps set up its Studio Primavera, Le Louvre set up Studium Louvre, Au Bon Marché set up Pomone, and Galeries Lafayette set up La Maîtrise. Customers soon realized that at these shops they could buy the most modern furniture at a reasonable price.

The further advantage of the studio system was that craftsmen were also allowed to accept private customers, as long as this did not interfere with the studio's work.

The whole furniture industry had a surprising openness of attitude, and ideas and skills were generously shared. In Ruhlmann's "Hôtel d'un Collectionneur" at the 1925 Exposition des Arts Décoratifs et Industriels, he included the work of sculptor Antoine Bourdelle, animal sculptor François Pompon, Jean Dupas, metalworker Edgar Brandt, silver designer Jean Puiforcat, lacquer expert Jean Dunand, and Pierre Legrain. It was an act of consolidation, an appeal for unity, which must also have displayed Ruhlmann's talents as an interior designer.

There are two matching Ruhlmann cabinets dating from 1925 in the Metropolitan Museum of Art in New York and in the Musée des Arts Decoratifs in Paris which show an absolute synthesis of his ideas at work and amply demonstrate his absolute mastery of the medium. Made from rosewood, the cabinets are inlaid with macassar ebony and ivory. The floral display on the front is highly reminiscent of Art Nouveau, yet the strictly spartan lines of the vase containing the flowers displays a sensibility well in advance of the turn-of-the-century style. It is in all the detailing around the edges of the pieces

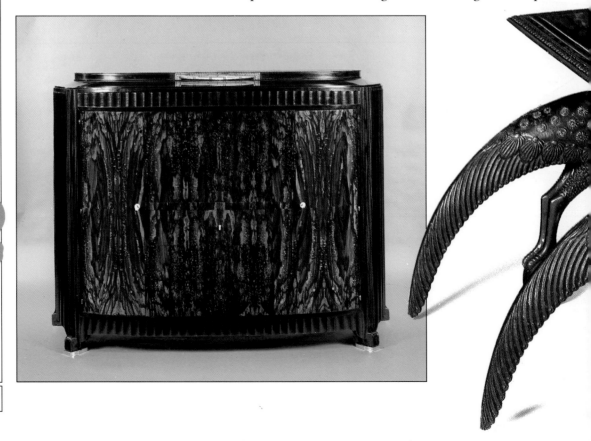

LEFT The famous
Zebra chaise-longue in
black lacquer by Pierre
Legrain of 1925.

BELOW LEFT Bizarre bronze
and marble table by
Armand J. Rateau, with
four encrusted stylized
birds used as supports.

RIGHT Elegant mahogany
and inlaid ivory petit
armoire in the style of
Emile Jacques Ruhlmann,
with the characteristic
splayed sword legs,
geometric inlay and piano
key motif on the top of
the cabinet.

that the Art Deco spirit comes to the fore. On the top edge, the ivory keys set into the macassar ebony suggest a modernized Greek decoration, or even a piano. The pieces are quite classical but in a modern vein. The slightly-offset and angled edging strips that run from the short legs to the white top edge are carefully finished with a small strip of ivory. The back legs, double the width of those at the front, are squared off, while the front legs taper elegantly down hexagonally. The pin-prick detailing on the front in ebony works as an open edge, marking out the floral pattern, but at the same time allowing the character of the rose-wood grain to show through. It is the detailing on the front legs that exemplifies Ruhlmann at his best. The legs are clearly supports, but the scrolls stand proud of the cabinet and are also inlaid with ivory. They are pure ornament, extraneous to the functionality of the cabinet, decorative yet discreet. The cabinet in the Félix Marcilhac collection in Paris also reveals Ruhlmann's ingenuity. As a complete object there is little novelty in the piece. It is a classical bombe shape, a form perhaps perfected by 18th

LEFT Painted wooden cabinet by Otto Prutscher, restrained in its simple, sophisticated elegance.

BELOW LEFT Suite of furniture in bronze, marble, wrought iron, corduroy and silk by Raymond Subes. A detail that is particularly unique is the swag in corduroy cloth over the armrest of the chair, which is purely decorative. Note also the gentle sweeping arch containing the tall mirror behind the table, and its echo in reverse on the table legs.

RIGHT Pair of chairs from 1927 by the architect Robert Mallet Stevens. The use of wood and fabric is a clever rethinking of the deckchair concept.

century Dutch cabinet makers, and works on the same lines as most French Louis XVI furniture. The framework of the cabinet is hidden behind sensual tortoiseshell squares – the surface is all-important. The shaping is curved and voluptuous, with only the key plate and the toes on the feet projecting. Ruhlmann's furniture always allows for an uncomplicated appreciation of the qualities of each material. If not necessarily a strict follower of the truth to material ethic, his best pieces never disguise themselves. In this way his work was very different from the eccentricities of Pierre Legrain, who made the African chairs for Mme Tachard.

Born in 1887, Legrain initially made his mark as a designer of book covers for his wealthy patron Jacques Doucet. Legrain was like many of the other Art Deco designers in that he seemed to be able to apply himself with equal success to designing for a wide range of craft disciplines. It is important to stress again the value of having access to experts in many different fields, which

set designers like Legrain free to experiment at will. One of Legrain's most famous pieces of furniture was the "Zebra" chair, or chaise longue. His clear affinity to all things African could hardly be more explicit than in this piece made in 1925. Compared to such representations of the opposite extreme of Art Deco as Eileen Gray's experiments in metals or, more directly, Le Corbusier's own chaise longue, Legrain's is nothing short of bizarre. The zebra skin is imitated in velvet, the armrest which logic tells you should be against a wall is decorated on the reverse with abstract patterns, expensively executed in mother of pearl. The overall design is almost crude, appearing both clumsy and uncomfortable, the exact opposite to the Le Corbusier chair, which is probably the most comfortable piece of furniture ever invented. The arm rest is left open from the front in order to house a small shelf whose purpose could be nothing more than aesthetic. The whole chair exudes a feeling of gratuitous luxury and

decadence, the kind of chaise longue that Nancy Cunard or some other wealthy aesthete might have possessed, on which to lie back elegantly while puffing on an opium pipe.

Another equally eccentric furniture designer and one who was often used by others for his designs incorporating lacquer work was Jean Dunand. Both Dunand and Eileen Gray used the talents of the Japanese lacquer master Sougawara. Dunand was another of the designers who executed major commissions for the liners *Ile de France* and *Normandie*. His most famous single piece, however, was a bed made in 1930 for Mme Bertholet, in lacquer and mother-of-pearl. It is a beautiful yet almost completely absurd object. So beautiful, in fact, that it verges on the hideous. The actual construction must have been a nightmare of intricate modelling and shaping. There is no sense here of truth to material, yet curiously enough lacquer is one of the very few materials that would work successfully. Inlaid wood would have lifted in any centrally-heated house, while paint would have cracked and chipped. The small fish bubbling away at the foot end are almost comical compared with the serene still life of water lilies on the curved headboard, derived no doubt from Monet's water lily paintings, or oriental examples.

Following Art Deco furniture to its other extreme, it is worth noting the great influence of Frank Lloyd Wright, Hoffman, the Dutchman Gerrit Rietveld, and the Bauhaus School. The strong move against unnecessary ornament, and the desire to provide functional furniture, were inseparable from the need to provide new forms in the most economical way at the cheapest possible price. Designers like Eliel Saarinen, famous for Dulles Airport, Washington DC, Alvar Aalto and the Americans Donald Deskey, the architect of Radio City Music Hall, and Ken Weber, all pushed the design of furniture in a more "rational" direction using stark, uncluttered streamlining that also left its stamp on the Art Deco age.

LEFT Reproduction by Cassina of the famous chaise-longue by Le Corbusier. This chair is the absolute ultimate in luxury and comfort.

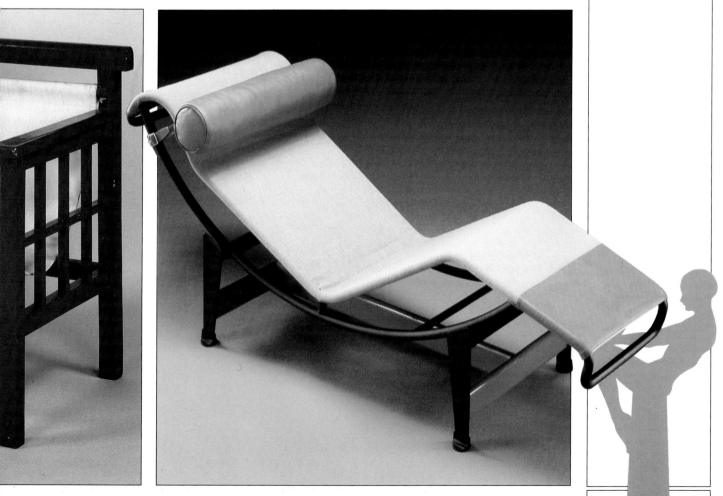

RIGHT Sycamore sideboard by Jacques Adnet. The heaviness is lightened and relieved only by the chrome fittings, and by the drawers which look as if they were somehow magically held in suspension.

BELOW RIGHT One of the most exquisite and sensational examples in the whole canon of Art Deco furniture, this lacquered bed by Jean Dunand is the ultimate in design for luxury living between the two great wars.

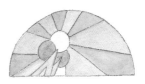

LEFT Reproduction by Cassina of the original Red-Blue Chair of 1918 by the Dutch *de Stijl* architect-craftsman Gerrit Rietveld. If there is one piece of furniture in the history of modern art that can be said to have had an influence beyond the discipline of furniture-making, then it must be Rietveld's chair.

BELOW LEFT Unusual decorated cabinet bombe in japoniste style by Clément Mère, partner in the Süe et Mare collaboration.

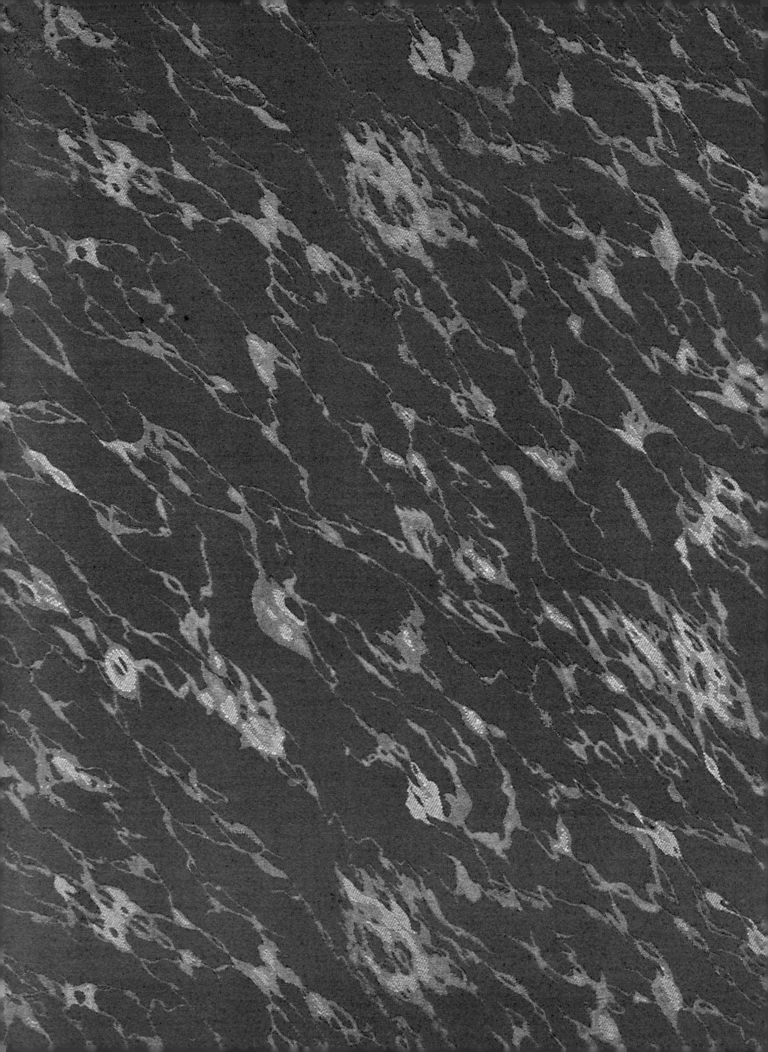

CHAPTER FIVE

METALWORK

A wrought iron and grey granite centre table by
Raymond Subes, 1925, which fully utilises the flexible
strength and malleability of the material. The image on
the surface, a nude with fruit bowl, is highlighted in
reverse in red ochre.

RIGHT Pair of bronze jardinières with cobras by Edgar Brandt.

CENTRE Rustic 1920s marriage between glass and wrought iron. The wrought ironwork is by Majorelle and the glass bowl by the firm of Daum, Nancy.

Adaptability and inventiveness flourished in Art Deco metalwork. Metal was often used on its own for gates and doors, but it could also be employed in conjunction with almost any of the other favoured materials. The history of Art Deco metalwork is also the history of changing materials. The 1920s was the period of wrought iron, bronze and copper. By the early 1930s these had not been completely replaced, but designers favoured the more modern aluminium, steel and chrome. The '30s were remarkable, not for any single colour preference, but for the lack of any colour at all. Glass and shiny metals complemented each other; both were reflecting and anonymous, sparkling and transparent. The typical '30s room had mirrored walls, with discreet metal borders, repeated in the bent metal furniture. It was stark, and ideally suited to university professors in pursuit of the pleasures of the mind. There were no distractions, except for their own reflections, twice or even ten times at the corners where the mirrors met. Such ideas were a long way from those involved in the initial resurgence of metalcraft, promoted most notably by the craftsman Edgar Brandt.

Walking round any Victorian square in London, as in many other cities, the uniformity of the cast ironwork and plaster mouldings is one of the most striking aspects of the period style. Houses had to be built quickly and cheaply to meet the needs of a growing population, and mass-produced, hastily constructed housing spread across urban areas; detailing and ornament were still preferred, but the result for the metalwork trade was an almost complete poverty of design. Builders used pattern manuals provided by the foundries that picked out the required effect and repeated it. In effect, the skilled craftsman had become almost entirely redundant. Into this vacuum stepped men like Edgar Brandt, Armand Albert Rateau, Raymond Henri Subes, Jacques Adnet, Louis Sognot, Adelbert Szabo and Paul Kiss.

As wrought iron has few limitations beyond that of the craftsman's skill, it broke through the confines of use in one specific area. Art Deco Metalwork pieces ranged from the intimacy of a commemorative medallion or a small mantel-piece clock, to the huge entrance gates for the Exposition des Arts Décoratifs et Industriels. Almost all these outstanding craftsmen/designers worked across this wide range, spreading their time and creativity between all the possible applications of the material.

Edgar Brandt was born in Paris in 1880 and, through his father's involvement in an engineering firm, he very early on developed an interest in working with metal. Most of his early work came from direct commissions by

LEFT Stone and wrought iron column supporting a glass vase and a wrought iron vase by Edgar Brandt and Daum, Nancy.

architects, who needed metal fixtures for private houses and hotels. Brandt never lost that willingness to work with others, and his best work was almost always the result of direct collaboration. Many of his commissions demanded a highly developed sense of detail and the ability to work to a very strict set of limitations. At the same time as sets of monumental doors, or wrought iron staircases for the liners *Paris, Ile de France* and *Normandie*, Brandt would be designing more mundane work: grilles for indoor heating, radiator covers and other everyday objects. Some of his finest work was with the glass expert Antoine Daum. Standard lamps of great elegance came out of this partnership. The most famous lamp, the "Cobra", showed Brandt's genius at its most quirky, bizarre and stylish. In contrast to Art Nouveau, Art Deco used animal themes far more readily. The "Cobra" lamp is the most powerful and vibrant of Brandt's creations. Brandt has caught and frozen the image at its highest point of potential. The snake is ready to lunge forward and strike; its head and coiled body cradle the alabaster shade. Stylistically and technically, Brandt continually invented and reinvented his ideas. The "Cobra" lamp was almost only possible as a structure because of the malleability and strength of bronze; in wood, or other materials, the snake would have been unable to support its

RIGHT Chrome hatstand in the shape of a woman's head by the Italian designer Bazzi. Note the contemporary, marcel-waved hairstyle which fixes it irrevocably in the 1930s era.

CENTRE RIGHT Elevator door of the Chrysler Building, by William van Alen, the most distinctively Art Deco of the New York skyscrapers. Recently threatened with destruction, the building has passed through several hands, including those of a religious cult, but is now the subject of a preservation order.

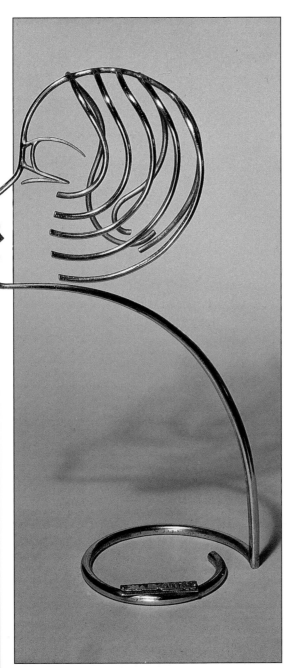

own weight, let alone that of the shade. In the same way, Brandt exploited the tensile strengths of the material he used when designing furniture. Console tables, instead of standing solidly on four squat legs, could be treated more as open sculptures. Legs could be opened out with delicate filigree mouldings of fans and thistles filling the gaps, yet still have enough strength to support the heavy weight of a thick slab of marble. Fire screens and doors could be reinterpreted to look almost like drawings suspended in air. Curling lines and leaves in door fronts seemed exquisitely delicate but had a strength and solidity fit for the purpose. Brandt also collaborated with Henri Favier on a series of screens for which he provided the framework.

Although Brandt was clearly the leader of the more traditional metal workers, men like Subes, Adnet, Kiss, Rateau, and Szabo produced work of great beauty. The most eccentric of this group by far was Armand Albert Rateau. He constructed a bronze chaise longue for Jeanne Lanvin's boudoir

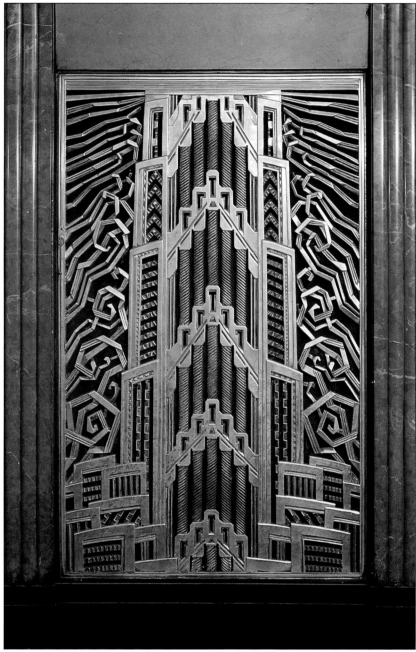

LEFT Radiator grille reproducing the exterior of the building in brass by Jacques Delamane, for the Chanin Building, New York, 1929.

that rested, almost comically, on the backs of four deer. A washstand and mirror was modelled from two peacocks standing back to back, their two heads holding the mirror. With metal, anything was possible, but the bizarre examples of Rateau were way out of keeping with the clean and practical furniture of Le Corbusier or the Irish designer Eileen Gray.

Elegance was not just the domain of the intricate foliage of a Brandt screen, a Kiss cabinet, or a Subes mantelpiece clock: it could be seen to even greater effect in an oak table top supported by just two sheets of bent metal by Louis Sognot. It was minimal, reduced to the contrast between the two materials used; the shiny cold metal, and the rich patina and grain of the wood.

The battle between a revamped French traditional approach to metalwork and the modernist tendency was short-lived. It started and finished with Art Deco, which, for a brief moment, managed to contain both opposing forces. The modernists, however, won the day.

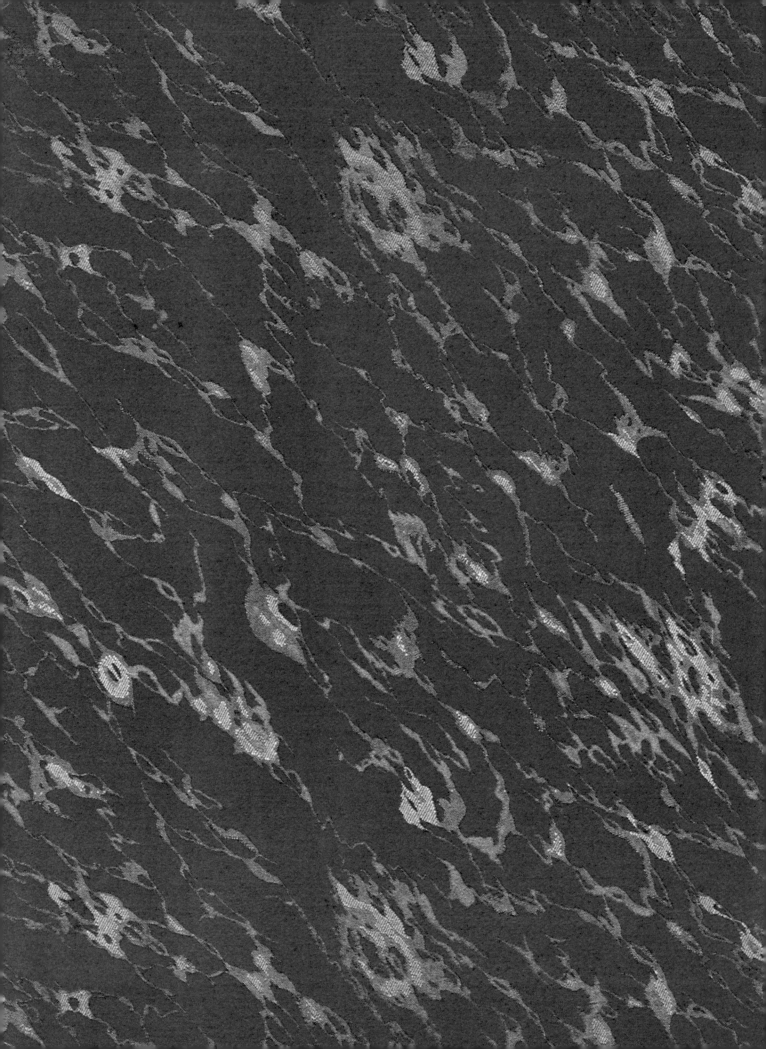

TABLEWARE, CERAMICS AND GLASS

'Sunburst' by Demetre Chiparus in cold painted
bronze and ivory. The sun symbol is often used in Art
Deco design, and here sits boldly on the sheet of drapery
falling from the woman's outstretched arm.

RIGHT A delicate enamelled silver box produced in 1928 by the master Jean Goulden, combines elements of Russian constructivism and French abstract art. The lustre of enamel works particularly well with the sharp and snappy demarcation lines inset in silver.

CENTRE Designed in 1915 by Johan Rohde, this 180-piece 'Acorn' pattern table service was manufactured by the Danish firm of Georg Jensen based in Copenhagen, proving that not all good things or even the best designs originate in France.

Tableware and objets d'art in the Art Deco style were designed for a far larger market than its furniture or high-class metalwork could hope to reach. Tableware consists of tea or coffee services, dishes, salt-cellars and cutlery (flatware), while objets d'art include clocks, ornaments, statuettes, boxes, candlesticks, ice buckets, cocktail shakers, some vases, ashtrays, fans, travelling sets, vanity cases, table lamps and scent bottles.

If any single area of Art Deco could be said to have been responsible for the spreading of the style, then the honours should go to objets d'art. Today, these everyday items can still be found in flea markets and antique fairs, and at a price that does not involve notifying the bank manager in advance. Art Deco ashtrays, pin-boxes and powder compacts were produced in their hundreds of thousands. Ten years ago, these items were deemed almost worthless; even now they are well within the range of all amateur collectors. One of the main reasons for this is mass production, but it also has a great deal to do with the materials that were used.

The 1930s, in particular, saw the emergence of new materials like Bakelite, Vitrolite, Vitroflex, urea formaldehyde, phenolic resin and other plastics. Cheap and manmade, these had a flexibility which particularly suited them to the small everyday object. Later forms of plastics had the added advantage that they were no longer brittle, and were thus almost unbreakable. This is

why so much has survived.

A further reason for their proliferation in Art Deco style was the novelty of the material. Initially, manufacturers were worried about their use for such consumer items as food and cosmetics containers; but, as soon as fears proved unfounded, whole industries turned toward their use. Mass production and the use of innovative designers do not always go hand in hand. What happened was that plastics producers merely copied the style of the day, taking its designs second hand. Purists would say that examples of such mass production were clearly second rate, but it is because of these applications that Art Deco became available to all. This is why it became such a universal style. Design, it must be remembered, is not necessarily debased by multiplication. Moreover, within the area of the plastic or resin pieces, there are oddities that are original in themselves, yet are typical, encapsulating the period. The "Tennis Ball"

LEFT Stylish but somehow impractical cubist tea set in silver from the 1930s.

BELOW LEFT A 1925 simple and stylish silver dish by Jean Puiforcat.

ashtray, made for the Dunlop company from phenolic resin with a lead weight insert in the base, is both witty and practical. Plastic allowed for the invention and production of many such items which are both tacky and vulgar that are representative of the humour of the time. Not necessarily beautiful, or crafted to a superb finish, they are unmistakably Art Deco. Plastic has become so much *the* material of the second half of the 20th century, used for anything from car bumpers to furniture, that it is forgotten that there is a history of style revealed in its uses. Deco began it all.

While the potential of plastics was explored for household objects, luxury materials were used in display items and ornaments. Perhaps the most representative of the luxury items were the Chryselephantine statuettes by artists like Gerdago, Otto Poerzl, Josef Lorenzl, Alexandre Kelety, Demetre Chiparus, and the master of them all, Ferdinand Preiss. Derived from the

Greek, 'Chryselephantine' was used to describe a sculpture of gold and ivory. What it meant in Art Deco terms was the combination of many different materials, including not only gold and ivory, but tortoiseshell, lacquerwork, silver and bronze.

The production of these sculptures was not a Parisian monopoly. Ferdinand Preiss set up his partnership with Arthur Kessler in Berlin, and was well enough known. and collected, to work from Germany. His most famous series of sculptures is on the theme of dance. Usually made from cold-painted bronze with tinted ivory, the dancers are little masterpieces of their type. Titles like *Flame Leaper*, *Charleston Dancer*, *Autumn Dancer* and *Con Brio*, reveal Preiss's interest both in contemporary dance and sculpture as a vehicle for his talent to depict the female form in action. Semi-erotic, the dancers are elegantly frozen in mid-flight. In these turning hips and shoulders, outstretched arms, figures on

■

RIGHT 'The Archer' by
Ferdinand Preiss in
bronze and ivory. The
amazonian yet
androgynous quality and
pose of this updated
classical figure is a perfect
excuse for showing off
technical virtuosity.

their tip-toes. Preiss used a wealth of new forms that are far distanced from the poses of classical sculpture. The rapt, faraway gaze of these dancers also creates a sense of distance: haughty goddesses so gracefully prancing through their exercises; and Preiss statuettes, as much as any item of fashion, reveal, on idealized figures, the dress that was typical of the day.

Gerdago, Chiparus, Kelety, Lorenzl and Poerzl all distinguished themselves by reinterpreting the female muse, as Preiss had done. Demetre Chiparus, a Rumanian who had settled in Paris, concentrated more on the costume of the dancer. Extending themselves in balletic poses, Chiparus dancers were often covered from head to toe in exotic finery. Using the bronze patina technique, he gave his dancers a far greater sense of texture than those of Preiss. Exotic costumes and poses reflected the great interest that the Ballets Russes provided for designers and craftsman alike. Their sculptures could be theatrical, modern, reflecting what was in vogue, but they did not need to concern themselves with the banalities of everyday life. They were exquisite pieces of escapism that, though not cheap, sold in large quantities in the more select shops in Paris, London, Berlin and New York. Sometimes the work of Kelety or Lorenzl might sink to the level of chocolate box lids, but the craftsmanship could not be faulted. The work of Bruno Zach verged even closer to the level of vulgar camp. The sculptures and statuettes of Art Deco are often misunderstood, because they are judged against serious sculpture that demands rigorous critical standards. These light, entertaining pieces never pretended to be any more or less than that.

In the application of Art Deco to mantelpiece clocks, the craftsman/designer was free to produce objects both entirely functional and as elitist as he wished. There could be no criticism, except in stylistic terms, of rounded off or stepped clocks that hinted at Aztec influences made from the uninspiring, yet immensely useful, phenolic resin. They shared much with the designs for the first wireless sets. Built to contain the latest in technological design, the cases for the radios now look curiously antiquated. Of course they had to be solid and robust to house the valves (tubes) which warmed up slowly, and became very hot. Consequently they also needed ventilation. The design often resembles a car radiator, but that is hardly surprising when car

CHAPTER 6

■

LEFT Examples from a discreetly designed, understated and highly functional silver cutlery service by the Art Deco genius Jean Puiforcat.

design was developing along parallel lines. If radiators and radios often had those heavy, curved edges that look like comic-strip speed-lines, or force-lines, the designs for electric clocks were more inventive. Flat diamonds or lozenges of brushed steel, with only the hour and minute hand disturbing the reflective beauty, were the very latest in clock design. A clock could also be traditionally round in chromed brass, set on a metal base like a vanity mirror. Perhaps the most typical clocks of the period were those made from stepped marble blocks, surmounted by a reclining nude by a sculptor like Preiss. Using cheap materials, a mass market could be reached; but there were still craftsmen and silversmiths such as Georg Jensen and Albert Cheuret who refused to accept loss of quality, and produced clock designs of distinctive beauty.

Another technique that was used in the 1920s and 30s was the making of vases in beaten copper. Once the copper had been laboriously hand-hammered, it could be decorated with enamel, painted, etched, or left plain. The master of this technique was Jean Dunand, who also created the decorative lacquerwork screens for the *Normandie*. One of his vases employed the

device of snakes wriggling up its side, reminiscent of Edgar Brandt's interest in the motif. Dunand could switch from the realistic and the natural to the completely abstract with relative ease and a high degree of success. Even at their most abstract, Dunand's vases looked Grecian, Etruscan, or Oriental; enveloped by rich patterns, they ignored modern austerity.

Where the modern austerity and the new clean line came into its own was with the art of the silversmith. Since the invention of silverplating in the mid-19th century, the required look could be achieved for a less discerning audience at a more attractive price. Apart from the advantage that electroplating gave to the trade, high quality silverwork is a skill that seems never to have suffered, especially as the demand for jewellery has always kept the craft alive. The greatest of all the silversmiths was Jean Puiforcat who, along with Ruhlmann and Lalique, will be remembered not just as a practitioner of the Art Deco style, but as a true master of his respective crafts. Puiforcat, Georg Jensen, the Danish silversmith, and the American Kem Weber, each in their own way, extended the craft of silversmithing, and the language of Art Deco.

Puiforcat learnt his trade at his father's workshop; through Art Nouveau on to Art Deco, he rapidly outgrew him. The precursors to Puiforcat's mature style were Josef Hoffmann and the other members of the Wiener Werkstätte. He adopted their example of radical austerity and perfected it into a new sensuous simplicity. After having seen the beauty and lustre of a plain sheet of silver, it is difficult to imagine that anything could improve it. Puiforcat recognized this, but also saw that the minimum of sophisticated detailing in another element could enhance the material's outstanding beauty through the power of contrast. The best examples of this were also the most minimal. Puiforcat produced dish after dish that was highlighted just by thick ivory handles, an ebony knob, or a ring-pull made from pale jade. The result was luxurious, made doubly so by the fact that the materials themselves that seemed to do all the work; only seemed, because it was Puiforcat's inherent sense of the correctness of form that made it all possible. He was not just a craftsman but also a highly sensitive aesthete; he believed that, ultimately, some forms are right and others wrong. With his work it is possible to sense that he, above all the other contemporary designers, came the closest to that elusive goal.

Other important craftsmen in silver were promoted in Paris by Christofle goldsmiths, who encouraged, among others, the talents of Cazes, and Süe, of the Süe et Mare workshops. Two outstanding examples in particular are the ice-bucket and champagne cooler modelled by Luc Lanel for the Normandie. They are not only superbly functional; they are, quite simply, right.

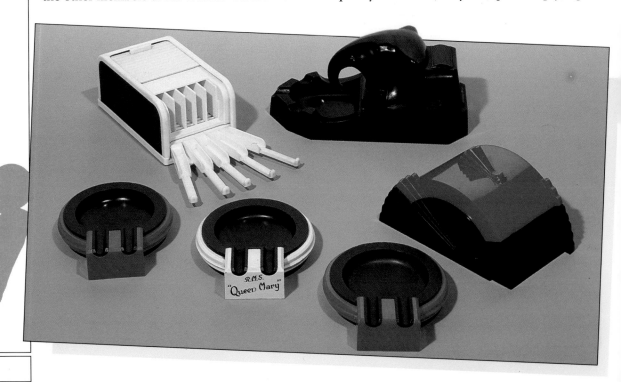

LEFT 'Kora' a gilt and cold
painted bronze and ivory
figure of an exotic dancer
by Demetre Chiparus. His
speciality was the heavily-
worked detailing of
costume that this figure
so aptly reveals.

RIGHT Art Deco clock from
the firm of Van Cleef and
Arpels, Paris. The
Japanese temple design is
a fine example of 20th
century japonaiserie.

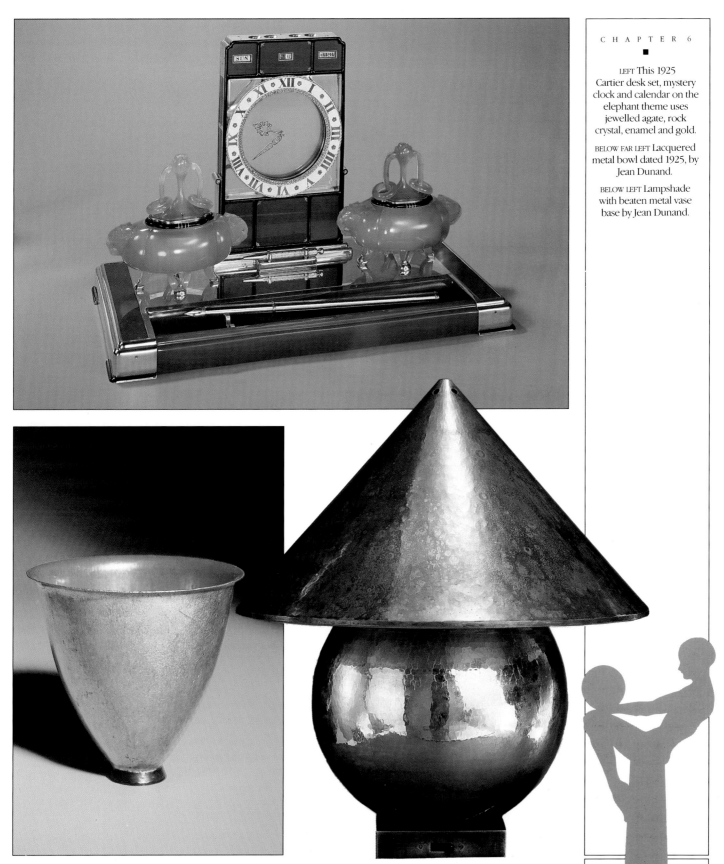

LEFT This 1925
Cartier desk set, mystery
clock and calendar on the
elephant theme uses
jewelled agate, rock
crystal, enamel and gold.

BELOW FAR LEFT Lacquered
metal bowl dated 1925, by
Jean Dunand.

BELOW LEFT Lampshade
with beaten metal vase
base by Jean Dunand.

RIGHT Terracotta cup designed by the English craftsman Keith Murray for Wedgwood & Sons in 1935. A pale blue outer glaze is accentuated by the four sets of indented bands that pick out the cream-coloured interior of the cup.

FAR RIGHT Porcelain Art Deco lamp designed by Henri Rapin for production by the Sèvres porcelain works.

BELOW RIGHT Saxbo stoneware vase, c. 1930 from Denmark. The oriental inspiration is evident in the shape and glazing. The return to simple, almost crude, craft pottery was as evident in Scandinavia as it was in Great Britain.

CERAMICS

Of all the applications of Art Deco, ceramics was without a doubt the most widespread. Every country had a pottery or porcelain factory and workshops that at some time in the 1920s or '30s employed some variation on the Art Deco style. The ceramics' place in society had long been central to the question of what role art should play in relation to industry. Apart from the rare instances of studio potters adapting the style, ceramic design was usually an automatic transformation of a design into a mass marketable product. Of course there would always be expensive porcelain statuettes, but even these need not be limited to numbered editions. The production of ceramics, porcelain and plaster models was as vast as it was various. Each country developed its own adaptation of the style and its own speciality.

It may have been that the material qualities of pottery and ceramics were not particularly suited to Art Deco's more rectilinear tendencies, but solutions were quickly found. More often than not, the basic shape of plates, vases, cups and saucers, was left alone. The undecorated object could then be used like an artist's canvas, and novel decorations could be painted or stencilled on. The blank, creamy, off-white surface was an ideal starting point, and for some designers was almost an end in itself.

What manufacturers had discovered of particular significance was that dinner and tea services were as essential to the Art Deco look required by their clients as furniture, glass, clothes, wireless sets, and jewellery. They had to keep up with the changing taste, so that they could provide another addition to the entire Art Deco environment. A set of Clarice Cliff "Bizarre" ware would look as out of place in a Louis Seize room as a Delft Blue plate or Wedgwood tea service would look on an Eileen Gray sidetable. With the ability to transfer design after design onto the same basic form they had always used, the ceramics industry was able to change over to new designs in a matter of weeks, if necessary.

The scale of the ceramics industry in Weimar Germany has already been discussed. In the 1920s a new development in taste had evolved. In 1930, the Berlin State Porcelain Factory held an exhibition in order to discover the preferences of the public. Of the 150 designs from all periods on display the two most popular were plain white pieces. The love of simplicity in Germany may have been out of keeping with the rest of Europe and America, but it was clearly indicative of a trend. The growth of interest in non-Western art forms also had repercussions for the ceramics industry. Examples of Ming porcelain from China and Japanese ceramics had become appreciated for its no-nonsense simplicity, its unique finish. This attitude, when it prevailed, scraped the creative palette back to virtually nothing, and the designer could start all over again, becoming either heavily decorative like Clarice Cliff, or pure and elemental.

The most interesting development of all in modern ceramic design took place in post-revolutionary Russia. Only two months after the Revolution the State Porcelain factory was reorganised completely in order to meet the new requirements of the people. The designer S V Chekhonin played a central part in the renaissance of Russian ceramics, helping to plan the new State works. Not even the most simple and homely of objects could be ignored, as far as its importance to the people was concerned. Even *Pravda*, the communist party newspaper, organized questionnaires on the lines of "What do we require from a plate?" The state wanted all its artists to be involved in production of work that was useful to the masses. Artists of the stature of Tatlin, Puni, Malevich, Suetin and Chasnik readily became involved in meeting the demands of new design. A plate could be appreciated on aesthetic grounds, but it was also beautiful in a political sense. As crockery is something that almost everyone uses it could be adapted to carry a political message. Many of the motifs and symbols that were incorporated into the designs – the hammer and sickle, the cogwheel, the factory worker, the healthy, robust farmworker – suggested that advance could be achieved through hard work and allegiance to the doctrines of the Party. They were ideal propaganda vehicles. Following on from that idea, the concept of mass production was promoted wholeheartedly; design was to be spread as wide as possible, its success measured in part by its popularity. Far from being mass-produced junk, such work equalled French, Dutch and English Art Deco in quality and often surpassed them in its novelty.

Other centres of production around the cities of Moscow and Leningrad concentrated heavily on borrowing the new design ideas of Petrograd

and other experimental stations, and churned out vast quantities of plates and cups adorned with the new patterns. The success of the industry was very obvious at the stands in the Russian pavilion at the Exposition des Arts Décoratifs et Industriels. If it had been expected that the political situation in Russia would give rise to a dull uniformity, the opposite was true. Ceramics produced from the designs of the Suprematist group were radically inventive. Futurist vases were displayed that looked as exciting and revolutionary as a Boccione sculpture or Picasso's sculpture of the absinthe glass. Malevich had designed a tea cup that was cut in half and completely solid, thus technically useless. It was nevertheless a response to the questionnaires and discussions on the purpose of ceramics. In spirit, the Russians had come very close to the concerns of the French master Jean Puiforcat, who wished to produce articles that were platonic in their beauty, with an ideal simplicity and elegance. If the advances achieved in Russian industry were stimulated from the top downwards, in Europe the individual designer, working for a factory like Sèvres or Wedgwood, was as much in tune with the new spirit.

In France, the designers responsible for the new style were mainly Suzanne Lalique, the daughter of the glass expert René Lalique, René Buthaud, Jean Luce and Marcel Goupy. It was of course important that factories of the calibre of Sèvres and Limoges involved themselves actively in the new style, and yet again the large Paris stores provided the best outlet for the resulting work. René Buthaud was made the artistic director of the Printemps' Primavera studio works at Tours. Many of the designers mentioned previously in relation to furniture and metalwork also experimented in this medium. Sèvres, which had set up its *faïence* department in 1920, allowed Emile-Jacques Ruhlmann and Jean Dupas to carry out work for them. Another development was the rise in importance of porcelain statuettes and figurines. The advantage of porcelain was that it was particularly suited to creating cheap ornaments for a clientèle that could not afford, or did not appreciate, the finesse of work by Preiss or Gerdago. Ceramic figures also had a different quality to them. Smooth and glossy, they accentuated the glorious, sensual curves of aspects of Art Deco design. People could have a group of ornaments on the mantelpiece or in their display cabinets

for a fraction of the price of a one-off statuette in expensive materials like gold, bronze, ivory, or silver.

The more rectilinear tendency in Art Deco was also responsible for some novel, if not always successful, reinterpretations of established ideas about design of household objects. Teacups could be square, oval, conical – pretty well any shape that could contain liquid – teapots could be playfully disguised as motor cars, or have their spouts shaped like the prow of an ocean liner. A functional object could be ornamental as well. They were, and still are, delightful objects to have around.

In Holland, the Art Deco style also caught on, not so much in the area of the traditional Delft blue output from the Porceleyne Fles, but in other studios like the works in Gouda that produced Gouds Plateel. In Denmark, Royal Copenhagen also responded quickly to the developing taste. Most of the factories in Europe moved with the fashion but also continued to produce their old and tested traditional designs for the less adventurous.

The relationship of the factory to the designer, and in particular the studio potter, was often problematical. England provided a good case history that must have had equal relevance to the situation in other countries. When factories like Royal Doulton, Carlton, Wedgwood, and the Shelley Potteries in Staffordshire started to produce and popularize Art Deco design they began to endanger the survival and integrity of the individual craftsman potter. Potters of the calibre of Michael Cardew, William Staite Murray and, most notably, Bernard Leach found a lot wrong with the new direction ceramics were going in. The production of the straight-sided vases of the "Midwinter" range from Shelley Potteries, were considered by Leach, in particular, to be perverse and untenable. In 1934, Leach actually closed down his pottery and went to Japan where he felt tradition and expertise were still highly regarded and appreciated. There were, however, still some designers who could find inspiration from their individual work and not be overly snobbish about the idea of having copies made. Richard Joyce, the main designer for the Pilkington works throughout the 1920s, was a case in point. His favourite motifs were animals and in this he helped to bring the craft potter and Art Deco closer together.

The most individual of all the ceramic

CENTRE LEFT Stark yet successful design for a porcelain cup and saucer by the Russian Ilya Chashnik.

BELOW LEFT Suprematist porcelain cup and saucer from Russia by the designer Nikolai Suetin.

RIGHT Plate in primitive
style, featuring jungle
animals and foliage.

BELOW RIGHT A collection of
the highly decorative
pottery by Clarice Cliff.
Simple forms are jazzed
up through daring
though sometimes less-
than-successful colour
combinations.

designers, however, and now the most sought
after and collected, is Clarice Cliff. She was born
in 1900 and, after a long apprenticeship, rose to
the post of art director of the Wilkinson and
Newport Companies. Her most famous designs
were the "Bizarre" range which were strongly-
coloured and abstract. Often loosely based on
flower motifs and landscapes, her work was
highly innovative. The designs for her plates
were sometimes hexagonal and sometimes even
square. Cliff also managed to tempt artists to
work on designs that she then manufactured. The
artist Graham Sutherland designed a limited
edition table set for Cliff, and others that she
worked with included Ben Nicholson, Barbara
Hepworth, Paul Nash and the Bloomsbury artists
Duncan Grant and Vanessa Bell, whose earlier
experiments at the Omega Workshops made
them particularly suited to the job. It was odd
how artists who worked with ceramics seemed
to flourish in that medium, while craft potters
themselves did not.

Ceramics throughout the '20s and '30s
enjoyed a great period of success; even the
arrival of materials such as plastics, bakelite and
phenolic resin made few inroads on the market.
Art Deco ceramics provided the style with a huge
boost, because they were attractive and readily
available, and even now the best designs do not
look particularly dated.

LEFT Eccentric
oriental interpretation of
an animal vase from the
Sèvres porcelain factory.

BELOW LEFT Three silver
and thickly enamelled
vases by Camille Faure,
that owe much to abstract
painting, and arguably
manage to cross the slim
dividing line between
vulgarity and beauty.

RIGHT Pâte-de-verre vase of 1925 by Gabriel Argy-Rousseau on the theme of fishes playing in the sea diving in and out of the waves.

FAR RIGHT Deeply-etched example of a glass bowl by Daum, Nancy, with an almost mediaeval feeling.

GLASS

The importance of glass to the development of taste in the 1920s and '30s is often overlooked. The Art Deco glass that is collected by connoisseurs is often limited to the vases, glasses and lamps designed by René Lalique and Daum. Those pieces are of course particularly rare and beautiful, but they only represent a small percentage of the glass produced, and do not give a full picture of all the uses to which glass could be put. Glass was not only used for table ornaments or vases, or even jewellery, but was also an important part of a whole architectural project on the grandest scale. At its plainest, a glass sheet is transparent – almost invisible. It was that particular quality of glass that many of the modernist architects exploited. Le Corbusier's Pavillon de L'Esprit Nouveau at the Exposition des Arts Décoratifs et Industriels stood as a statement against superfluous decoration. It also showed how to use the window as the only ornament and break in the structure of the building. Many architects, including Robert Mallet Stevens, Mies van der Rohe, Walter Gropius and Le Corbusier himself used glass for its properties of transparency. The modern buildings of the 1930s started off the boom in what we now call curtain

walling, that is floor to ceiling glass walls in which the division between the interior and exterior space is minimised as far as possible.

Newly-invented types of glass compound allowed for a greater range of applications. Vitroflex could be bent round pillars and curved walls in ways that would be difficult to imitate with plain standard glass. The fragility of glass could also be overcome. Not only was glass used for mirrors and larger furniture ensembles, but some new types of glass would stand up to high heat. In the late '30s, the designers Raymond McGrath and Elizabeth Craig worked on various oven to tableware prototypes for the British Heat Resisting Glass Company. The designs themselves were hardly novel, but showed that the traditional limitations of glass need no longer be so restricting. Even within the traditional areas of glass usage such as for vases and lamps the Art Deco period saw a revival of many old techniques and the invention of some new ones. René Lalique, the master of glass manufacture, began to use moulds and casts in order to be able to manufacture large numbers of glass sculptures. Maurice Marinot discovered methods of catching bubbles between skins of glass in his vases, other makers used the etching and engraving techniques, while yet others exploited the *pâte*

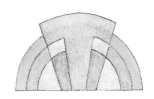

de verre technique.

Two of the largest projects during the period to use glass extensively, apart from the Exposition des Arts Décoratifs et Industriels, were the Grand Hotel at Dax in France, and the bathroom designed for Tilly Losch by Paul Nash. The entrance hall to the hotel was a dynamic extravaganza, its hundreds of plates of glass giving the visitor the impression of walking into the heart of a diamond as big as the Ritz. The Tilly Losch bathroom, which James Clark, Eaton and Son, constructed for Nash, was up to the minute in its use of mirrored walls, chrome and glass. It looks as modern today as it must have looked precociously ahead of its time. In America the designers Joseph Urban and Donald Deskey also used glass panels extensively in their interior designs. The precedent for abstract patterned or stained glass in America had already been set by Frank Lloyd Wright in the Avery Coonley Playhouse, and later in his mammoth project for the Midway Gardens in Chicago. If many of the modernist practitioners favoured the clear aspect of sheets

of plain glass, there was still great support and understanding of the decorative potential of worked glass.

France had kept alive the skill of working glass throughout the 19th century with the most exciting contributions to the medium coming from Baccarat and Emile Gallé. Gallé was the master of the Art Nouveau style, and René Lalique was his direct heir. Born in Ay-sur-Marne in 1860 Lalique was one of the oldest practitioners of the Art Deco style. Turning to glass manufacture in 1902 he quickly recognized its expressive potential. Lalique was particularly important because not only did he achieve total mastery of the small ornament, vase and statuette, but in the 1920s he started to design glass furniture. Following the example of Baccarat's etched glass furniture in the mid 19th century Lalique reinvented the form in a totally modern way. He was followed in this by other designers, most notably Robert Block and Serge Roche.

The highpoints of Lalique's career were his designs for the Exposition des Arts Décoratifs et Industriels

LEFT Vaguely cubist-inspired eight piece liqueur or water service, employing the pâte-de-verre technique, by Gabriel Argy-Rousseau.

RIGHT Delicately-shaped rectangular vase by E. Rousseau, with an image on the side of a grotesque figure.

and the large *Normandie* commission. As well as having his own stand Lalique also participated in others. At his own, which was designed by the architect Marc Ducluzand, Lalique displayed examples of his work covering the complete range of his output. He was also asked to provide a glass fountain for the Exposition. Like a transparent Cleopatra's needle it rose with geometric ease through fifteen layers to an astonishing height for a glass construction. For the Primavera pavilion designed by Sauvage and Vybo, Lalique supplied the glass "cobblestones" that diffused the light into the central space through the ceiling canopy. Lalique also provided a dining-room setting for the Sèvres pavilion in which he displayed his glassware on a glass table, lit from above through squares of glass set into the ceiling.

In Lalique's work other designers could see the unification of the disparate strains of Art Deco design. He was at once luxurious, elegant, practical, interested in abstract design, showy, intimate and, above all, the supreme craftsman. Among his smaller pieces, he created delicately-coloured scent bottles, small glass plaques of nude bathers, statuettes of sleeping muses, and glass mascots for cars. The eagle mascot he produced later adorned the cars of Hitler's favoured staff members, a use that Lalique and other Frenchmen must have abhorred.

The method of working that Lalique favoured for his ornamental pieces soon found wider favour. He would first shape the object in another material and then take a plaster cast and pour molten glass into the mould. Apart from the advantage of being able to cast shapes that could not be blown, moulds could be employed for mass production. The results could be varied slightly by using variously coloured glass, or in the finishing process. Another designer who used this method was Marius Ernest Sabino, who favoured the nymph and animal motifs popular in Art Deco. The quality of pieces by Lalique, Sabino, Marcel Goupy and Alméric Walter is almost always a clarity that resulted from the use of few and discreet colours, but there were other designers who experimented with a far greater range, giving their work a heavier, opaque feel.

The revival of the *pâte de verre* and *pâte de cristal* techniques brought back the art of sculpting in glass. The method produced a cold glass compound that could be modelled like clay and coloured easily. Foremost proponents of this technique were Gabriel Argy-Rousseau, Alméric Walter and François-Emile Décorchemont. In comparison to that of Lalique, their work has a heightened sense of luxury and colour. Rich reds, oranges, mauves and blues blend delicately into each other without the strict demarcation lines that appear in other types of glassware.

Daum and Maurice Marinot specialized in the etching and enamelling of glass. By starting off with a thick glass vase, for example, they would cut back layer after layer with the application of acids, until the pattern was left as a deep relief. The Daum Frères factory at Nancy was quick to pick up on the experiments of Marinot in this field, and they mass-produced variations on the theme.

Glass had many possible applications, but one of its most inspired was when used in conjunction with the metalwork of Edgar Brandt. The screens, vases and lamps that Brandt constructed were beautifully illuminated by the glasswork of Daum and sometimes Schneider. The famous "Cobra" lamp discussed earlier could not only be bought in three sizes, but had a variety of coloured glass lampshades by Daum, enabling it to fit into the overall decorative and colour scheme of the client's home. The contrast of translucence and opacity was further heightened by the tactile contrast of solid metal supporting fragile glass. When Edgar Brandt manufactured doors and gates for specific settings such as the Paris shop for Paul Poiret, clear glass filled the spaces, so that the metalwork looked like sculpture suspended in air. When Brandt designed overhead lighting and chandeliers he would also draw on the talents and expertise of René Lalique.

Other European countries, as well as the United States, produced Art Deco glass of merit. The Leerdam company in Holland carried out designs for the architects Henry van de Velde and Frank Lloyd Wright, while the Orrefors company in Scandinavia also produced simple, good design. In America, the Steuben company, in collaboration with the Corning Glass works, produced many pieces that are on view at the whaling port of New Bedford. The most important designer for Steuben was Walter Dorwin Teague.

In England, the design and manufacture of glassware was carried out in much the same way as ceramics. The companies of Stuart and Sons, and Thomas Webb and Sons of Stourbridge invited the artists Graham Sutherland and Paul Nash to create new forms in glass. Another highly talented designer was Keith Murray, whose work for the Stevens and Williams company at Brierley Hill created new standards in Art Deco design. English glassware was never as inventive as that of the French, but what it lost in complexity, or colour, it made up for in simplicity. Where the English might engrave a vase with clear-cut lines, with the occasional ornamental motif, the French would burn or scour deep into the glass. Both were equally viable, and good examples of the fluid diversity of the Art Deco style, and of the new techniques available to designers in glass.

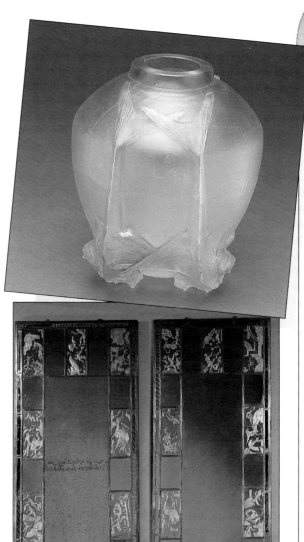

TOP LEFT A 1923 semi-translucent glass vase using the lost wax method by René Lalique. The common fish motif that is seen on the famous lacquered bed by Jean Dunand, and the playful pâte-de-verre vase by Gabriel Argy Rousseau, is here transformed into an extremely elegant, yet somehow disquieting image of disappearing fish. Frozen for that split second before they dive.

CENTRE LEFT Pair of 1936 Orrefors mirrored doors by Simon Gate, depicting eighteen scenes based on the circus theme, including knife throwing, juggling, trapeze artists, lion-taming, snake-charming, weightlifting, displays of strength by an elephant and a man, and the more unlikely pastimes of ostrich and tortoise racing.

BOTTOM LEFT Elegant, streamlined glass bowl by the Steuben Glass Works, United States, from 1939. The glass is engraved with a design of acrobats, which results in an astonishing play of perspective by Pavel Tchelitchev, sometime companion of the poet Edith Sitwell.

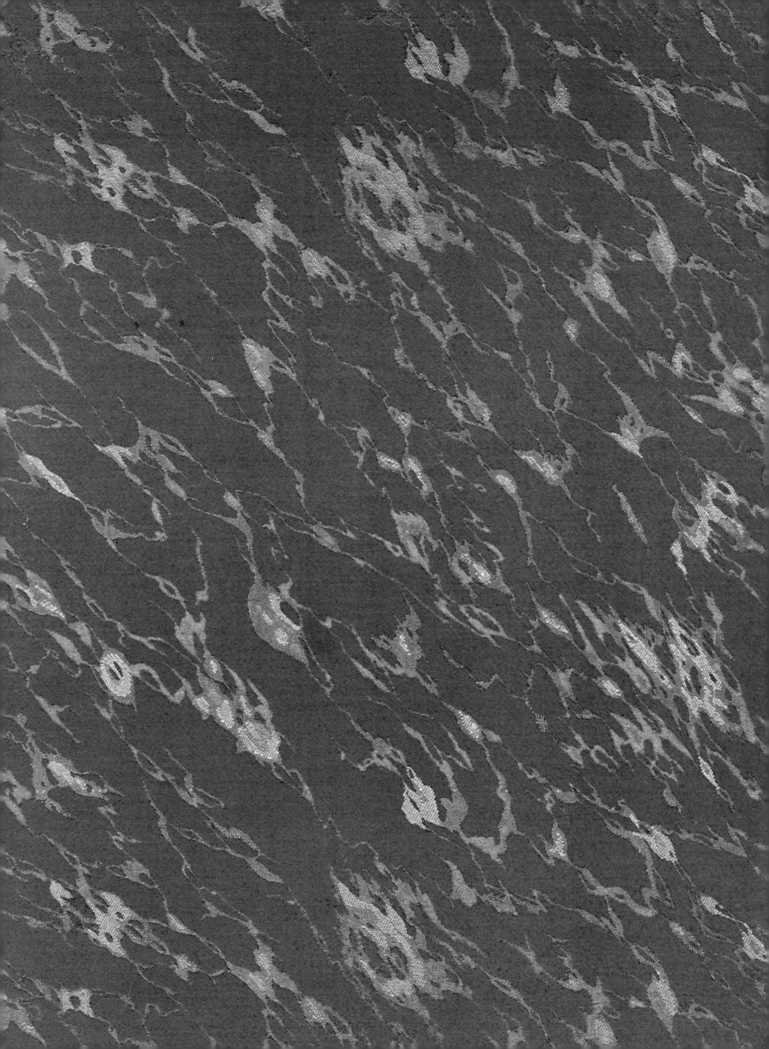

CHAPTER SEVEN

FASHION

Witty sketch in pencil and gouache by Ernest
Deutsch Dryden dated 1926. An angelic lady of fashion
refreshes her appearance in her motor car laden with
gifts as the bemused chauffeur and dog look on.

RIGHT A morocco crêpe day dress, and pâletot by Lucien Lelong, illustrated for Art-Gout-Beauté in 1922.

The world of fashion clothing and accessories is always quick to pick up on the latest changes in taste, even though it is fleeting and changeable as weather. The fashion that appeared in the 1920s and '30s is well known to anyone that has ever looked at films of the period. It has been repeated and diluted so many times since that it becomes difficult to place it historically, to see where it came from, or to notice how subtle modifications point to a dress being a '60s replica or the original. In itself, fashion may only be as important to people as the amount of care they take in clothing themselves. For the elegant Parisian or New Yorker of the '20s and '30s, fashion was a vital part of life. The reason for the rapid success of Art Deco was that it was essentially a fashionable style. All styles have their day, but in the 20th century the fashion industry moved in response to public taste quicker than ever before. This has as much to do with built-in obsolescence as with a sense of style and finesse; both feed off each other. Tastes fluctuate quickly, so the industry has to come up with something new, as clients try to stay one ahead of the rest of the pack. Fashion is always to do with snobbishness and the desire to outstrip the Joneses. With Art Deco, this was particularly important, since it was a total style. If your collector lived amongst Ruhlmann tables, Lalique sculptures, African chairs by Pierre Legrain, lights by Brandt and Daum, a coffee service by Sèvres or Clarice Cliff, place settings by Jean Puiforcat; if he or she lit your cigarette with a lighter designed by George Sandoz to the strains of Paul Robeson or a jazz number on the gramophone, as you examined the bizarre portrait by Tamara de Lempicka, or waited to hear from the travel agent as to whether he had managed to beat the waiting list for his or her forthcoming trip on the *Ile de France* across to New York, to spend a weekend with Scott Fitzgerald and crazy Zelda at one of their notoriously wild Long Island parties, before nipping over to Hollywood to set up a film contract – then you can guarantee that the cut of the husband's suit, the length and sharpness of his lapels, the width of tie, and the wife's dress by Schiaparelli worn for dinner at the Algonquin, or the Pierre, would be precisely in keeping. If so much effort in intellect, taste and money had been expended on creating the home environment, then the only things that could travel out of the door, clothes and jewellery, had to be as

Art - Go

important; it had to complement the overall effect. In terms of design, the effect of fashion items on the other applications of Art Deco was fairly minimal; as a mirror to hold up and see the speed of the change, however, fashion was unrivalled.

Sometimes, of course, the converse was true. The statuettes and Chryselephantine figures of Otto Poerzl and Ferdinand Preiss were direct reflections of the opera and ballet costumes, and the ballroom clothes, of the period. They were – if you like – knowing little nods; small elegant gestures of recognition that the owner appreciated the essence of what it was to be fashionable.

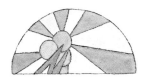

LEFT The Hindustan design by Paul Poiret of 1920 from the Gazette du Bon Ton.

té

It is not difficult to build up an accurate, if superficial, overview of fashion in the '20s and '30s from the statuettes by Preiss, the photo of Nancy Cunard in her African bangles, or photos of Picasso, Jean Cocteau and other *flâneurs* and poseurs in your mind.

There is a perverse rule in fashion that the poorer the economic climate is for the majority of people the more ostentatious the select, wealthy few become. The double standards of the "Roaring Twenties" in America particularly, where Prohibition cast a depressing cloud of double-dealing, suspicion and crime, reflected itself in the sexless, androgynous short skirts, bob cuts, and shapeless tops worn by the flappers. By

the beginning of the '30s, when the reality was far more depressing and the comforting pedestal of wealth had been kicked away from under their feet of the erstwhile bootleggers, the fashion became fuller, the jewellery – even if it were paste – far more startling.

The top designers of the day included Schiaparelli, who at times courted the ludicrous inventions of the Surrealists, Coco Chanel, Jean Patou, Jeanne Lanvin, Worth, Nina Ricci, Paquin, Christian Berard and Mainbocher. Paul Poiret spread his influence and taste far wider than most of the other fashion designers. At the Exposition des Arts Décoratifs et Industriels, Poiret exhibited his designs on decorated barges just

■

RIGHT *L'heure du Thé*
("Teatime"), fashion plate
from the *Gazette du Bon
Ton, Paris.* The coat and
veiled cloche hat are
designed by Benito, 1920.
Exaggerated high collars,
already popular in
Edwardian times, were
still in vogue, but the
plainness of the hat and
figure-disguising shape of
the coat are pointers to
Art Deco fashion taste.

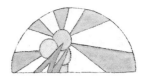

under the Alexander III Bridge. When he needed an architect for his fashion house in Paris he used the firm of Perret Frères. The entrance door into the premises was one of Edgar Brandt's masterpieces in metalwork. Poiret recognized the importance of creating a suitable environment for displaying his talents and impressing his wealthy clientele. He was, above all, a man of taste.

One of the more jokey and humorous contributions to the Paris fashion scene was made by Sonia Delaunay. Her "Orphist" car was decorated in checks of bright colour; the matching coats, hats and interior were impressive adaptations of her husband's serious high art. They reflected the heady *joie de vivre* of the show. Delaunay was quite serious about the whole enterprise: it was hard work creating fun; it was spirited, uplifting work. Her Orphist car, in particular, captured all the contradictions of Art Deco in one energetic leap into the machinery of the modern world. It was a remarkable feat of far-sightedness.

The contributions of other European countries and America were mostly reactions and pale reflections of what Paris was offering. Russia was deadly serious about the use of clothes design in relation to the people, as it was in ceramic design; but it was not any less inventive for that. Again, artists like Tatlin and Rodchenko applied themselves to the design of clothes fit for the average working Russian. The results were not elegant, but the stark frugality of the cut and material would have looked completely in place in a pavilion dedicated to L'Esprit Nouveau. The modernist Art Deco contingency never quite managed to make ideals and reality meet; if it met at all it was in the area of Robert Delaunay's "Simultanist" designs.

BELOW Art Deco carpet by De Silva Bruhns. Carpets like these were often used to give a feeling of warmth and comfort to interiors that were otherwise fashionably stark and austere.

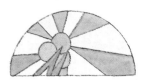

TEXTILE DESIGN

ABOVE LEFT
Knaresborough, a silk
tissue designed in 1926
by Bertrand Whittaker
and used in the
decoration of what was
then London's newest
and most luxurious hotel,
Claridges.

ABOVE CENTRE **Tideswell**, a
turquoise and cream
coloured textile by
Warner & Sons.

ABOVE RIGHT
Roller-printed cotton
textile, designed by J. S.
Tunnard for the Warners,
the British furnishing
fabric manufacturers,
1922.

RIGHT **Seaham**, a wool-
and-cotton damask
designed by Alec Hunter
in July, 1935.

CENTRE RIGHT **Cranwell**, a
block printed figured silk
fabric, based on a French
design, 1928.

ABOVE **Braintree**, a cotton, cotton gimp and jute tissue designed by Alec Hunter in 1932.

Textile design was another area in which fine artists taught the established trade a great deal. In England, the ever-flexible Paul Nash and Duncan Grant produced dashing new pastel-coloured textiles. They were a direct attack on the heavy colours used in Art Nouveau Liberty designs and the work of William Morris and Co.

In France in the early 1920s the textile manufacturers and the tapestry weavers based in Aubusson found their industry in decline. Its revival in the 1930s was due in part to the large commissions for the liners *Ile de France* and *Normandie*, and the inspiration of a Madame Cuttoli. What she did was to invite France's greatest artists to produce painted designs that would then be faithfully copied by the tapestry weavers. The project clearly touched a chord with such artists as Pablo Picasso, Henri Matisse, Georges Rouault, Fernand Léger, Georges Braque, Jean Lurçat, André Derain and Raoul Dufy, all of whom contributed to the venture.

Dufy played an extremely important role in textile design. The fashion designer Paul Poiret had set up the Atelier Martine before the First World War, and it was Dufy who produced the most inspired designs for the workshop. The diluted character of his post-Fauvist style proved to be well-suited to textile work. Other designers like Emile-Jacques Ruhlmann also found it necessary to work in the medium in order to provide coverings for their furniture. In England, the American husband and wife team of Edward McKnight Kauffer and Marion Dorn produced work that typified the taste of the period. As in so many other things, the most outlandish and original designs were produced by Sonia Delaunay. The vivacity of her designs was matched only by the work of some of the best Russian textile designers.

RIGHT ("The Sweet Night"), fashion plate from the *Gazette du Bon Ton, Paris*. Clothes designed by Charles Worth, 1920. Note the skirt length which had already risen well above the ankles, even for formal evening wear, and the draping over bust and hips, obscuring the natural female shape.

FAR RIGHT 1922 drawing from Art-Gout-Beauté of a model wearing a white crêpe cocktail dress from the fashion house of Worth. Note also the furniture, which is a ragbag of Afro-Egyptian and neo-classical styles.

BELOW RIGHT Colourful 1925, Japanese-inspired textile design by the artist designer Raoul Dufy.

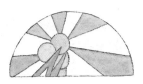

FRANCE XXᵉ SIÈCLE

GEORGE BARBIER 1921

Le Cadran Solaire

LEFT Fashion plate by
Georges Barbier
(1882–1932). Fashions for
the 1921 'Le Cadran
Solaire', stencil print from
Falbalas et Fanfreluches,
Almanach des Modes.

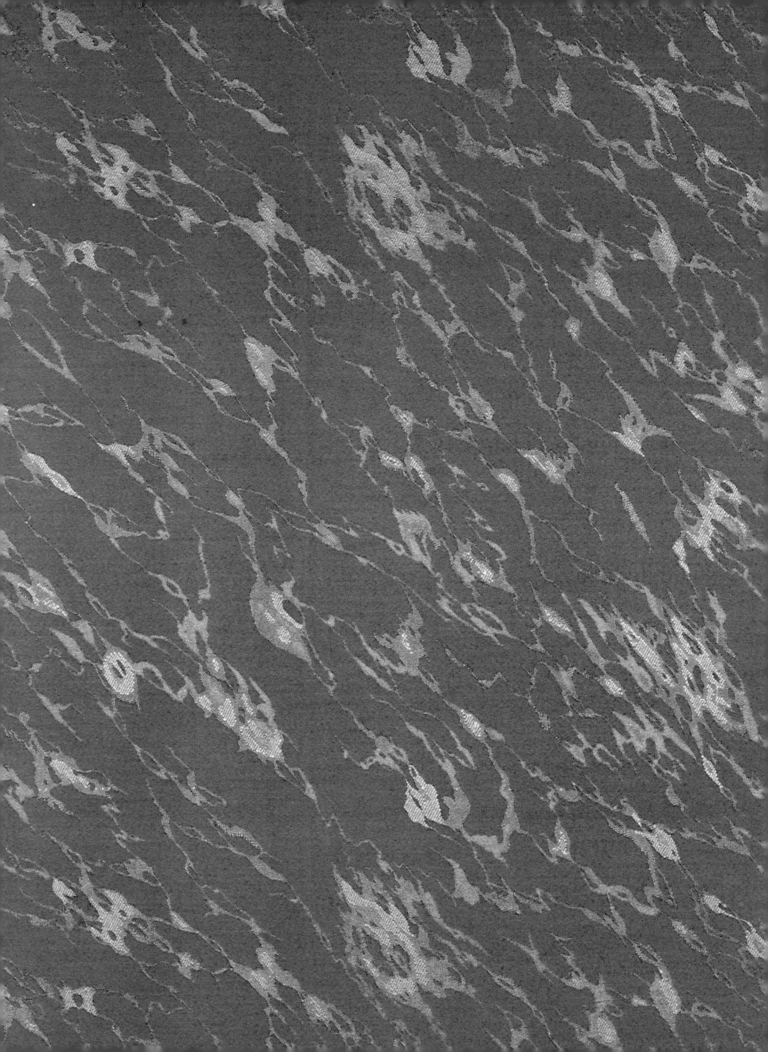

CHAPTER EIGHT

PAINTING AND DESIGN

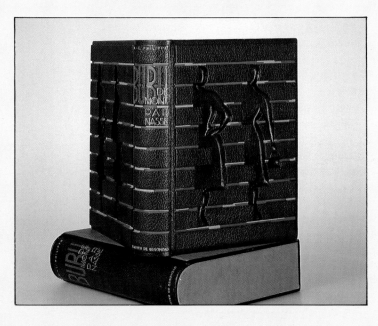

Highly rare and lavishly-bound copy of Charles L.
Philippe's book 'Bubu de Montparnasse', with slip case.
The design by Paul Bonet utilises the craft of leather
tooling in relief to depict women silhouetted against
multi-coloured stripes. The illustrations are by Dunoyer
de Segonzac.

There is really no such thing as specifically Art Deco painting. It is possible to talk of Cubism, Surrealism, and Expressionism as coherent styles, but Art Deco painting never really existed in any convincing way. Strictly speaking, Art Deco derived its name from the Exposition des Arts Décoratifs et Industriels, which did not allow for a painting pavilion. Although the distance between the decorative arts and fine art is not as great as many people think, the best painting of the 1920s and 1930s certainly had little to do with the Art Deco style – if anything, the best painting and sculpture produced in Paris, Germany and Russia was itself an influence. What does still exist are examples of work by particular individuals that describe, or record in some way, the spirit of Art Deco.

Art historians looking back at the art between the wars find examples of the best art in the work of Picasso, Matisse and the Surrealists. There is really very little question that artists of the stature of Picasso, Mondrian, Kandinsky, and others pushed forward the limits of painting, enriching the visual language beyond a stale academicism. Although these artists are now seen as the giants of 20th century art, it would be wrong to disregard the contributions of less well-known artists who communicated their message more readily, and illustrated the taste of the age. Between the two extremes there is no contest on the grounds of quality, but minor art is often a more accurate indicator of public taste than works of geniuses ahead of their time.

The history books almost totally ignore the work of Tamara de Lempicka – surely the most representative of the period's portrait painters – the murals of Jean Dupas, the portraits of Kees van Dongen, or the later works of Raoul Dufy, reproducing instead the abstract innovations of Paul Klee, Pablo Picasso's classic nudes of immediately after the First World War, or the rigidly thought-out and constructed canvases of Piet Mondrian. This actually misrepresents the prevailing taste of the period. The artists commanding the highest prices at auction in Paris between the wars were Maurice Utrillo and Maurice Vlaminck. In retrospect, we can see that the host of canvases they produced then were just watered-down versions of their early work, but that was what the public wanted. There is no use either in being highbrow or snobbish about the decorative arts of the period – even artists as

LEFT One of the most exciting examples of Art Deco design. This two-part lacquered wood screen, dated 1928 by Leon Jannot, is an enormously successful solution to the problem of juxtaposing highly naturalistic subject matter with bold striking abstract design. The tails of each ape are dramatically employed to both contain and energise the complex design.

great as Picasso turned their hand to stage design, pottery and furniture.

What is perhaps curious about the painting that reflected the taste of the period most accurately was that it was almost always figurative, and in particular there are a great number of portraits that, even if dismissed as vulgar and modish, gave a clear insight into the character and taste of their sitters. The many portraits or figure studies in the Art Deco style were really just illustrations of the period. It is in poster design, where there is no question of high or low art, that a style could truly be said to exist. Graphic artists of the calibre of Rockwell Kent and Cassandre could employ all the devices of Deco design, without needing to feel guilty. Their success relied directly upon their ability to reach the largest audience, to produce a popular image. Abstract art, which had taught so many designers the advantage of using clear form, and strong bold design, was not itself strengthened by Art Deco. It was, rather, watered down and made acceptable in its application to consumer items. Although there was generally little place for abstraction in Art Deco-style painting, there were exceptions to the rule.

Robert Delaunay and his wife Sonia had been deeply involved with the most advanced art in Paris since before the First World War. Quickly adopting the lessons of Cubism from Picasso, Braque, Juan Gris and Fernand Léger, Robert Delaunay produced paintings of Paris, the Eiffel Tower, Saint-Séverin church and other motifs of the modern world such as the aeroplane and the motor car. By the outbreak of the war he had distilled his art into pure abstraction, where fields of intense colour collided with one another. Developing a style that was called Orphism, Robert Delaunay's work provided inspiration for Art Deco design. The sweeping circular curves and fields of intense colour could be easily adapted to almost any other medium. It was his wife, however, who really developed and used the possibilities of the Simultanist style to the full. Photos of Sonia Delaunay-Terk at the 1925 Exposition show her in Simultanist dresses sitting on a motor car also painted in the house colours. Her designs were all the rage, becoming *the* look for the wealthy, sophisticated and avant-garde culture vulture. Bright and pleasing to the eye, her style brought a refreshing change after the heavy, exotic palette made popular by Bakst and Erté costume designs for the Ballets Russes.

The cut was also far more practical, severe, and modern.

Another painter who is still regarded as important, and could be said to reflect Art Deco preoccupations was Fernand Léger. A friend and ally of Le Corbusier and Amédée Ozenfant, his pictures hung in the Pavillon de l'Esprit Nouveau at the 1925 Exposition. If Le Corbusier's architectural preferences were to provide a house that was a machine for living in, Léger painted large murals and canvases that reflected the age's obsession with machinery. His canvases are peopled with robot-like figures in the brightest of colour combinations. What he aimed to do was personalize the machine and employ it as subject matter, an attitude that ran throughout Art Deco in its more modernist vein.

The painters Henri Matisse and Raoul Dufy also contributed to Art Deco influence. Matisse's interest in exotic subject matter, inspired by his visits to Morocco, reflected the contemporary French obsession with the colonies. Oriental art had been in vogue since the mid-19th century, but Matisse's exquisite sense of decoration reinstilled it with a vigorous modern feel. Dufy, who had failed to win a commission for a large mural for the swimming pool of the *Normandie*, produced painting after painting of the Côte d'Azur and Marseilles and its sailors. The South of France became the playground of the rich.

The many-faceted nature of Jean Dupas' talent was also applied to painting. In Emile-Jacques Ruhlmann's "Hotel d'un Collectionneur" at the 1925 Exposition, Dupas displayed a large mural entitled *Les Perruches* (the parakeets), a theme that was equally dear to Matisse. His many murals and folding screens for the *Normandie* and other private commissions, although executed in lacquer among other media, were in essence large paintings. Exotic and rich in subject matter, they were fine examples of the decorative tendencies of painting in the Art Deco style.

Tamara de Lempicka, who had been a pupil of André Lhotte, was probably the most typically Art Deco of all the portrait painters. De Lempicka's portraits of women, in vogue again, are garishly hideous studies in eroticism. The Folies Bergères, Ziegfeld's follies, Josephine Baker dancing in the nude are all highly suggestive and informative portraits of the risqué fast set that Nancy Cunard was part of. Semi-clad nudes provoke with pointed breasts behind thin layers of diaphanous silk, or thin coverings of black

LEFT Late four-part painted screen by the French Master Jean Dunand, dated 1941 of two deer drinking at a watering hole in a snowy forestscape.

331

Spanish lace. Like Foujita's sitters or the hermaphrodite little girls in Balthus paintings, de Lempicka's sitters look at the spectator with a coy, langorous look. Other painters of this sort of genre were Otto Dix and Christian Schad, who did for Berlin what de Lempicka had done for Paris, but better. Interesting and anecdotal, no Art Deco style painting is ever great art, it is more an example of entertaining camp.

POSTERS, GRAPHICS AND BOOK DESIGN

The history of poster design really started in the late 19th century. Before that, posters had been used to illustrate the ambitions and aspirations of political parties, or on a more intimate scale limited edition prints by Rowlandson, Gillray and Honoré Daumier had provided a forum for acid and biting criticism of the hypocrisies of the Establishment. By the end of the nineteenth century artists like Steinlen, Henri de Toulouse-Lautrec, Aubrey Beardsley and Edward Penfield produced works that truly understood the limitations and advantages of the poster medium. From them other graphic artists learnt the skills of successful poster design, and its role in 20th century society. A poster had to be inexpensive to mass-produce, striking in design, and arresting enough to catch the viewer's attention for long enough to tempt him to read the accompanying text. This latter attribute was not even essential, as the poster could work on the same level as a mediaeval stained glass window, educating and informing an illiterate audience and suggesting to them what they might like to acquire. Although the message was more mundane and down to earth than that of the mediaeval craftsman, the result in terms of beauty was not necessarily less. The best posters were equal to if not better than a lot of so-called fine art, and this was especially the case with Art Deco.

The Art Deco poster was the first full-blown example of a sophisticated understanding of the advantages and idiosyncracies of the world of advertising. This was hardly surprising as the growth of the advertising industry and the medium of poster design were inseparable. Art Deco, the style of the consumer age, was applied with great success to the promotion of all the

new consumer items; the gramophone (phonograph), radio set, the motor car (automobile), aeroplane, ocean-going liner, cosmetics, household appliances and, of course, the Hollywood movies. The one lasting theme and motif that ran throughout the Art Deco poster and illustration was that of the modish, chic, self-possessed and highly energetic woman. She would be the role model that any woman bent on self-improvement would have to emulate. Ever changing, she inspired people to part with their money in order to keep up with her. Unlike all the idealized nudes and nymphs that peopled Art Deco sculptures the women in posters were modern in every sense of the word. The sketches of Ernest Deutsch Dryden are a superb contemporary record. Women in the latest fashions stand with their companions around a Bugatti motor car ready to step in and set off to where? Deauville, Cannes, Long Island, or a weekend party at a country house?

The two greatest Art Deco poster designers were without a doubt Paul Colin and Cassandre. Both produced outstanding posters advertising rail travel and luxury liner voyages. Cassandre's most famous single work was the poster for the liner *Normandie*. The prow of the ship pushes forward out of the picture, as the majestic giant dwarfs the small tug beneath it. The stark outlines of the design and the stylized realism of the picture suggest to the viewer qualities that the *Normandie* certainly had, strength and elegance. Colin also produced posters to advertise the visiting Jazz giants at the Folies Bergères and other venues. It is with posters like these that the Art Deco style comes closest to gaining the name the Jazz Style. Deriving loosely from cubist painting with its disjointed sense of perspective, the colours are jazzed up, as unlikely combinations of electric blue are juxtaposed with reds and livid greens. The overall effect was initially jarring but then resolved itself into an energetic and fully comprehensible pictorial logic.

One of the most exciting areas of graphic Art Deco was the book jacket. Pierre Legrain, the furniture designer, had started his career designing book covers for Jacques Doucet. Other well-known designers were Paul Bonet, Louis Creuzevelt, Robert Bonfils and René Kieffer. Paris in the 1920s was the period of the small presses, but as well as this there was still a strong tradition of wealthy people, like Huysmans' hero des Esseintes in *Against Nature*, who had their

BELOW LEFT Pair of matching Carvacraft bookends, a Dickinson Product.

favourite books specially bound. Although book design may seem in some ways superfluous to the actual purpose of a book, no one who has held a fine-tooled morocco leather binding in the hand, and turned the pages of handmade paper can deny the sensual delights of sight, touch and smell, and the pleasure of good design and craftsmanship, that such a book can give. A particularly fine example was the collaboration on the book *Bubu du Montparnasse* in 1929 by Charles L Phillipe. The binding designed by Paul Bonet was accompanied by illustrations by the artist Dunoyer de Segonzac.

In America, the best designers of posters, books and illustrations were Rockwell Kent and Edward McKnight Kauffer. McKnight Kauffer also worked for Hollywood; his poster for Fritz Lang's masterpiece *Metropolis* is one of his best-known works. The common ground that all the best designers shared was simplicity, the use of a bold image, and a clear legible typeface that got the message across at a single glance.

ARNOLD CONSTABLE
COMMEMORATING THE MODE OF YESTERDAY
PRESENTING THE MODE OF TO-DAY
FORECASTING THE MODE OF TO-MORROW

CHAPTER 8

■

LEFT Limited edition
lithograph and poster by
Jean Dupas of 1928.

RIGHT Poster by Cassandre
advertising the French
Line service from New
York to Europe.

FAR RIGHT Poster by Paul
Colin advertising the
Black Review that was
then all the rage.

COLLECTORS AND COLLECTING

There are very few people nowadays who can afford to put together a comprehensive collection of top-quality Art Deco pieces. The best examples of work are still in the museums, notably the Metropolitan Museum in New York and the Musée des Arts Décoratifs in Paris. The three greatest private collections at the moment are those of Mr and Mrs Peter M Brant, and, in Paris, the collections of Alain Lesieutre and Felix Marcilhac. The depth and range of the last two collections is so astonishing, and the quality so consistently high, that any full-blown show of Art Deco could hardly take place without borrowing examples from these Deco connoisseurs.

Fortunately, the state of contemporary collecting in the Art Deco period was healthy. The major collectors and patrons then were the fashion designers Jeanne Lanvin and Jacques Doucet. Both of these promoted Art Deco by ordering the designs for complete interiors. Doucet, like most converts to the style, was passionate about his new interest. His patronage was particularly important for the furniture designer Pierre Legrain who, early in his career, was commissioned by Doucet to design book covers for him. The relationship between Lanvin and her favourite designer, Armand-Albert

ABOVE Cutlery service designed by Jean Puiforcat.

FAR LEFT Tea service in silver with wooden knobs and handles designed by the Christian and Dell metal workshop of the Bauhaus. Although more traditional in style than much of the work of the Bauhaus metalworking department, note the originality of the totally unmatched handles on each piece.

BELOW, FAR LEFT
Stoneware vase with mirror-black and rust-red iron glaze decoration by Charles Vyse, working in Chelsea, 1934. Note the Japanese influence.

SECOND FROM|LEFT Swedish tufted carpet handwoven and designed by Marta Måås-Fjetterström, 1923. Båstad, Sweden.

LEFT Writing case, wallet and match-case, designed as a matching set in gold-blocked, tooled black leather by the Austrian architect, Josef Hoffmann (c. 1925). Hoffmann was a leading member of the avant-garde group of Viennese artists known as the *Wiener Werkstätte*.

Rateau, was equally stimulating for both parties. In 1922, after decorating Lanvin's Paris apartment, Rateau joined her decorating firm as a director. America also produced two collectors of note, the Blumenthals and Templeton Crocker.

Although the major collections are now firmly established, and almost certainly destined to enter national museums eventually, Art Deco collecting is not out of reach of the average pocket. To build up a collection that is specialized in a single area is satisfying in itself. A collection of the mass-produced items, posters or Bakelite vanity sets is still possible to put together. What it needs is the same application and attuned eye that Marcilhac and Lesieutre have, and the bravery to buy on instinct and if necessary the willingness to spend just a little bit more for a special piece than the collector feels he can afford. Collecting can always be a gamble, but if the prime motivating force is the pursuit of objects that are beautiful, then the collector will never feel that his hobby has been worthless. The developing passion for the artefacts of the period teach the collector a great deal about a time that is not very far distant. It is also exciting to see at first hand the recurrence of aspects of Art Deco design in today's architecture, as well as every other aspect of the visual arts. Collecting can be a serious business, but it should never cease to be fun.

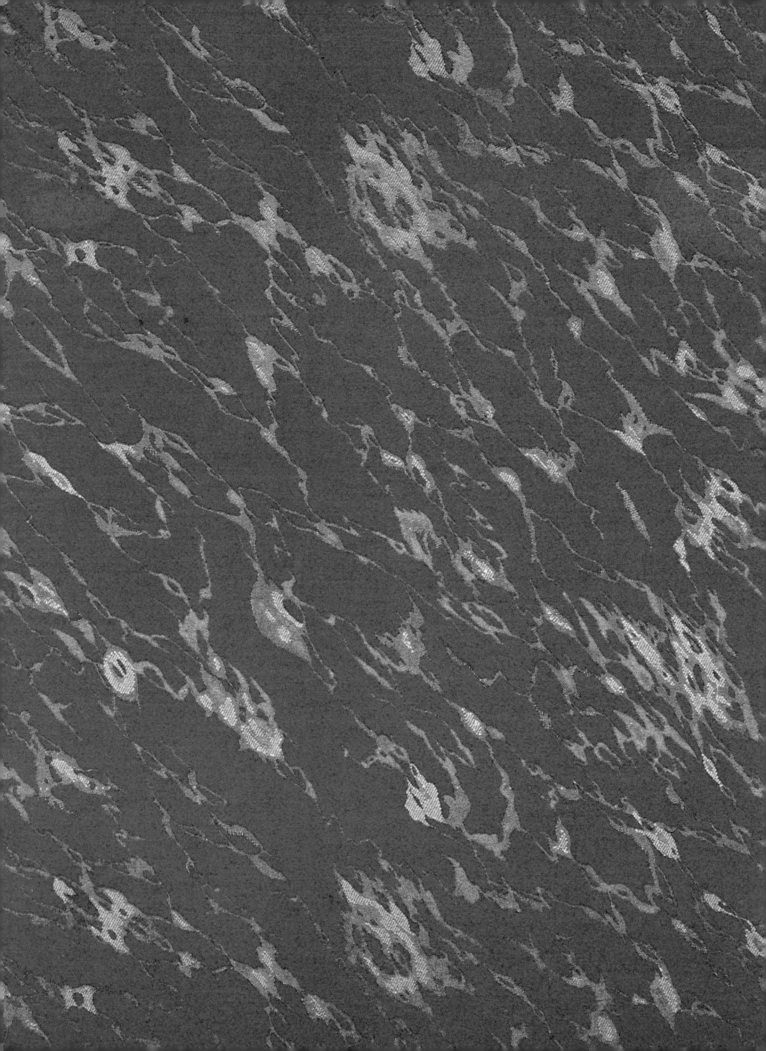

CHAPTER NINE

JEWELLERY

Diamond pendant brooch, a diamond calibre, ruby
and enamel Coldstream badge brooch by Cartier, and a
diamond and emerald bracelet and brooch by Lacloche.

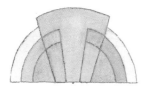

RIGHT Stunning example of an Art Deco brooch by Georges Fouquet that is timeless in its elegance.

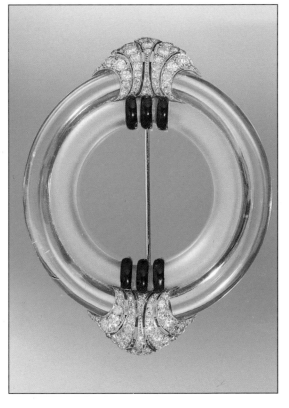

Jewellery is often regarded as a trivial luxury, a little extra touch that sets off an article of clothing. Apart from the wonderful creations by Jean Puiforcat in the area of tableware, it is in the field of jewellery that Art Deco reaches the very zenith of its stylishness. That is perhaps not so surprising when one considers the detailing on a Ruhlmann chest, or the fine finish of a Jean Dunand lacquerwork screen. Even though they were working in different materials, with a different sense of scale and purpose, they were really applying the care and craftsmanship to their work that is normally associated with the making of jewellery. If the designs for furniture or building interiors sometimes looked clumsy or not quite right, the intimate scale of jewellery could disguise those shortcomings.

The great names of Art Deco jewellery are now household words: Cartier, Boucheron, Lalique, Templier, Chaumet, Fouquet, Sandoz, van Cleef and Arpels, and Mauboussin. The established jewellers, Chaumet, Boucheron and Cartier, soon set the standard of the new jewellery.

The changes that took place in the field of jewellery in the 1920s and '30s occurred for several reasons. Firstly, the new style in women's clothing had changed the type of jewellery that was required to set it off. Sleeveless, low-cut dresses accentuated the two main areas where jewels could be worn, the neck and the wrists. A vogue that was to have little effect on the top-class jewellers was the wearing of heavy primitive bangles, although Jean Fouquet was one of the few to exploit the fashion with African-style bracelets. The short hair styles that became fashionable also did away with the demand for elaborate extras like combs and hat pins. If hats were worn they were usually small cloches that sat securely on the wearers' heads. The simple dresses, in contrast to turn-of-the-century styles, and the simple hats could be decorated with small brooches (pins) and clasps. The most important single innovation to take place was the invention of the double-sided clip or clasp. The clips could be used in pairs to hold together material, or separately as brooches and pins. The finest examples came from the major jewellery houses but they were quickly imitated in less expensive materials to cater for the larger market. At the cheaper end of the scale, hundreds of different designs were brought out for the buttons used on everyday wear.

As with furniture, the use of exotic new stones and metals was promoted. No longer limited to the traditional precious stones and metals, the jewellery designers made full use of new materials. The adoption of platinum as a setting meant that the other elements could be accentuated. Platinum is a far stronger metal than gold or silver and the settings for stones could therefore be reduced to just two or three retaining teeth. Other new materials were onyx, ebony, chrome, plastic, lapis lazuli, lacquered metals, agate, coral, Bakelite, rhinestones, jade, tortoiseshell, jet and moonstone. Used in conjunction, these materials offered up a riot of colour and contrasting textures. The types of jewellery produced were as various as the materials available: cigarette holders, rings, geometric necklaces, diamond and jet pins, glass pendants and wristwatches for day and evening wear.

The most beautiful objects of all were the small boxes, cigarette cases and notepads produced by Sandoz and Chaumet. Exactly the right size to support their simple abstract designs, the slim elegance of these containers makes much of the other Art Deco produced look tasteless in comparison.

LEFT Pearl and diamond
necklace by Cartier, and a
delicate pair of Art Deco
emerald and diamond
earrings by Van Cleef and
Arpels.

INDEX

PICTURE CREDITS

Picture credits abbreviation key: a=above, b=below, c=centre, l=left, r=right, t=top